VICE AND NARCOTICS CONTROL

GLENCOE PRESS CRIMINAL JUSTICE SERIES

Allen/Simonsen: **Corrections in America: An Introduction**

Bloomquist: **Marijuana: The Second Trip**

Brandstatter/Hyman: **Fundamentals of Law Enforcement**

Brandstatter/Radelet: **Police and Community Relations**

Eldefonso: **Issues in Corrections**

Eldefonso: **Readings in Criminal Justice**

Eldefonso/Coffey: **Process and Impact of Justice**

Eldefonso/Coffey: **Process and Impact of Juvenile Justice System**

Eldefonso/Hartinger: **Control, Treatment, and Rehabilitation of Juvenile Offenders**

Engel/DeGreen/Rebo: **The Justice Game: A Simulation**

Gourley: **Effective Municipal Police Organization**

Koga/Nelson: **The Koga Method: Police Weaponless Control and Defense Techniques**

Koga/Nelson: **The Koga Method: Police Baton Techniques**

LeGrande: **The Basic Processes of Criminal Justice**

Lentini: **Vice and Narcotics Control**

McArthur: **Police Patrol Pointers**

Melnicoe/Mennig: **Elements of Police Supervision**

Nelson: **Preliminary Investigation and Police Reporting: A Complete Guide to Police Written Communication**

Radelet: **The Police and the Community**

Radelet: **The Police and the Community: Studies**

Roberts/Bristow: **An Introduction to Modern Police Firearms**

Waddington: **Arrest, Search, and Seizure**

Williams: **Narcotics and Drug Dependence**

General Editor:

G. DOUGLAS GOURLEY

Inspector (Ret.), LA Police Department
Chairman, Department of Criminal Justice
California State University at Los Angeles
Los Angeles, California

VICE AND NARCOTICS CONTROL

Joseph R. Lentini
The University of Akron

GLENCOE PRESS
A division of Benziger Bruce & Glencoe, Inc.
Beverly Hills

Collier Macmillan Publishers
London

Dedication

To Joan, my wife, and mother of all the J's. . . . To Jay and Jim, who are following in the footsteps, Jorie, who did the typing, and Jamie, who did the proofreading; and to Judy, Jeff, Jerry, Janice, and Justin, who constantly provide motivation. To Joey, who should be here but isn't; and to Joseph G., who started it all back in 1932.

GLENCOE PRESS
A division of Benziger Bruce & Glencoe, Inc.
8701 Wilshire Boulevard
Beverly Hills, California 90211
Collier Macmillan Canada, Ltd.

Library of Congress Catalog Card Number: 75-14924

First printing 1977

Contents

Preface

VICE AND NARCOTICS CONTROL covers the broad area of consensual crime, those crimes in which the victim willingly participates and thus is an accessory to the vice act. Topics in this book include gambling, loan sharking, prostitution, sex offenses, and narcotics. These vice activities are dealt with from both a practical and a philosophical viewpoint—practical because hundreds of thousands of police hours are spent in attempts to suppress these activities, and these hours should be made to bear more affirmative results than they have in the past; philosophical because the main roadblock to effective control of these crimes lies in the ambivalence exhibited by the general public and even by the police themselves when confronted by widespread vice crime.

Hopefully, the reader will gain from this text a basic knowledge of vice activities and the various methods used to suppress them. He or she should also be able to place these crimes in perspective among the activities of professional, organized criminals.

When one attempts to write a textbook on vice and narcotics control, one immediately is faced with the fact of fifty individual criminal codes. The definitions used in this book are meant to be generally descriptive of a specific group of acts which have been defined as criminal in most states. They do not conform specifically to the laws of any state. The same may be said of the slang terms which appear throughout the book. A term may be in general use over a wide area and not used at all in another part of the country. It is expected that the student will learn the street language of the area in which he or she is working.

The author wishes to acknowledge with gratitude the contributions of the following: the Fund for the City of New York, for permission to use their extensive research on gambling in New York City; the New York State Commission of Investigation, for permission to use material from their 1965 study of loan sharking; the Federal Bureau of Investigation, for permission to use their training material on sex crimes; the State of Georgia Crime Laboratory, for permission to use photographs of various narcotics; my colleagues, Professor Ken McCormick of the University of Akron, who read and commented on the chapters dealing with investigative methods, and Bill Bickett, who took most of the narcotics photographs; my editor, Judy Ziajka of Glencoe Press, a person of infinite patience and goodwill who rode herd on my instinct to procrastinate; and, finally, to my students, whose needs prompted the writing of this book.

University of Akron
Akron, Ohio
July, 1975

Chapter 1

The "Victimless" Crimes

Each day in the United States millions of dollars and large blocks of police time are spent enforcing the laws against gambling, loan sharking, prostitution, obscenity, and narcotics. This work is largely carried out by police officers who are members of vice and narcotics squads or organized crime strike forces.

Crimes against Public Morality

As we study the acts that constitute the crimes that threaten public morality, we find that they all have one characteristic in common: they do not have victims, at least not in the same sense that crimes involving robbery, burglary, rape, or murder have victims. In each case, those whom the law defines as criminals—that is, the bookie, the loan shark, the prostitute, and the pusher— all have accomplices without whom the crime could not be carried to its conclusion. These accomplices are simply the citizens of the community, those who purchase the particular commodity being offered for sale. Thus, the term *victimless crime* has been coined to describe this unique variety of offenses. In contrast to most crimes wherein the victim complains bitterly (confidence games are sometimes the exception), vice offenses depend upon the willing participation of a customer who does not consider himself a victim unless, of course, he becomes ill as a result of his action or discovers that he has been dealt with fraudulently (Wilson 1950). Although this point of view reflects a somewhat superficial interpretation of vice activity, it may be logically argued that most vice crime is indeed victimless. The main problem with this interpretation, however, is that it tends to ignore the ''behind-the-scenes'' victim, the family who suffers because food or rent money has been gambled away; the victims of robberies and burglaries committed by addicts who have to support a sixty-dollar-a-day habit; the individuals who despair at the loss of a family member or close friend whose death is the result of an overdose of narcotics; the debtor who is unmercifully beaten or forced into crime because he is unable to pay his debt to a loan shark. Perhaps a better term for describing the activities of those involved in vice crime—both the entrepreneur and his or her customer—would be *consensual crime,* that is, crime in which all participating parties become involved of their own volition. Using this approach, we can view the matter of vice crime from the standpoint of the police, who must enforce the law.

1

The Official View vs. the Public Perspective

Attempts to distinguish between vice crime and other types of crime have led to two completely opposing points of view with regard to the enforcement of the laws which define certain acts as vice crimes. The official viewpoint is perhaps best articulated by Leonard and More (1971, p. 288):

> No halfway measure or concession is compatible [in vice control] with good police administration. It has been demonstrated that where the people of a city lend their support to this type of policy, police administration can carry out its functions in this area with an extraordinarily high degree of efficiency. Vice-free communities in this country are not altogether unknown.

This point of view is the one that has been adopted by the majority of our governmental units and their police forces. It has long been an axiom in police circles that "the police do not make the law; they just enforce it." And because this is the official attitude toward vice control, police officers are required to work within its guidelines, even though they may not always agree with it. Many individual officers have ambivalent feelings about some or all of the vice crime laws and therefore use discretion in selectively enforcing these statutes.

That ambivalent feelings do exist on the part of individual police officers is evidenced by the fact that most official corruption takes place in the area of vice control. In fact, most of the major police scandals of the past few years have occurred as a result of attempts by police officers to protect illegal gambling and vice operations; many of these officers try to rationalize their acceptance of bribes by calling it "clean graft."

The opposing point of view, which opts for the legalization or decriminalization of the vice crimes, is espoused by Morris and Hawkins (1970, pp. 4–5) in a controversial book titled *The Honest Politician's Guide to Crime Control:*

> The function, as we see it, of the criminal law is to protect the citizen's person and property and to prevent the exploitation or corruption of the young and others in need of special care or protection. We think it improper, impolitic, and usually socially harmful for the law to intervene or attempt to regulate the private moral conduct of the citizen. In this country we have a highly moralistic criminal law and a long tradition of using it as an instrument of coercing men toward virtue. It is a singularly inept instrument for that purpose. It is also an unduly costly one, both in terms of harm done and in terms of the neglect of the proper tasks of law enforcement.

There are several indications that the views expressed by Morris and Hawkins are being taken seriously. For example, thirteen states have already established limited forms of legalized gambling through their state lotteries. Eight states have changed their sex laws to read that, in effect, private sexual activity between consenting adults is no crime. Prostitution is legal by local option in the state of Nevada, and the Gay Liberation movement is rapidly making homosexuals just another minority group. Private-interest groups throughout the country are lobbying for the decriminalization and/or legalization of many of the activities that are currently the subject of laws which govern public morality or public order.

On the other hand, church groups, school groups, conservative reformers, and others are demanding more loudly than ever that the laws governing all vice crimes be strictly enforced by police agencies. This, of course, places the police directly in the middle of the controversy. The law exists and therefore must be enforced, regardless of how large a segment of the public pays lip service to enforcement yet participates in these crimes as gamblers, "Johns," borrowers, and in some cases, as users of narcotics. Many of those demanding enforcement of these laws, while themselves participating (either actively or peripherally) in the crimes the laws are meant to deter, have sufficient political clout to make them relatively immune to the law. This state of affairs inevitably leads to discretionary enforcement of the law, discretionary in the sense that the prostitute, for example, is arrested in all states, but in most states her customer is allowed to go free. The bookie is taken into custody, yet his customer is not. And the loan shark is arrested (when we can apprehend him), while the borrower is held blameless. Similarly, forty-two states define as criminal certain sexual activities between spouses, yet were the laws pertaining to these activities actually enforced, roughly 75 percent of all the married couples in this country would have been, at one time or another, technically guilty of a felony. McLaren and Wilson (1974) seem to take a step backward from the stand taken earlier by Wilson (1950). In one statement they claim that "there can be no compromise with vice any more than there can be compromise with other crime." Yet they also state that "the proportion of police effort to be directed into the several fields of police control [of vice] is a matter of administrative judgment, based in part on the interpretation of public opinion."

These two contradictory statements taken from the same page of a book written by two highly regarded experts in the field of police administration clearly exemplify the ambivalence that is felt by police officers everywhere as they are faced with the dilemma of when to enforce the laws and when not to enforce them. Either we compromise or we don't. Either we respond to public opinion or we don't. Of course, any attempt to respond to public opinion must necessarily involve compromise since the influential public does not always practice what it preaches. In fact, strict enforcement of the letter of the law would undoubtedly produce an outcry that would topple most city administrations. On the other hand, no enforcement at all would have a similar outcome. Therefore, elected politicians, police chiefs, and police officers are invariably forced to walk the fine line between full enforcement of the vice statutes and a permissiveness that sometimes borders on the criminal.

Price (1974) notes that in 1970 almost one-half of all the arrests made in the United States were related to "victimless" crimes. Included in this group were prostitution, pornography, gambling, marijuana use, and drunkenness. In relation to arrests for drunkenness Price notes that taxpayers in Washington, D.C., spent $600,000 prosecuting six chronic drinkers who had been arrested a total of 1,400 times for public drunkenness and who had collectively served a total of 125 years in the city's jails.

Price questions whether law-enforcement agencies, given the current yearly increase in serious crimes, can afford to spend as much time as they are presently spending dealing with public drunks, whose arrests in 1967 alone constituted almost 40 percent of all nontraffic arrests in the United States. He also emphasizes the harmful effects of processing offenders of this type as criminals, and goes on to suggest that diversion and treatment might well be more effective than the revolving-door policies presently being employed by the criminal justice system.

Schwartz and Goldstein (1970) postulate that the ambivalence inherent in society's views of these crimes often leads law-enforcement officers to such undesirable practices as entrapment, illegal searches, and unauthorized audio-surveillance in their efforts to combat the so-called private crimes.

The following statement by Pace (1971, p. vii), however, indicates that he shares the point of view of this author:

> The enforcement of statutes dealing with vice has been the subject of much criticism by the public. Many police officers, aware of this criticism, know that mere punitive enforcement is not the final answer for the elimination of vice crimes. A police agency does not purport to be totally effective in vice control. The best that may be expected of law enforcement is stop-gap repression until more enlightened preventive and rehabilitative methods are put into practice. Although some policemen may disagree, it is not the prerogative of the law enforcement officer to make individual decisions condoning vice violations. *Because if a given act is a violation of a statute, the enforcement officer is required to take some positive action against the violator.*

Most of the arguments for and against strict enforcement of the laws against consensual crimes are perfectly valid when considered only in terms of the individual citizen's right to "go to hell" in his own fashion, but there is more to the issue of vice crime than meets the eye. The problem with many of these arguments is that they ignore the important fact that the revenue derived from the sale of most illegal activities and services does not, in most cases, go into the pockets of the individual bookie, prostitute, loan shark, or pusher. Granted, each receives a small share of the profits, but the bulk of the money eventually finds its way into the treasuries of organized crime. The President's Commission on Law Enforcement and the Administration of Justice in its *Report on Organized Crime* (1967) quotes Peterson (1963) on the implications of the role of organized crime in vice activities:

It is organized crime's accumulation of money, not the individual transactions by which the money is accumulated, that has a great and threatening impact on America. A quarter in a jukebox means nothing and results in nothing. But millions of quarters in thousands of jukeboxes can provide both a strong motive for murder and the means to commit murder with impunity.

In other words, the nickels, dimes, and dollars accumulated from gambling, loan sharking, and drug imports buy power—power to elect judges, power to subvert law enforcement, power to invest in legitimate business, and power to force honest businessmen out of the marketplace. The twenty-five-cent bet on a number means nothing in itself, but that same twenty-five-cent bet multiplied hundreds of thousands of times every day across the country adds up to millions of dollars and the power that those dollars can buy.

Criminal Sanctions in Consensual Crime

The approach taken by our criminal justice system to the enforcement of the laws against these various crimes has been a provincial one, with individual communities treating each vice offense as an isolated case. Only in recent years have attempts been made to view the vice crimes as a collective problem. And several of the states have yet to adapt their laws to handle the "organization concept." Contrary to what was once believed, the bookie, the loan shark, the drug peddler, and sometimes the prostitute are not independent operatives but rather, in many instances, are merely small cogs in a much larger machine. The judge who hands down a fifty-dollar fine to a bookie may feel that he is punishing the individual offender; because he is unable to see the organization behind the bookie, he fails to realize that he has merely added a very small amount to the bookie's cost of doing business. The fault lies even more heavily within the state legislatures, which have defined most of the vice crimes as misdemeanors. Indeed, the time has come for comprehensive, organized crime legislation at the state level, legislation that would define individual vice crimes committed in furtherance of organized crime as felonies. Such legislation would have at least two positive effects: first, stiffer penalties would probably alter the public's attitude toward the seriousness of vice crime as it relates to organized crime; and second, such legislation would do much to eliminate the dichotomy that exists in the minds of police officers about the desire of society to rid itself of organized crime.

An alternate solution would be to adopt the position of Morris and Hawkins (1969), who postulate that organized crime, as it is presently defined, does not exist and that most vice crime should either be decriminalized or legalized and controlled. Regardless of whether one agrees or disagrees about the existence of the crime syndicates, legalization may well be a viable alternative to strict repression. As stated earlier, the thrust of this text is that "as long as the laws exist, let's enforce them.'' We cannot solve the problems inherent in vice crimes by merely vacillating between enforcement and nonenforcement.

As stated by the proponents of legalization, we do spend millions of dollars and hundreds of thousands of police hours trying to enforce the laws against vice crime. To a large extent, these efforts are wasted because we have failed to eliminate vice crimes and cannot even claim to have put an appreciable dent in the frequency of their occurrence. If we—and by we I mean not just the police or others engaged in the criminal justice system—really want to rid ourselves of vice crime in the community, then we have only to demand of our legislators and our judges the necessary laws and then insist that the police enforce those laws; only in this way can we achieve optimum efficiency in combating vice crime. If we are going to spend the money and time, then let us receive what we are paying for—an all-out housecleaning.

If we decide that we do not wish to go all out in eliminating vice crime, then we should move toward legalization, decriminalization, and control in much the same manner that we once dealt with the problems of alcohol and cigarette smoking. For the time being, however, we must accept the former method of enforcement—arrest and prosecution—and, despite the shortcomings of the laws, bring to bear on the problem the proper methods and strategies necessary to at least maintain the status quo.

The following chapters will deal in detail with the nature of vice crime, its place in the structure of organized crime, and the strategies that have proved most successful in carrying out the enforcement role. In all instances we will look at alternatives to the current strategies. Each chapter will cover one specific type of vice crime, with the exception of chapter 5, which deals with sex crimes. That chapter has been included because some of the activities described as "sex crimes" are legislated against as "crimes against morality and decency," and though unenforceable, carry with them significant social stigma and sanctions ranging up to twenty years in prison. Those sex crimes which do not fall into the unenforceable category are usually "crimes against the person" and as such are not technically vice crimes.

REFERENCES

Leonard, V. A., and More, Harry W. *Police Organization and Management.* Mineola, N.Y.: The Foundation Press, 1971.

Morris, Norval, and Hawkins, Gordon. *The Honest Politician's Guide to Crime Control.* Chicago: University of Chicago Press, 1970.

Pace, Denny F. *Handbook of Vice Control.* Englewood Cliffs, N.J.: Prentice-Hall, 1971.

President's Commission on Law Enforcement and the Administration of Justice. *Task Force Report: Organized Crime.* Washington, D.C.: U.S. Government Printing Office, 1967.

Schwartz, Louis B., and Goldstein, Stephen R. *Law Enforcement Handbook for Police.* St. Paul, Minn.: West Publishing Co., 1970.

Wilson, O. W. *Police Administration.* New York: McGraw-Hill, 1950.

Wilson, O. W., and McLaren, Roy C. *Police Administration.* New York: McGraw-Hill, 1972.

Chapter 2

Gambling

Gambling, the lifeblood of organized crime, is one of the largest and most profitable industries in the United States. During the 1950s, the Kefauver Commission estimated gambling to be a twenty-billion-dollar-a-year business. More recent studies place the figure at between thirty and fifty billion dollars. Without this formidable income, organized crime could not operate.

It is axiomatic to state that whenever there is a strong consumer demand for an illegal service or commodity, racketeers and criminals will step forward to fill the vacuum and to satisfy the demand. Gambling is a prime example. It has been estimated that roughly 60 percent of the adult population of the United States have gambled at one time or another. In a study conducted in 1972, titled *Legal Gambling in New York,* the Fund for the City of New York (Appendix, Study 1458-A, 1972, p. 36) reported the following:

1. Eight in ten adult residents of New York City report betting money at some time on games of chance and sporting events.
2. Three-quarters have played the New York and other state lotteries.
3. Some 36 percent in total say they bet on sports such as football, baseball, basketball, and horse racing. Betting on the horses is most popular—30 percent of adults have bet.
4. A quarter of the city's population plays the numbers. If the game were legalized, almost half of all adults with an opinion (45 percent) say they would be probable or almost certain legal numbers players. Virtually every current numbers player would play the legal game if it were convenient for him to play.*

Although this particular study was conducted in a large, eastern, liberal city, its results could probably be replicated in almost every large and medium-sized city in the country. The conclusions reached in the New York study suggest that there are certain inherent contradictions in the general public's attitude toward gambling (see the addendum to this chapter). As one of the vice crimes, gambling in itself is a relatively innocuous activity. It poses no threat to the

---

*See the addendum to this chapter for a more complete report of the Fund's findings.

health or moral character of the bettor; it attaches little or no moral stigma to the bettor; and any financial injury that is incurred affects only the individual bettor.

Moreover, because a double standard is practiced in the enforcement of gambling laws, the general public can easily rationalize the act of betting. "Why," the bettor asks, "should it be legal for me to bet at the race track yet illegal for me to bet with a bookie? If gambling *is* in fact illegal, then why do the police arrest only the bookie and not the player?" This latter question might be applied to prostitution, loan sharking, and obscenity, as well.

It is difficult to convince the average, small-time bettor that a nickel or dime bet on the numbers or a two-dollar bet on a horse feeds the coffers of organized crime. Such bettors see the local bookie as merely another small businessman who provides a service (albeit an illegal one) and would be insulted if they themselves were referred to as criminals.

The fact remains, however, that gambling is illegal in most states—except under certain specified conditions—and as long as it is illegal, we can formulate a logical rationale for the enforcement of the laws against it.

1. Gambling profits are used to further the activities of organized crime syndicates.

2. Crime rates are significantly higher in areas in which gambling abounds.

3. An atmosphere conducive to gambling tends to attract criminals to the area. Rates of robberies, burglaries, and narcotics violations increase when gambling and vice are not controlled.

4. The presence of gambling operations casts a shadow of doubt on the honesty and integrity of the police.

5. Gambling is, after all, against the laws which the police have sworn to uphold (Lentini and France 1972).

People will bet on almost anything, and thus part of the gambler's code is to provide the average bettor with the opportunity to place his bets. The most popular games of chance include the numbers or "policy wheel," off-track horse betting, football, baseball, and basketball pools, boxing matches, hockey games, and golf matches. In the more rural areas bets are placed on cockfights and dogfights. The fact that, in most cases, the bets placed on these various activities are small and seemingly innocent is one of the major reasons that illegal gambling survives so successfully. The average bettor is a small bettor: nickel and dime bets on the numbers, two-dollar bets on the horses, a dollar for a treasury balance ticket, or a quarter on a baseball pool. And although each small bet seems harmless in itself, when added together on a national scale, they form a multibillion-dollar business.

In the major cities, gambling is not an independent venture. Contrary to what most people might think, the local bookie is not merely a small businessman but rather an employee of a much larger interest. He gets his cut from the bets he takes and passes the rest on to another, higher up in the organization. No independent operator survives for very long in a large city; eventually he is either taken in by those in control or he is put out of business permanently.

The Numbers Game

At one time, the numbers game was referred to as "poor man's roulette," since the game was largely confined to the poor. Today, it is estimated that 55 percent of all numbers players are white and belong to the working and middle classes; however, in terms of percentage of the population, a disproportionate number of these players live in the poor, ghetto areas of our large cities. The numbers game is particularly attractive to the poor because it imposes no minimum on the amount that can be bet. A bettor may bet any amount from a few cents upward.

The player in the numbers game may choose any three-digit number from 000 through 999. Since there are 1,000 three-digit numbers in this span, the odds against picking the winning number are 1,000 to 1. The player may also play a "bolida," or "bleeder," which is a bet on the last two digits or the first two digits of the winning number, in which case the odds against him are 100 to 1 and the payoff is 60 to 1. The payoff for picking the winning three-digit number is 600 to 1. The player also has the option of playing "single action," or the "lead"—that is, betting on the first number of the winning three-digit number. In this case, the odds against him are 10 to 1 and the payoff is 6 to 1. (See figure 2.1 for an example of a typical numbers-play marker.)

Players can also "box" their numbers; in other words, they can bet all the possible combinations of a three-digit number. For example, if a player "boxes" 569, he is, in effect, betting the following numbers at the same time: 596, 659, 695, 965, and 956. "Boxing" increases the player's chances of winning, but the payoff odds are reduced to 100 to 1. If a player "boxes" a three-digit number having a double digit like 771, he only has three numbers in his box. The odds should be 333 to 1 in this case, but most bookies hold the payoff to 100 to 1.

The numbers operator also protects himself from a heavy hit by designating certain numbers as "half numbers" or "cut numbers." These are numbers

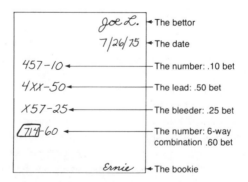

Figure 2.1 A typical numbers-play marker.

which receive a consistently heavy play from the bettors—round numbers such as 100, 200, 300, and so forth; triple numbers such as 111, 222, or 333; traditionally lucky numbers, such as 711 (the winning numbers in craps), 317 (heavily played on St. Patrick's Day), and usually the date—on June 15, for example, 615 would be a typical cut number. Numbers players tend to play the date heavily. The odds on cut numbers result in a 400 to 1 payoff. In some cities the cut number pays only 300 to 1.

The winning number is determined in several arbitrary ways. One method is simply to add up the betting totals for selected races at various designated race tracks. For example, the totals for the third, fifth, and seventh races might be used to determine the winning number in Boston and New York. Until a short time ago, one of the local newspapers in Boston always printed the winning number in the following "concealed" manner:

Third Race—134.60

Fifth Race—207.20

Seventh Race—277.40

In order to determine what the winning number was, the bettor had only to read the three numbers to the left of each decimal point. Thus, in the example given above, the winning number would be 477. The only reason that this particular newspaper printed the betting totals for those three races out of context was to cater to the numbers players among their subscribers.

In the New York area, the same system is used but the player must work a little harder to locate the winning number. In Brooklyn, the winning number is designated as the last three digits of the total mutuel handle at the designated track. The designated race track is usually a local track. When the local track is closed, another track located anywhere in the country may be substituted, as long as the local newspapers report the results from the chosen track.

The winning number may be found in the following manner. The win, place, and show payoff figures for the winning horse in the first race are added to the place and show payoffs for the second horse in the race plus the show payoff for the third horse in the race to produce a first race total payoff. The same is done for the first, second, and third horses in the second race to produce a second-race total. This process is repeated for the third race to produce a third-race total. The three totals are then added to produce a total for the first three races. Let us suppose the sum to be 134.60. The 4 to the left of the decimal point becomes the first digit of the winning number. This process is repeated for the fourth and fifth races to produce a two-race total of, for example, 207.20. In this case the 7 to the left of the decimal point becomes the second digit of the winning number. Next, the payoff figures for the first three horses in the sixth and seventh races are added together. Let us suppose this total to be 277.40. The 7 to the left of the decimal point becomes the third digit of the winning number. Therefore, the winning number is 477.

The winning number is not always taken from the mutuel handle at a race track. In the city of Cleveland, for example, the number is taken from the financial pages of the local paper. (See figure 2.2.) In another city, the number is taken from the last three digits of the United States treasury balance, which is printed daily. It really makes no difference from what source the winning number is drawn so long as it is one that is published each day in the local paper. Since in most states the tracks and stock exchanges do not operate on Sunday, the numbers are played only six days a week.

The player bets his numbers with a bookie, runner, collector, or writer (the title varies in different sections of the country). In most cities, this individual also takes off-track bets on the horses. The player usually bets in his own neighborhood, although large numbers of bets are placed in offices, factories, bars, and other legitimate business establishments.

The numbers collector works in one of two ways. He either travels around his "beat" or neighborhood, stopping at various prearranged locations to take bets from his customers, or he is a stationary collector who establishes himself in one location so that his customers can come to him. He may make himself accessible to customers by hanging out in a local bar, a barbershop, or even on a street corner. Many stationary collectors are actually legitimate businessmen who book numbers on the side as an extra source of revenue or as a convenience to their customers. Barbers, bartenders, cabdrivers, candy-store proprietors, and tobacconists are examples of this type of collector.

Collectors in factories and offices are usually people whose jobs allow them to move freely around the various areas of the building—for example, messengers, mail clerks, shop stewards, office boys, and so forth.

Collectors typically take bets up until a certain time of the day (the deadline is usually just before post time for the first race at the designated track). The bets are then collected by a controller who is the equivalent of a district manager. A single controller may be collecting bets from a large number of bookies. The controller sends all the bets to a banker, who is the central operator of the numbers game. The banker finances the payments to the winners and absorbs the losses incurred on winning numbers. It is he who decides on the winning numbers and sends the players' winnings back down the chain to the collector, who, in turn, pays off the winners. The banker is also responsible for hiring the controllers, settling disputes, and paying for protection either directly or through the controllers.

The banker has the additional responsibility of having to protect his operations from large hits and heavy losses. He does this by "laying off" bets; in other words, by betting heavily favored numbers with other operators in order to minimize his losses in the event that a heavily played number should win. The lay-off bank is usually operated by organized crime syndicates that have large amounts of cash available for this type of operation. The banker is usually in the direct employ of the syndicate, or he pays a franchise fee to be allowed to operate his territory without outside interference. The syndicate sets the odds for payoffs and often arranges protection from the law. A table of organization for an illegal numbers game is shown in figure 2.3.

NYSE STOCK AVERAGES

1975-76 HIGH	LOW		HIGH	LOW	CLOSE	NET CHANGE Points	Percent
54.24	35.06	Composite......53.93		52.94	53.27	+ 0.30	+ 0.56
60.41	36.76	Industrials......60.10		59.07	59.28	+ 0.35	+ 0.59
37.93	26.76	Transportation..38.37		37.51	38.06	+ 0.78	+ 2.09
36.67	27.77	Utilities........36.01		35.70	35.83	+ 0.06	+ 0.16
54.18	41.16	Finance.........52.23		51.32	51.50	+ 0.25	+ 0.48

DOW JONES WEEKLY STOCK AVERAGES

1975-76 HIGH	LOW		SALES	HIGH	LOW	CLOSE	NET CHANGE Points	Percent
976.62	632.05	30 Indus....	8,742,700	971.90	957.18	958.36	+ 3.46	+ 0.36
201.94	146.47	20 Trans...	3,325,100	202.73	199.94	200.93	+ 2.60	+ 1.31
91.90	72.07	15 Utils....	1,847,000	89.60	88.03	88.03	− 1.79	− 1.99
299.50	205.30	65 Stocks	13,914,800	297.73	293.96	293.96	+ 0.80	+ 0.27

STANDARD & POOR'S WEEKLY STOCK INDEX

1975-76 HIGH	LOW		HIGH	LOW	CLOSE	NET CHG.	P.E. RATIO	YIELD
101.91	70.04	500 Index.....	100.77	99.62	96.67	+ 0.21	11.71	3.67
114.31	72.41	425 Indus.....	113.10	111.73	111.84	+ 0.31	12.71	3.35
43.67	34.09	15 Rails......	43.67	43.03	43.03	+ 0.17	7.71	4.89
48.37	35.31	60 Utils......	47.26	46.93	46.93	− 0.29	5.94	7.79

Highs and Lows for the Week are Highest and Lowest Daily Closing Figures for Each Index.

THE WEEK'S LEADERS

	SALES	CLOSE	CHANGE
Ramada Inn....	1,673,300	6¼	+ 1¾
Pan Am.......	1,408,200	6⅜	+ ⅞
Texaco Inc	1,363,100	25	− ⅝
Penn Cent.....	1,356,300	2⅝	+ ⅛
Singer Co.....	1,255,200	16⅝	+ 2¾
Citicorp.......	1,120,900	32¼	− ⅞
Evans Pd.......	984,300	7¾	+ ¾
Polaroid........	956,900	40⅜	+ 2⅛
A T & T.......	902,400	55⅛	+ ⅝
Westghuse Elec..	834,000	15¾	+ ⅜
Coast States Gas	825,700	10⅞	− ⅝
Inmont Op......	804,100	11⅞	+ 1⅛
Gulf Oil........	759,400	24¼	− ⅛
RCA...........	734,700	25½	+ ⅛
Gen Motors.....	730,600	63¼	+ ⅛

TOTAL WEEKLY TRANSACTIONS*

Last Week..................	137,787,770
Week Ago..................	157,490,000
Year Ago	128,365,030
Two Years Ago.............	69,549,090

NYSE ADVANCE-DECLINE VOLUME*
(Thousands of Shares)

	LAST WEEK	WEEK AGO	YEAR AGO
Advances	74,606	73,298	67,638
Declines	44,656	66,027	45,311
Unchanged	18,518	18,165	16,001

VOLUME ON OTHER MARKETS

	SHARES
NYSE......................	137,780,000
Pacific	4,941,400
Midwest	5,766,400
NASD	6,593,930
Boston	903,600
Cincinnati	359,100
Detroit	48,200
PBW	2,054,580
Intinet System	412,600

WHAT THE MARKET DID*

	LAST WEEK	PRIOR WEEK	YEAR AGO	2 YRS. AGO
Issues Traded	2,069	2,087	2,012	1,972
Advances....	1,267	1,086	1,174	813
Declines......	631	822	634	900
Unchanged....	171	179	204	259
New Highs ...	526	652	87	22
New Lows 4		3	3	122

VOLUME JAN. 1 TO DATE*

This Year	931,155,159
Year Ago	670,715,940
Two Years Ago.............	500,865,780

*NYSE Volume only—Thousands of shares

Figure 2.2 An example of a financial page from a newspaper from which the winning number might be taken. First number in the circled area is the winning number.

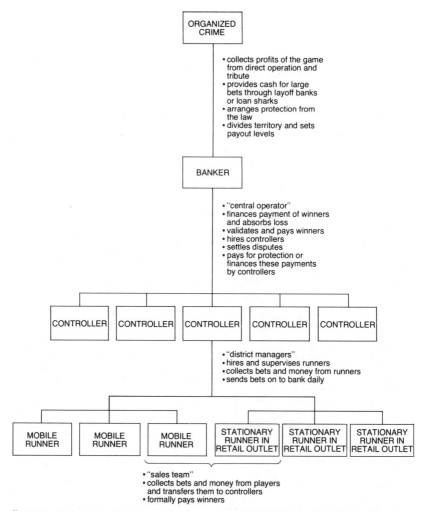

From *Legal Gambling in New York: A Discussion of Numbers and Sports Betting.*
Copyright 1972 by Fund for the City of New York. Reprinted by permission.
Figure 2.3 Numbers game structure.

All numbers players have their own favorite numbers; they might play their birthdates, addresses, employee badge numbers, license plate numbers, or practically any other number that strikes their fancy. Within the fraternity of numbers players, "hot numbers" are passed around by word of mouth. Many players buy a "dream book" which lists numbers for every category of dreams. For example, if a player dreams about a bullfrog, he might look up bullfrog in his dream book and be advised to play the number 112. Dream books are sold on local newsstands and are not illegal. However, many of these books are published by the numbers operators themselves. (See figures 2.4, 2.5, and 2.6.)

PRICE $1.25

IT'S BIGGER AND BETTER
NEW 1974 EDITION

THE ORIGINAL

LUCKY

Three Wise Men

A REAL COMBINATION

Dream Book

Edited by PROF. ZONITE

YOUR HOROSCOPE READING

THE SCIENCE OF NUMBERS REVEALED

Vibration Is Life—Without It There Would Be No Life.
The study of the law of vibrations through Numerology
points the way to recording mans vibrations and expres-
sing them in numerical values.

This book contains a popular list of daily number vibrations for the entire year.

PLUS THEIR MONTHLY
DIGIT CALENDARS

*Figure 2.4 The cover of a typical dream book. Dream books are sold legally on local
newsstands and are frequently consulted by avid numbers players.*

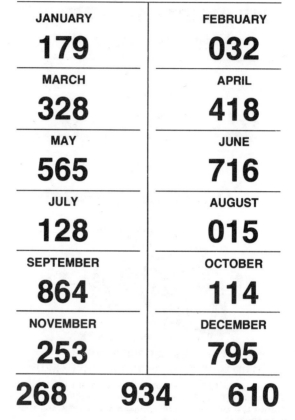

SUPER SPECIALS
COMPILED BY PROF. ZONITE
They are due to "HIT" according to the law
of averages in all the "Totals"

JANUARY	FEBRUARY
179	**032**
MARCH	APRIL
328	**418**
MAY	JUNE
565	**716**
JULY	AUGUST
128	**015**
SEPTEMBER	OCTOBER
864	**114**
NOVEMBER	DECEMBER
253	**795**

268   934   610

Figure 2.5 Most dream books compile lists of "lucky" numbers which claim to be based on the "law of averages." These "super special" numbers correspond to the months of the year.

Since numbers is a very "open" game, it is almost impossible for the racket to be carried on in a neighborhood without the knowledge of law-enforcement officials. In an article titled "The Private Government of Crime," Daniel Moynihan (1961) poses the following question: "If the average citizen knows where to go to place an illegal bet, why is it so difficult for the police to get the same information?" This is clearly a valid question; because it stands to reason that if the general public knows that gambling abounds in a certain locality, then the police must also have access to this knowledge. If the police consistently fail to take action, does the general public not have the right to question their

426—Brewery-472	10-38-58	176—Butterfly-287	13-14-15
538—Brandy-683	3- 8-38	544—Buttermilk-545	7-11-71
999—Broadcloth-998	7-69-70	437—Buttons-834	34-44-58
833—Bronchitis-623	6-17-18	420—Buying-124	11-22-40
777—Brass-767	16-52-60	357—Buzzing-563	40-46-47
741—Bread-819	20-34-62	369—Buzzard-496	52-73-75
210—Bribery-301	3- 9-39		
278—Bricks-873	8-15-17	369 C—3-9-19	
567—Brick mason-658	14-33-42	481—Cab-411	40-46-71
180—Brick house	17-21-50	638—Cabbage-453	3-16-45
380—Brick wall-802	7-17-71	189—Cabaret-829	7-11-44
391—Brickwork-219	8-15-17-39	986—Cabaretting-987	1-11-22
485—Bride-507	1- 2-27	841—Cabin-248	18-21-51
584—Bridegroom	48-49-50	579—Cablegram-687	41-56-65
814—Bridge-518	13-19-24	242—Cage-324	2- 4-22
497—Bridle-379	47-49-66	186—Calomel-862	8-13-68
813—Bright-931	43-44-45	562—Calamity-185	3- 9-61
182—Broach-280	34-48-49	168—California-167	6-10-71
973—Brook-837	5-11-60	360—Calipers-640	30-50-70
155—Broom-951	39-62-73	694—Calling-965	49-56-73
341—Brother-421	1- 3-50	548—Calm-486	4-48-75
288—Brother-in-law-218	8-24-32	487—Calf-923	11-35-53
155—Brown-156	5- 6- 7	110—Cake-100	10-11-38-59
697—Burial-687	7- 9-21	870—Calendar-781	6-12-52
713—Burning-741	5-15-55	183—Camphor-283	18-32-63
719—Bubbles-891	59-65-68	689—Camp-798	15-46-69
212—Bust-211	12-15-50	961—Camel-951	22-69-70
390—Bucket-409	9-10-20	852—Can-842	29-32-78
159—Buffalo-941	46-64-67	924—Canada-914	21-31-41
150—Bug-500	8-28-38	839—Canal-849	6- 7- 8
416—Buggy-651	12-15-50	722—Canary Birds-723	2-24-36
347—Builder-348	27-29-40	378—Cancer-750	3-27-40
722—Building-712	1-17-25	259—Candidate-195	9-57-59
459—Bulb-485	54-59-70	162—Candle-620	6-16-66
504—Bull-305	6-11-66	597—Candle burning	6-51-66
816—Bull-head'd-851	58-60-67	116—Candy-683	38-51-56
749—Bullet-894	4- 7-29	996—Canker-986	1-11-22
112—Bullfrog-120	69-71-73	621—Cannon-601	16-21-57
323—Bulletin-223	32-38-49	13—Cancer-103	11-33-45
358—Bumble-bee-458	25-28-37	107—Cannonball-810	10-17-70
816—Bumps-617	46-57-59	110—Cantaloupe-201	1-10-21
819—Bumper-692	69-71-73	147—Canvas-274	12-25-69
211—Bundle-210	12-16-40	529—Canvassing-924	15-29-39
259—Bunions-953	5- 7-77	814—Cap-413	13-16-20
050—Business-550	3-17-21	218—Capacity-381	11-32-38
815—Busy-618	32-48-50	851—Capital-861	1- 8-15
975—Busybody-497	53-54-73	289—Capture-398	28-29-73
591—Butcher-850	1-32-74	441—Car-213	5- 6-17
174—Butter-544	4- 7-15	236—Carbuncle-163	36-52-78

Figure 2.6 An excerpt from a typical dream book in which certain "lucky numbers are associated with various subjects of dreams. Numbers players often consult dream books to decide which numbers to play.

honesty and integrity? When in the line of duty an officer submits routine reports on gambling activities and then learns that for no apparent reason he is being transferred, is there not room for doubt about the integrity of his superiors or the elected officials of the community? Of course, deliberately failing to take action is quite different from being unable to act because of the peculiar legal obstacles in the area of vice control that prevent effective police action. Although the police may be fully aware of an ongoing illegal gambling operation, the requirements for taking action are much the same as those for dealing with a major felony. Before they can raid an establishment, they must have accurate information, probable cause, a search warrant, willing witnesses, and a court that will penalize the operatives to the fullest extent of the law. In many instances, gambling operations are carried on behind barred steel doors. And by the time the police are prepared to enter one of these establishments, their evidence may have completely disappeared. Several states have tried to combat this problem by passing legislation that makes it an additional crime to construct unusual barriers in buildings used for vice purposes. But the fact remains that it is one thing for the police to know that vice activity is taking place and another thing to prove it in a court of law.

Off-Track Betting

The individual who takes bets on the numbers will typically take bets on the horses as well. Through the bookie, the horse player may bet on races being run anywhere in the country. This service affords the player a number of advantages that he would have were he to actually go to the racetrack himself.

Off-Track Betting	*Betting at the Track*
• May bet on credit	• Cash bets only
• Pays no taxes on winnings	• Must pay taxes on large winnings
• May bet in own neighborhood	• Must go to track to bet
• Minimum $.50 bet	• Minimum $2 bet
• May bet parlays in one bet	• Must arrange parlay bets himself

One of the disadvantages of betting with a bookie is that very often the bookie does not pay track odds. For instance, if a particular horse wins the first race and pays 6 to 1, the bookie may only pay 4 to 1. In addition, it has become almost a tradition for a winner to tip the bookie 10 percent of his winnings.

The parlay bet mentioned above involves a player picking two, three, or more horses—one in each race he is parlaying. If his horse wins in the first race, his winnings are automatically placed on the horse he has chosen in the next race. Should this horse win, all of the player's winnings are automatically placed on his choice in the next race and so on until his parlay is completed. If any of the horses in the parlay loses, the bettor loses his entire bet.

The same hierarchical organization that exists within the numbers-game racket is also present in horse betting (see figure 2.3). Revenue passes from collector to controller to banker to organized crime. The lay-off action by the banker is the same in both cases; excessive bets on heavy favorites are laid off in order to protect the banker's operation from heavy hits.

The heart of the bookmaking operation is the "office," the central location to which bets are brought from the writer or collector. Here running totals of all bets are kept, lay-off action is arranged, and odds and point spreads are changed and modified to reflect local conditions, as well as the number and types of bets being made by the players. The office is usually run by the controller and his employees, including an accountant, telephone men, and office help. Communication between the office and the bookie is usually a one-way operation, with all calls being made from the office to the bookies. However, in some operations, the bookie may call in his bets to the office from a public phone. When this happens, the bookie is in possession of a phone number that is not directly connected to the office but rather to an electronic switching device, which is attached to a phone that may be located three blocks or so from the office. In some cases, the bookie may call a relay phone ''spot'' located in an apartment and leave his number. Then the relay operator in turn contacts the office through the ''cheese box,'' and the office telephone man returns the bookie's call. In another variation, the relay-phone-spot operator calls a stationary agent at a specified time and is given all the plays. The office telephone man then calls the relay phone spot and the plays are passed on. In this way, the office is protected. The office also receives communications from the wire service, which provides information on out-of-town races and sporting events.

Occasionally, the bettor will have a phone number at which he can contact the bookie. This may be a public phone or a phone in a bar, restaurant, or other small business. Because the bettor and the bookie are the weakest links in the communication chain, they seldom have direct phone contact with the office. (See figure 2.7.)

The office is generally run by the controller, who acts as office manager and is usually a salaried employee, although some independent operators maintain their own offices and pay a franchise fee to the syndicate in whose territory they operate. A medium-sized office may have from twenty to thirty collectors taking bets on the street and may handle a total play of approximately $200,000 a week. (See figure 2.7.)

As previously stated, the bettor and the bookie are the weakest links in the gambling chain. It is at these two points that the police are most likely to be able to make contact; successful contact at this level can lead to the office and hopefully to the banker. Undercover officers posing as bettors can often become friendly with the bookie, or at least keep him under surveillance. When the bookie transports his collections to the office or when a runner picks up the bets from the bookie, either one or both may be followed to the office. When there is probable cause for an arrest or a search warrant, officers should be on the alert for any evidence that might support the gambling charge. Most often this evidence is in the form of betting markers, which list the numbers to be played or the bettor's choice of horses. Also listed will be the track, the bettor's initials, the race, and the amount of money bet. When taking the bet, the bookie will often write the bets on ''flash paper'' or water soluble paper. These devices are also used by telephone men in the offices. Flash paper is a magician's gimmick.

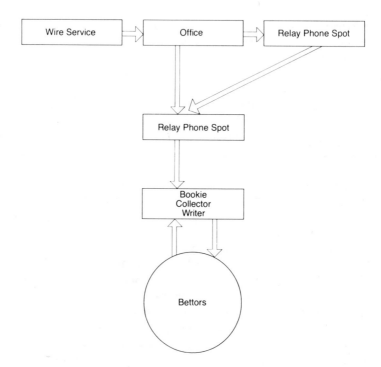

Figure 2.7 Off-track betting communication system.

When touched by a lighted cigarette or a match, it disappears in a flash and a puff of white smoke. Anything written on the paper is lost as evidence. Water-soluble paper is used almost exclusively in offices. At the onset of a police raid, the markers are swept into a bucket of water where they dissolve immediately. (See figure 2.8.)

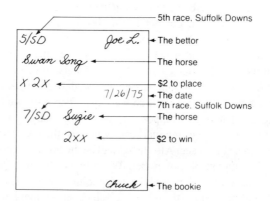

Figure 2.8 A typical horse-betting marker.

The most difficult bookie to apprehend with evidence is the one who commits all bets to memory and then phones them in from a public phone. He has no markers on his person. He will, however, have possession of the money paid by the bettor, and if vice officers have managed to bet with him and have used marked money, this will serve as evidence.

Pools: Sports Wagering

The selling of pool tickets on various sporting events, such as football, baseball, basketball, and sometimes hockey games, is the second largest form of illegal gambling in the United States. During any given sports season, thousands of pool tickets are distributed each week in factories, business establishments, schools, offices, and on the street. Each ticket lists about thirty professional and college games, including the point spread, which refers to the handicap awarded to the underdog team to balance both teams competing in the contest. The pool operator generally establishes the point spread in such a way that a tie game will result. In tie games the player loses. The more tie games, the more the operator wins. The player must choose three or more games and must indicate his selections. If any of his teams loses or ties, he automatically loses his bet. The pool seller usually makes about 90 percent profit on all bets taken, paying out only 10 percent of the bets to winners. (See figure 2.9.)

Pools do not produce much "heat" from the police and are usually left alone by organized gamblers, who tend to think of these operations as too small to be worthwhile. However, next to numbers, pools produce the highest revenue to the operators, even more than horse betting.

Lotteries

If one were to combine all the different definitions of lotteries found in the statutes of the various states, the final definition would read something like this: *A lottery is a scheme for the awarding of prizes by chance for a consideration (price), and chance rather than skill must be the predominant element in such award.* According to this definition, a lottery would have to include all the following elements in order to be considered illegal:

1. The awarding of prizes
2. Chance (random drawing or some other random method)
3. Payment by the player to participate in the drawing
4. No special skill required on the part of the player

An Example of an Illegal Lottery

A local grocery store announces that it will give away a boat and a trailer. Each customer who purchases five dollars' worth of groceries will be given a ticket to fill out and drop into a revolving drum. On a specified date, one ticket

COLLEGE SCHEDULE

35 49 516 630 740 860 9100 10150 971025

OCTOBER 27

1	N. Carol. St.	2	Clemson	10
3	Harvard	4	Dartmouth	13
5	Miami (Fla.)	6	Syracuse	17
7	Pittsburgh	8	Navy	8
9	Pennsylvania	10	Princeton	6
11	Virginia	12	Wake Forest	14
13	Houston	14	Auburn	3
15	Yale	16	Cornell	4
17	Maryland	18	Duke	10
19	Georgia	20	Kentucky	11
21	Notre Dame	22	Southern Cal.	1
23	Tennessee	24	Tex. Christ.	20
25	Texas A & M	26	Baylor	7
27	Illinois	28	Iowa	13
29	Wisconsin	30	Indiana	7
31	Kansas	32	Iowa St.	7
33	Purdue	34	Michigan St.	7
35	Michigan	36	Minnesota	20
37	Mississippi	38	Vanderbilt	14
39	Nebraska	40	Oklahoma St.	10
41	Missouri	42	Colorado	3
43	Oregon	44	Wash.	7
45	Stanford	46	Wash. St.	E
47	L.S.U.	48	So. Carolina	13
49	Tulane	50	Geo. Tech.	7
51	Arizona State	52	Oregon St.	17

OCTOBER 27

①	2	3	4	5	6	7	8	9	10
11	12	13	14	15	16	17	18	19	20
21	22	23	24	25	26	27	28	29	30
31	32	33	34	35	36	37	38	39	40
41	42	43	44	45	46	47	48	49	50
51	52	53	54						

Figure 2.9 A typical football pool ticket. Tickets such as this are sold by the hundreds of thousands each week during the football season. Note the point spread for each pair of teams in the extreme right-hand column.

will be drawn to determine the winner. Note that in this example all of the elements of the crime are present: a prize will be awarded by random drawing (chance), participants have to purchase something in order to be eligible, and no special skill is required.

An Example of a Legal Lottery

A national magazine mails lottery tickets to millions of homes around the country announcing that it will award thousands of prizes in a random drawing. Participants are asked to indicate whether they wish to subscribe to the magazine and are assured that whether they decide to subscribe or not, their tickets will have an equal chance of winning. On a specified date the drawing is held and all the prizes are awarded. Note that in this example all of the elements but one are present: an award of prizes, a random drawing, and no special skill required. What makes this particular type of lottery legal is the fact that no price is charged to participate. The fact that this activity results in thousands of new subscribers to the magazine has no bearing on the legality of the operation.

Another Example of a Legal Lottery

A national organization sends contest blanks to homes all over the country. The contest consists of unscrambling the names of U.S. presidents. From the names of those who successfully identify all of the presidents, a drawing will be held and prizes awarded. Each contestant pays one dollar to enter the contest. Again, all of the elements but one are present: a random drawing, the awarding of prizes, an entry fee. In this case, the element of skill has been interjected (the contestant must unscramble the names of presidents). The fact that a certain amount of skill is required to participate in the contest is what makes this lottery legal.

Among the more common illegal lotteries in the United States are the Irish Sweepstakes, the Treasury Balance Lottery, bingo (illegal only in certain states), church penny sales, and various automobile giveaways. Numbers and policy, treated elsewhere in this chapter, are also illegal lotteries.

Betting Information

In order for the organized gambler to operate successfully, he must have quick access to betting information from all over the country—odds, post times at the track, scratched horses, jockeys, winners (win, place, and show horses in each race), pari-mutuel handles, and so on. Without this information at his fingertips, the organized gambler could not operate the horsebook. This information is available through legitimate sources, but usually not until late in the evening or early the next day. If a bookmaker or controller is interested in obtaining information about the odds, horses, races, or track conditions at a particular track, he must make arrangements to receive the information through other than legitimate channels. To obtain the needed information, bookmakers usually subscribe to an illegal wire service which provides gamblers with up-to-date information from all of the racetracks around the country. Wire services of the illegal variety are usually operated by organized criminals. Transmission of gambling information in interstate or foreign commerce is a federal crime, and because the risk is great and obtaining the information difficult, the subscriber to the illegal wire service pays a premium for the service.

Title 18 of the U.S. Code, Section 1084, says that it is a federal felony offense for any person:

- To engage in the business of betting or wagering.
- To knowingly use a wire communication facility for the transmission of gambling information in interstate or foreign commerce, including bets or wagers, information assisting in the placing of bets on any sporting event or contest which entitles the recipient to receive money or credit as a result of bets or wagers, or any information assisting in any of the above.

One would expect that it would be a simple matter to obtain information from a particular track by having a confederate who is stationed at the track go to the nearest public telephone and call in the information. In order to prevent such occurrences, public telephones at racetracks are shut off prior to the opening of betting windows for the first race. No phone calls may be made from local tracks during the running of the race. In the event of emergencies, calls may be made only from carefully controlled and monitored phones. Bookmakers have developed many elaborate schemes to get around this prohibition. In cities where the track is located near high buildings, confederates inside the track relay betting information to others stationed outside, but within view of, the track by means of hand signals. The information is then relayed to the illegal wire service for interstate transmission or for conveyance to a local bookmaker. In other instances, entire teams of spotters have been sent to the track. As each race is run, a team member leaves the track and relays the information by phone or radio to those waiting for the information. The advent of sophisticated electronic equipment has made it much easier for gamblers to relay information from the track to their cohorts on the outside.

Legalized Gambling

The American people are fond of gambling. In fact, roughly 60 percent of the population of this country has at one time or another gambled on some game of chance. Despite the fact that we take pride in our reputation as hardworking people who achieve by doing, we tend to believe in luck, and all have within us the desire to get something for nothing. For this reason most Americans have extremely ambivalent attitudes toward gambling and the existing antigambling laws. These attitudes have been manifested in a number of ways in recent years: the growing popularity of the gambling spas of Nevada, the only state in which gambling in its many forms is legal; the passage of legislation in thirteen states establishing state-run lotteries; the legalization of off-track betting in New York, and the continuing study of ways to establish legal numbers games in that state. Of course, we must not forget bingo, penny sales, automobile giveaways, and other forms of gambling conducted by churches and other charitable organizations as a means of fund raising. Although most of the latter games are technically illegal in every state, both the public and the law-enforcement establishment close their eyes to this type of gambling.

Legalized gambling might well be the answer to the problem that law-enforcement agencies face when attempting to enforce the unenforceable. It might also serve as a means of removing from organized crime the monopoly created by law that has afforded criminals the funds to finance other nefarious rackets, such as loan sharking and narcotics. Logical arguments have been put forth by both the proponents and the opponents of legalized gambling. In 1950, the late O. W. Wilson (1950, p. 303) wrote:

> At the outset it must be said that the discussion of this police problem will strictly adhere to the principle of absolute repression of vice conditions. No half-way measure or concession is compatible with good police administration. Legalizing vice operations only multiplies the evils, and official sanction and regulation do not solve the problem. The police administrator must treat vice offenses in the same manner as other criminal offenses. There can be no compromise with commercialized vice.

During its 1972 investigation of police corruption (mainly in connection with gambling) in New York City, the Knapp Commission (1972, p. 18) made the following proposal:

> The criminal laws against gambling should be repealed. To the extent that the legislature deems that some control over gambling is appropriate, such regulation should be by civil rather than criminal process. The police should in any event be relieved from any responsibility for the enforcement of gambling laws or regulations.

Organized crime takes millions of dollars annually from those communities in which illegal gambling enterprises are operated. State-run or -licensed gambling could funnel these funds back into the coffers of our financially hard-pressed cities and counties. Money which now finances narcotics and loan-sharking operations might conceivably be used to institute much needed educational and health programs; likewise, the hundreds of thousands of police hours currently being devoted to the suppression of illegal gambling might better be used in the prevention of crimes that constitute a much greater threat to our people.

Despite the fact that there appears to be a trend toward the legalization of gambling, the antigambling laws do still exist and thus it is the responsibility of the police to try to enforce them.

Enforcement Techniques

As has been stated above, the single, most satisfactory enforcement method against organized gambling appears to be legalization. If, on the other hand, we become convinced that gambling should be stamped out, perhaps an addition to our present gambling laws should be considered. Under the antigambling laws of most states, any person who participates in any activity which furthers gambling is culpable. If police departments let it be known that individual players would be arrested and prosecuted as well as the bookies, many of organized gambling's customers would disappear. In those states in which the player is not included in the law, a section pertaining to the bettor should be added. Publicity to this effect should greatly reduce the number of players.

As one looks at the table of organization for the typical gambling operation, it becomes clear that several weak points exist within the organizational structure. First, the most vulnerable figure in the operation is the runner; this person is particularly visible, whether mobile or stationary, because it is he who moves about the neighborhood collecting bets from customers. Thus, the runner is most susceptible to surveillance and apprehension. Properly conducted surveillance can lead police to the controller and eventually to the office. Although the office is usually well hidden and is sometimes disguised in ingenious ways and moved regularly, a well-conducted surveillance, plus the cooperation of the local telephone company, can nevertheless lead to its location. Once officers manage to locate the office, they should move in as quietly as possible. Office records are often kept on water-soluble paper or flash paper. At the slightest indication of a raid, records are stuffed into a bucket of water and disappear, or a lighted cigar is touched to them and they go up in a puff of smoke.

Entrance into the office should be made as quickly and as quietly as possible. Whenever possible, an undercover officer should be stationed inside the premises prior to the raid. The undercover officer's job is to open the doors (which are usually heavily barricaded). Once entrance is made, everyone present should be immobilized and placed in a location away from the papers and records. Everything in the office—records, papers, furniture, telephones—should be catalogued and seized as evidence. All paraphernalia used in the operation is admissible as evidence.

When arresting a mobile runner, everything he uses to carry out his part of the operation should be seized—betting slips, his car if he is using one, pens, paper, address books, anything that could possibly be relevant to his illegal activities. Sometimes these items can provide valuable information leading to the higher-ups in the organization.

Locating the stationary runner in a bar, candy store, gas station, and so on can usually be accomplished through an informer or an undercover officer. Surveillance should be set up to establish probable cause for a search warrant. Officers should be on the lookout for any unusual activity, such as an inappropriately large number of customers for the type of business being conducted, the presence of known gamblers, visits by a mobile runner or controller who is known to the police. If possible, an officer should try to place a bet in the establishment. Once the surveillance team is convinced that they have established probable cause to believe that the establishment is being used as a front for gambling, they should apply for a search warrant and set up a raid. Again, if evidence of gambling is found, everything in the shop should be catalogued and seized as evidence.

The penalties for gambling, in most jurisdictions, are relatively light, and, more often than not, those arrested and brought to trial are only required to pay a small fine or serve a short sentence. Among organized gamblers, these fines and short stays in jail are considered part of the overhead costs of doing business. It is fair to say that the types of penalties imposed on these individuals do not serve as a deterrent to the gambling operation.

After convictions in court, the police should not cease their antigambling activities. They must continue to arrest offenders time and time again, if necessary. After a number of convictions, an operator may decide to move out of town, but this is unlikely. The record of conviction can, however, be used by the police in another enforcement tactic that has often proved worthwhile. Mobile runners who take bets in bars, barbershops, and other places of business on their routes do so with the cooperation of the owners of these establishments. Almost every business in any city operates under a number of licenses administered by the state or local licensing authority. The police should bring notice of gambling violations and convictions to the attention of the licensing authority. In many instances, this will result in suspension or revocation of the owner's license and thus put the stationary runner and those who allow their premises to be used for gambling out of business for a while.

Recognizing an Illegal Gambling Operation

The Technical Assistance Division of the Law Enforcement Assistance Administration (1972, pp. 32–40) listed a number of routine observations made by uniformed patrolmen which could indicate the presence of an illegal gambling operation on an officer's beat.

1. A candy store, grocery store, drug store, or other retail establishment seems to be doing a brisk business—many customers coming and going. But the customers do not remain in the store very long and do not leave with packages or

other evidence that purchases were made. The store may have a meager selection of merchandise, which raises the question of how it can attract so many customers day after day. *This could indicate the presence of a policy or numbers operation at the writer level, or the place of business of a bookmaker's commissionman.*

2. At about the same time each day, a package is delivered to a newsstand, bar, or other location. Later the package is picked up by another individual. *The newsstand or whatever could be a policy or numbers drop—the place to which a numbers writer sends his slips and/or day's receipts.*

3. A number is chalked on a street-lamp pole. The same number is observed in other locations. *It might be the winning number for the day's number or policy play.*

4. A parked car—often double parked—is observed daily at the same location and at the same time. The driver remains in the vehicle while a number of "friends" come up to say hello. *Such a situation may indicate bet-taking activity.*

5. A well-dressed individual is often seen driving an expensive late model car in the area. No one seems to know what his occupation is. One patrolman pursued observations similar to this and found out that *the individual was a policy operator* and had been for 21 years, without so much as an arrest. On the basis of this information and further investigation, a special squad of detectives made a case against the operator and his employers.

6. Determining who the bettors are in your area can be as important as knowing who the bookmakers are—indeed, many times the identification of a bettor leads to the identification of a bookie. Patrolmen have identified bettors through conversations with those on their posts—sometimes even by observing who buys racing forms. In some instances, you may even get close enough to a bettor to observe the number dialed when the bet is placed. *Observations such as these could trigger an investigation leading to the prosecution of the upper echelon or organized crime's gambling hierarchy.*

7. Certain individuals always seem to frequent a certain bar although none of them live in the neighborhood. *Perhaps they use the bar as a bet-taking center.*

8. A club shuts down at irregular times—sometimes early in the afternoon, other times at mid-evening. Do these times coincide with the completion of racing or when the results of other sporting events become available? *If so, the club may be a base for gambling operations.*

Source: Technical Assistance Division of the Law Enforcement Assistance Administration, 1972.

While many of these observations may seem unimportant in themselves and alone may not constitute a case, when combined with information gathered by other officers, they may provide the missing link that will make the case. Do not worry about whether your observations are significant or important. Let those to whom your information is sent judge for themselves. In other words, let others do the evaluating. Always assume that others do not know what you are about to report. Report everything you believe might be somehow related to an organized crime operation.

ADDENDUM

During its studies in preparation for publication of *Legal Gambling in New York**, the Fund for the City of New York developed some interesting observations on the gambling habits of the residents of New York City:

1. Eight in ten adult residents of New York City report betting money at some time on games of chance and sporting events.
2. Three-quarters have played the New York or other state lotteries.
3. Some 36 percent in total say they bet on sports such as football, baseball, basketball, and horse racing. Betting on the horses is most popular—30 percent of adults have bet.
4. A quarter of the city's population plays the numbers. If the game were legalized, almost half of all adults with an opinion (45 percent) say they would be probable or almost certain legal numbers players. Virtually every current numbers player would play the legal game if it were convenient for him to play.
5. Very strong support also exists for legalizing the numbers game. Close to two-thirds of all adults, and over three-quarters with an opinion, say the numbers should be legalized.
6. Most numbers players play the game frequently. Over 40 percent play daily, and an additional 30 percent play two or three times a week. The most popular or typical amount bet per day is one dollar (35 percent), with far more of the remaining bets over a dollar (47 percent) per day than under a dollar (18 percent).
7. We estimate that at least 1.5 million dollars are bet on the numbers per day by New York City adults, or more than half a billion dollars per year.
8. Few numbers players have any difficulty placing bets—either in their own neighborhood or where they work. Most of them do, however, have to go someplace to meet their runner or collector.
9. Very few numbers players are extended credit by operators of the game. Even fewer are extended loans for purposes other than playing the numbers.
10. The numbers game is not the exclusively black or ghetto game it is so frequently portrayed. More whites (55 percent) than blacks and Puerto Ricans combined (45 percent) are numbers players at present. The num-

---

*Fund for the City of New York, *Legal Gambling in New York: A Discussion of Numbers and Sports Betting* (Appendix, Study 1458-A, March 1972), pp. 36–37.

bers game is more white and middle class than nonwhite and poor in terms of who the players are.

11. While higher percentages of Puerto Ricans and blacks both play the numbers now and are probable players in a legalized game, more whites are likely to play legalized numbers because whites are by far the largest racial group in the city's population.

In relation to betting on sports, the Fund for the City of New York found that*:

1. Some 1.4 million adults, which is one-fourth of the adult population, bet on football, basketball, or baseball last year.
2. Heavy sports bettors (500 dollars a year or more) constitute 5 percent of the adult population; moderate bettors (100 to 499 dollars) are 8 percent of the population; light bettors (less than 100 dollars per year) are 12 percent of the adult population.
3. More adults report placing bets on baseball (18 percent or 1.0 million people) than on football (15 percent or .86 million people) or basketball (13 percent or .77 million people).
4. Sports bettors also bet a good deal on other events such as horse racing, cards, and the numbers. They do not limit their betting to sports by any means.
5. The great majority of those who bet on football or basketball or baseball are men—80 percent or more for all three sports.
6. Betting on sports is primarily middle class behavior. Two-thirds of bettors on all three sports hold down white-collar or blue-collar jobs.
7. Football betting is a little bit more upscale in terms of who bets on it than either basketball or baseball, while basketball, the "city game," draws substantially more black bettors. While baseball now has more bettors in total, football and basketball are attracting more young bettors and would appear to be the growth sports as far as betting on sports is concerned.
8. Over 850,000 New Yorkers bet on football games last year. Fully 71 percent report that all or most of their bets were placed on pro games.
9. Two-thirds of those who bet on football games say that most or all of their bets are made strictly with friends or acquaintances—legal bets. But of the over 282 million dollars bet on football last year, 188 million, or two-thirds of all dollars, was bet with bookmakers. This is because heavy sports bettors account for 85 percent of all dollars bet on football, with three-

---

*Op cit., Appendix, Study 1493, pp. 49–51.

quarters of all their bets being placed with bookmakers. Few moderate or light bettors, on the other hand, bet much with bookmakers.

10. About 765,000 New Yorkers bet on basketball games last year. Again, the great majority were on pro games rather than college games, and again, most bets were legal ones made with friends. But when it comes to dollars, of the 193 million dollars bet, 118 million dollars were bet with bookmakers, or 61 percent of the total. As with football, heavy bettors account for a very high percentage of all dollars bet on basketball (81 percent), with most of these dollars (73 percent) bet with bookies.

11. Some 1,045,500 adult New York City residents bet two or more times on baseball games last year. Over 212 million dollars was bet, with bookies accounting for about 121 million dollars or 57 percent of all dollars bet. This is again due to a minority of baseball bettors—the heavy bettors who bet primarily with bookmakers.

12. In total, over 688 million dollars was wagered on the three sports last year in New York City by its adult residents. Over 60 percent of this sum, or about 428 million dollars, was bet with bookmakers. Private bets with friends account for a third of the total, or some 225 million dollars, with 5 percent or 35 million dollars being bet on cards or betting sheets. Most of this latter sum was bet on football cards.

13. More money is bet on football games (41 percent) than baseball (31 percent) or basketball (28 percent). This is because far more money is bet on football cards than basketball or baseball cards combined, and because considerably more money is bet with bookmakers on football than either of the other two sports.

14. The great majority of bettors say that they never bet on credit. Even among heavy bettors, only 31 percent say that half or more of their wagers are made on a credit basis. An even higher percentage say they never bet by telephone (84 percent), although this may well be due to bookmaker reluctance to transact business by phone. Most bets are not made at work, or going to and from work.

15. Sports bettors are all for legalizing sports betting in New York State. Over 90 percent support the idea, with 82 percent supporting legalization strongly. Their major reason for supporting it is that society would benefit from it—primarily in terms of increased revenue for the city and state, but also because it would eliminate corruption and cut into organized crime.

16. The vast majority of sports bettors say they would participate in a legalized sports betting operation. Fully 90 percent say they would either probably bet or be almost certain to bet. Among heavy bettors, and those who now bet with bookmakers, intention to "bet legal" is even higher: 85 percent in both groups say they would be almost certain to bet in a legalized sports operation.

19. These findings on intention to bet in a legalized sports betting operation are buttressed from our findings from sports bettors who also bet on horses.

Almost 50 percent of these bettors say that half or more of their bets used to be placed with bookies, with heavy horse bettors, who account for most dollars bet on horses, reporting that most of their betting used to be with bookmakers. Now, horse bettors report only a quarter of their current dollars going to bookmakers, with OTB and the tracks, in that order, getting the lion's share. Among those who still bet with bookmakers, almost 60 percent say they are betting less money with them than they did before OTB opened shop, while a third say they are betting about the same amount as before, and only 2 percent that they are now betting more with bookmakers on horses.

From "A Study of Betting on Sports in New York City," pp. 49–51, *Legal Gambling in New York: A Discussion of Numbers and Sports Betting.* Copyright 1972 by Fund for the City of New York. Reprinted by permission.

GLOSSARY OF GAMBLING TERMS

ACTION. Any type of gambling activity either by the bookmaker or by the bettor.

AGENT. A bookie, bookmaker, or runner. One who takes bets.

BANK. The central gambling office. Provides funds for payoffs.

BANKER. The biggest gambling operator in the city. Provides money to pay off all winners, validates all bets, settles disputes, pays for protection.

BET. The wager of money or property on a contest of speed, a game of chance, or any incident by which both parties stand to win or lose by chance.

BLEEDER. In numbers, to bet on the last two numbers of a three-digit number. For example, in the number 123 the bleeder would be 23.

BOLIDA. *See* BLEEDER.

BOOK, BOOKIE. An agent. One who takes bets on numbers, horses, pools.

BOX. In numbers, to bet on all the possible combinations of a three-digit number—for example, 123, 132, 231, 213, 312, 321. Indicated on the slip by writing the number inside a box.

BREAKAGE. The odd cents left in a betting pool at the race track. This money traditionally goes to the state.

CASH ROOM. The office where all bets are taken and computed before being sent to the bank.

CHEESE BOX. A small telephone switching device installed in the room containing the telephone whose number is given to bettors. The device automatically switches calls to another phone at another location. Used to protect the location of the office.

COLLECTOR. A bookie. One who collects bets and money from players.

CUT NUMBER. A number on which the bookie usually pays only half the standard odds such as the date, triple numbers, 711, and so forth.

DAILY DOUBLE. In horse racing, a bet in which the player attempts to choose the winners of the first two races.

FLASH PAPER. A special type of paper on which the bookie records bets. When touched by a lighted match or cigarette it explodes in a puff of white smoke and ashes.

GAMBLING DEVICE. Any equipment used in gambling, such as dice, cards, slot machine, pool card, and so on.

GAME OF CHANCE. Any game, the outcome of which is determined by chance and in which no element of skill is involved in determining the winner or loser.

HALF NUMBER. *See* CUT NUMBER.

HAND BOOK. The place or establishment where bets are made on horses, numbers, or sporting events.

IN. A contact. The person or method or code used to contact the bookie and to identify the bettor as one who can be trusted.

LAY-OFF. The process by which the bookie, controller, or banker rebets money originally bet on a heavy favorite. A method of insurance used by gambling operators to spread their risk.

LEAD. The first number of a three-digit number. A bet in which the player attempts to guess the first digit of the three-digit winning number. For example, in the number 123 the lead is 1.

LINE. The calculated odds on any gambling event.

LOTTERY. A scheme for the distribution of prizes by chance, for a consideration. Chance, rather than skill, must be the predominant element in an illegal lottery.

MARKER. A betting slip showing that one person owes money to another. An I.O.U. A promissory note.

MORNING LINE. A complete rundown of the odds on all gambling events distributed on the morning of the day on which the event is to take place.

NUMBERS. A gambling game in which the player attempts to choose the winning three-digit number each day.

ODDS. The amount by which the bet of one party to a wager exceeds the bet of the other party. For example, 2-to-1 odds means that if the bettor wins, the bookie will pay him two times the amount of his bet.

OFFICE. The place to which bets collected from the bookies are taken. The place of operation of the controller.

OFF-TRACK ODDS. The odds paid by the bookie to winning players who bet on horse races with him. Usually lower than the odds paid to winners at the track.

PARLAY. A type of horse-racing bet in which the bettor bets on a horse in an early race. If he wins, his winnings are automatically bet on a horse in a succeeding race. The bet is described by the number of succeeding bets made—for example, two-horse parlay, three-horse parlay, and so on.

PAST POSTING. A fraud in which a bettor tries to cheat the bookie by betting on a horse race in which he already knows the winner. Success depends on the bettor's obtaining information on the race before the bookie does.

PHONE SPOT. The location of a telephone at which a player may reach a bookie in order to place his bets.

PLACE. The second finishing position in a horse race. If a horse comes in second in a race, we say that he "placed."

POINT SPREAD. In sports betting, the number of points given to the underdog team in order to theoretically make the contest end in a draw. A bettor may choose a team and x points or choose a team and give points to the bookie.

POLICY. A numbers game in which certain numbers—usually about twelve or thirteen—are chosen from a possible seventy-eight numbers. Players choose numbers and bet any amount of money on their choices. Seventy-eight numbers are drawn. If any of their numbers are drawn they win.

POOLS. A betting strategy in which all bets are placed in a pool. Winners share the entire pool, less operating costs.

POOR MAN'S ROULETTE. The numbers or policy game.

POST TIME. In horse racing, the time when the horses are to be in the starting gate for the start of the race. At this time, the pari-mutuel windows are closed and no further bets are taken on that particular race.

RACING FORM. A newspaper devoted to horse racing. Prints results of all the previous day's races and the entries of today's races with past performance records of all horses entered in all races around the country.

RELAY SPOT. A location of the premises where bets are taken prior to their relay to the office. Also, the location of a phone to which a cheese box has been connected to relay phone bets to the location of the bookie.

RUNNER (MOBILE). A bookie who moves from place to place in order to pick up bets from his customers.

RUNNER (STATIONARY). A bookie who takes bets in a set location, such as a bar, barbershop, restaurant, cab stand, or candy store.

SCRATCH SHEET. A racing form which publishes results of yesterday's races and all entries in today's races, including past performances of the horses entered in races around the country.

SHOW. The third finishing position in a horse race. If a horse comes in third in a race, we say that he "showed."

SINGLE ACTION. *See* LEAD.

SLIPS. Betting slips on which both the bettor and the bookie record the bets.

SPOT. A location where bets may be made on the numbers, horses, or sporting events.

TOTE BOARD. A totalizer or totalizator. A large, lighted board set in the infield of a race track on which the numbers of the horses entered in a race and the odds on each horse are indicated. After the race, the tote board shows the win, place, and show horse, plus the amount of money that will be paid for each two-dollar bet on the first three horses.

TRACK ODDS. The odds that are paid to winners who bet on race horses at the track. Usually higher than the odds paid by a bookie.

WIN. The first finishing position in a horse race. If a horse comes in first in a race, he is designated as the "win" horse.

WIRE SERVICE. An agency or business that syndicates gambling information. Usually uses telephone lines. This type of operation is against federal law.

REFERENCES

Fund for the City of New York. *Legal Gambling in New York*. New York, 1972.

[Knapp] Commission to Investigate Allegations of Police Corruption. *Summary and Principal Recommendations*. New York, 1972.

Law Enforcement Assistance Administration. *Police Guide on Organized Crime*. Washington, D.C.: U.S. Government Printing Office, 1972.

Lentini, Joseph R., and France, James G. *Ohio Peace Officer's Manual*. Cincinnati: W. H. Anderson Co., 1972.

"Market Statistics at a Glance." *Cleveland Plain Dealer* (January 3, 1974).

Moynihan, Daniel P. "The Private Government of Crime." In *Crime in America,* edited by Bruce J. Cohen. Itasca, Ill.: F. E. Peacock, 1970.

Wilson, O. W. *Police Administration*. New York: McGraw-Hill, 1950.

Chapter 3

Loan Sharking

Charlie Taylor (the name is fictitious) works on the production line of a large East Coast manufacturing company. His take-home pay is $168.40 a week. Charlie's job is a dull, repetitive one, performed mechanically amid the din of machinery and the shouted conversations of his coworkers. One of the few pleasures in Charlie's life—other than his days off—is his daily bet on the horses running at the various tracks around the country. He places his bets with the company bookie, a "tool hustler" who pushes a cart of tools up and down the production line and generally has access to most sections of the plant. The bookie collects Charlie's bets each day, and the two settle accounts on payday. If Charlie wins, the money is a welcome addition to his paycheck. If he loses, he pays the tab. Usually the amount of money that changes hands ranges from $5 to $25. Charlie is a typical small bettor.

For the past two weeks, Charlie has been having a run of bad luck. At the end of the first week, he had lost $50 to the bookie. When payday came, he explained that he could not pay him because $50 from his pay envelope would be a hardship on his family and his wife would raise the roof. The bookie agreed to carry the account for another week. Charlie, of course, hoped to hit a few horses and break even, but his bad luck held, and at the end of the second week he owed $110 and was still unable to pay his gambling debts. The bookie suggested that they meet in the tavern across from the plant after work and discuss the matter.

That evening, over a couple of beers, the bookie explained that he could no longer carry the tab and suggested that Charlie get a loan to pay his debt. He convinced Charlie to pay him $10 in cash and to take a loan from a shark named Lew Gaylor, who just happens to be sitting down at the end of the bar. Lew joins the two in a booth and explains the loan to Charlie. He will lend Charlie $100 for a week. Charlie will be expected to pay back $6 for every $5 he borrows. If he can't pay back the loan plus the interest on time the interest will be compounded the following week. Lew will be glad to accept the interest payment at any time and carry the principal as long as Charlie understands that he must pay six for every five on the outstanding balance. Charlie, always the optimist, agrees to Lew's terms and accepts the loan. However, as each payday rolls around, he repeatedly finds himself unable to pay either the loan or the interest, or as Lew calls it "the vigorish."* At the end of four weeks Charlie is deeply in debt. The financial structure of the loan and the vigorish look like this:

Amount owed at beginning of week		Amount owed at end of week
First week	$100.00	$120.00
Second week	$120.00	$144.00
Third week	$144.00	$172.80
Fourth week	$172.80	$207.36

At the end of the fourth week, Charlie manages to make a payment of $100.00 leaving a balance of $107.36. He goes through another period of four weeks without making a payment and his debt builds. He makes another payment of $100 and still owes Lew the principal of the loan. If this process were to continue for six months, Charlie would have paid Lew $600 in vigorish and would still be in the same position he was in at the beginning of the first week. Lew, of course, is not interested in the principal amount of the loan so long as Charlie continues to pay the vigorish. In fact, he would be content to allow the loan to go on indefinitely.

After six months, Charlie, harried and worried, realizes that he has been taken by a loan shark. Unless he does something soon, he will spend the rest of his life trying to pay off his debts. He tells Lew that since he has already paid $600 interest on the $100 loan, he does not intend to pay anymore. Unlike most lenders, Lew does not begin to send dunning letters and he does not threaten to take Charlie to court to collect what is owed him. Lew doesn't do these things because he is in violation of the usury laws, which prohibit the lending of money at exorbitant rates of interest and which also prohibit making loans without being licensed to do so. His collection methods are more direct. One night as Charlie leaves the plant, two strangers fall into step beside him and he is led to a car parked at the curb. Inside the car Lew sits with a smile on his face. He calmly explains to Charlie that the vigorish has been doubled because of Charlie's refusal to pay. He also explains that if he allows Charlie to default, all of his other borrowers will try to renege as Charlie has done and that they must make an example of Charlie. When Charlie leaves the car, his face is a bloody mass of cuts and bruises and his head rings with threats of death and injury to his wife and children. Feeling that he has no other alternative, Charlie continues to pay on his loan. Lew manages to spread the word throughout the plant that Charlie's "accident" occurred because he failed to pay his loan. Lew's other customers promptly pay any arrears to keep themselves from having a similar "accident."

Vigorish is the underworld term for the interest and other penalties and charges imposed on a usurious loan.

Background of Loan Sharking

Charlie's plight is typical of what happens to the small borrower in the loan-shark operation, which has been estimated to be the second largest income producer for organized crime. The profits from loan-sharking are estimated to range from $20 to $50 billion a year. This is a far cry from the almost nonexistent racket of the twenties. In the 1930s—the years of the Great Depression— loan sharking grew to nationwide racket proportions in the major East Coast cities and in the industrial cities of the Midwest. By the end of World War II, loan sharking was an accepted racket in organized crime cities across the nation.

As the second largest income-producing activity of organized crime, loan sharking, or, as it is called in several sections of the country, "the juice racket" or "shylocking," is not a business in which an independent operator is allowed to make a living. Initial operating capital is provided by income from gambling. Territories are franchised to "family" employees, and competitors who are not "related" are discouraged from entering the operation in family-held territory. A small operator like Lew can make loans of up to $20,000 with interest rates ranging from the traditional six for five to as much as 100 percent for a specified time period. In the family hierarchy, Lew would probably be a "soldier," running his racket with the approval of the bosses and paying a percentage of his profits for the privilege. Lew would also be expected to provide a living for other, lesser lights in the family, using them as "enforcers" or collectors.

Lew's customers would include blue-collar workers like Charlie, small businessmen who are unable to borrow money from legitimate lending institutions, small-time gamblers seeking one more chance to hit it big, and small-time criminals needing funds to finance their schemes. Occasionally, someone who owes money to one loan shark will try to borrow from another to pay his debts. According to the rules, such action would be an infringement on territorial rights and is strictly prohibited. Even though the small shark may lend up to $20,000, there are times when he is expected to ask permission to make a specific loan. Those times occur when the prospective borrower is a person in whom the family might take an interest. Among these types of borrowers are labor union officials, public officials, employees of stock brokerage firms, and others having positions of prestige in legitimate business. Borrowers seeking amounts of more than $20,000 are referred to family representatives who handle the big-money loans. This type of control is enforced because loan sharking is one of the most common strategies for achieving family control of labor unions, immunity from prosecution, channels for redistributing hot money and securities, and legitimate business fronts for family rackets.

Loans made to union officials are often the "foot in the door" for underworld control of the unions. Should the official be unable to pay the usurious interest, he may be offered a deal. For example, his loan may be amortized in return for his support of particular candidates for union office—typically those offices which handle and control union pension, slush, and investment funds. From this type of base, the family can conduct many different types of profitable activities. These might include, for example, the use of union funds to finance family-owned real estate development in retirement or resort areas, "sweetheart" deals with employers whereby, for a specified fee, the family will guarantee that there will be no labor problems in the employer's business, outright theft from dues funds, the opportunity to provide jobs for family members, and extortion from rank-and-file union members in order for them to work.

Public officials, fearing that their applications for loans from legitimate lenders might become public and generate investigations into their finances, often borrow from illegal channels. Once caught in the web, they become easy prey for the sharks, who demand that city contracts be awarded to family-controlled construction companies, that judges protect family members accused of crime, or that police officials develop blind spots in regard to family activities in certain parts of the cities. Often the public official is forced to bring pressure against competitors to family-owned operations in an effort to put them out of business.

The Chamber of Commerce of the United States in a publication titled *White Collar Crime* (1974, pp. 48–49) describes the theft of securities from New York brokerage firms and the countermeasures which have been taken against the thieves:

> To avoid detection of thefts, cooperative employees (often pressured by loan sharks) can warn their outside contacts about impending audits. In one case a brokerage house employee alerted those who possessed ABC bonds stolen from the firm that an audit was scheduled covering securities in the A to M range. ABC bonds were returned and stolen N to Z securities substituted.

In other securities operations, employees in debt to loan sharks have amortized their loans by substituting counterfeit bonds for genuine securities and then turning the stolen bonds over to the loan sharks. Once they have committed a theft of this kind, they are further pressured to continue the thefts or to provide information on security precautions.

The loan shark is often engaged in providing funds for professional criminals. The President's Commission on Law Enforcement and the Administration of Justice (1967, *Task Force Report: Crime and Its Impact—An Assessment,* pp. 99–100) quotes Sutherland and Maurer in describing this practice:

> The loan shark . . . may meet the professional criminal's needs for cash in emergencies, but this activity often has secondary effects which tend to be detrimental to his clients.

Professional criminals may turn to the loan shark to finance crimes which require extra amounts of capital—to buy the tools, or whatever may be needed for the operation, or to bribe public officials. The professional criminal may be willing to pay usurious interest rates (sometimes reported to be as high as 100 percent per week for highly risky loans) if he expects his activities to be particularly lucrative. He may also need emergency financing when apprehended to pay bail and legal costs. To repay the money borrowed plus interest upon his release, the criminal will often engage in further criminal activities, often more risky than those he ordinarily undertakes. If rearrested he must post bond again and incur additional legal fees. This pattern may be repeated a number of times before he is finally brought to trial. The high interest charged by the loan shark may thus itself precipitate criminal activity.

In the same vein, a used-car dealer in a major East Coast city was selling "cream puffs" on his lot. He also had a number of "junkers" for sale. The junkers were a favorite dream of the teen-agers in the neighborhood. The dealer sold the junk cars to the kids for an extremely small down payment with the balance to be paid at six for five per week. Naturally, the young people could not pay their debts within the allotted time and were then pressured by collectors to pay off the loans by stealing late-model cars which were then disguised in the dealer's garage and shipped to Florida, where they were sold.

The president's commission also describes criminal groups that satisfy defaulted loans by taking over businesses, hiring professional arsonists to burn buildings and contents, and then collecting on the fire insurance. Another tactic was illustrated in the recent bankruptcy of a meat-packing firm in which control was secured as payment for gambling debts. With the original owners remaining in nominal management positions, extensive product orders were placed through established lines of credit, and the goods were immediately sold at low prices before the suppliers were paid. The organized criminal group made a quick profit of three-quarters of a million dollars by pocketing the receipts from the sale of the products ordered and placing the firm in bankruptcy without paying the suppliers. This same kind of operation has taken place many times to satisfy defaulted loans from the loan sharks. The process is called "a bankruptcy scam."

There are also indications that loan sharking may have significant effects on the rates of criminal recidivism. Paroled convicts, failing to find employment and in need of money to support their families, may borrow from the loan sharks. When they are unable to make their payments, they are pressured back into crime in order to satisfy the demands of the loan sharks.

In actual practice, the loan shark operates in several ways: first, in the manner in which our friend Charlie received his loan; and second, lending for a straight interest per week—for example 10 percent. This may seem more humane than the traditional six for five loan, but the payments on this type of loan are due each week at a specific time on a specific day. If the borrower is even ten minutes late with his payment, he automatically owes an additional week's interest. The larger loans, known as "classics," may be for a specific amount plus interest (usually 100 percent), and are due within thirty, sixty, or ninety days.

Problems arising from moneylending have vexed the banking industry from its earliest history. However, loan sharking—the charging of unconscionably high and onerous rates of interest on loans of money—as an organized criminal enterprise is a fairly recent development. The loan-shark racket as we know it today was developed by the same lawless elements that turned the streets of American cities into battlegrounds during the Prohibition era of the 1920s and early 1930s. There was a time when a "respectable" racketeer looked down his nose at the usurious moneylender. He was regarded with the same contempt accorded to the common procurer. The czars of the underworld and their highly organized minions were then engaged in other pursuits—first protection rackets (during the earlier part of the century) and then bootlegging (after the passage of the Volstead Act). It was not until the repeal of the Prohibition laws that the organized crime syndicates, with tremendous capital at their disposal, started looking around for new enterprises. Expansion of gambling, vice, and the traffic in narcotics took up the slack caused by repeal. This produced new and greater profits. The underworld sought a racket that would allow them to put this money to work in a way that would produce "legitimate" revenue. They found it in loan sharking.

By the end of the thirties, crime syndicates were fully engaged in usurious moneylending operations. This venture soon proved its tremendous potential for making money. Racket-controlled moneylending operations were not affected by the governmental regulations imposed on legitimate lenders, nor was organized criminal loan sharking ever encumbered by considerations of proper banking practices, procedures, or ethics. Competition for business—in the normally accepted sense—was never a factor. In the years that followed, the racket flourished.

The New York State Commission's investigation and hearing, conducted in 1964, revealed that loan sharking today has become one of the major and most lucrative operations in the criminal underworld. Moreover, loan sharking is a principal avenue by which crime syndicates have invaded legitimate businesses. These businesses, when taken over by loan sharks, are used to advance other criminal enterprises. With this growth of power, the loan shark has become a serious threat to our economy as well as a menace to society.

The New York State Commission of Investigation (1965, p. 13) elaborates on the need for more effective law enforcement in the area of loan sharking:

> Law enforcement officials have long recognized that one of the principal and most lucrative operations of the criminal underworld is the loan-shark racket. Together with gambling operations, labor racketeering and trafficking in narcotics, loan-sharking, in its various aspects, has engaged the major efforts of law enforcement

in the battle against organized crime. Yet comparatively little is known by the general public about loan-sharking. More disturbing is the fact that enforcement efforts in this area have been handicapped seriously by weak and confusing anti-usury laws under which the most nefarious and vicious practices are often legal.

Crime Syndicates in the Moneylending Business

The usurious moneylending business was particularly adaptable to successful operation through existing underworld organizational structures. Its potential for great profits presented an open avenue to the world of legitimate business and the means of turning racket revenues to usable, legitimate capital.

Organization of the loan-shark racket as a syndicate venture is composed generally of three principal echelons. (See figure 3.1.) On the first or top level is the underworld boss. He is the original source of money and the person to whom all others owe their absolute allegiance. Assistant District Attorney Frank Rogers of New York County, in his testimony about the hoodlum hierarchy of loan sharking, stated that the bosses distribute unlimited amounts of money; millions of dollars are entrusted to chief lieutenants and underbosses who comprise the second echelon. The amount of money these men receive from the top is determined by their stature, past performances, and volume capabilities. The

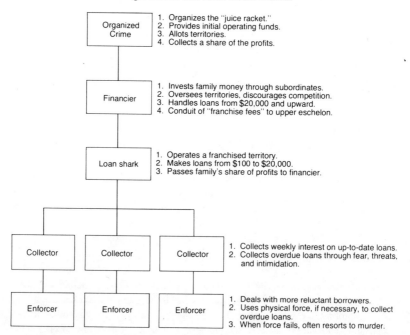

Figure 3.1 Organization of the loan-shark racket.

second echelon pays 1 percent vigorish, or interest, weekly for its money. There is absolute responsibility for the use of this money on all levels. This includes the distribution of funds to borrowers and the profitable return of capital and interest to each source. Each man is an independent contractor and knows that there are no excuses for failure to perform his part of the "contract."

The chief subordinates act as middlemen and lend monies to a third echelon composed of the hoodlums who deal with borrowers—the ultimate victims of this underworld financial empire. Rates charged to the third level are generally from 1½ to 2½ percent weekly. The third-level loan shark lends money to borrowers at rates of interest usually not less than 5 percent per week.

Distribution does not always follow the general pattern as outlined. In fact, there are several loan sharks who, law enforcement officials agree, are chief lieutenants in the second echelon and handle their own distribution. These are among the major loan sharks in New York City who can loan $1 million at a time to a borrower.

One such transaction has been described by the New York State Commission of Investigation (1965, p. 15) as follows: The borrower needed $1 million to finance a construction project. In his conference with the loan shark, who was a chief lieutenant of a syndicate and one of the most prominent loan sharks in New York City, the borrower talked about credentials and collateral. The loan shark clearly acquainted him with the facts of such a loan:

> And the loan shark quite frankly stated to him that he doesn't need any credentials, number one. The man who had sent the borrower, the prospective borrower, in to him, he was enough, his word that you, meaning the prospective borrower, are okay, is enough for me.
> And the borrower didn't require any collateral. The borrower couldn't understand this too well. He was simply told in no uncertain terms that "Your body is your collateral."

The borrower then understood the type of loan that he was getting.

It appears that either membership in or affiliation with one of the syndicates is necessary in order to move money into the usurious moneylending business. The "Newsboy" Moriarity case illustrates this fact. Moriarity, a professional gambler who operated a numbers or policy racket in Jersey City, was characterized as an "overlook." This term is used to refer to a criminal who operates on a larger scale than is generally recognized and who has escaped being absorbed by the syndicates. Consequently, ". . . he couldn't move money out without the assistance of the mob. Therefore he had to hide it." He did just that. In July 1962, approximately $2.5 million in cash was found crammed in a Jersey City garage and was generally acknowledged to represent the proceeds of Moriarity's illicit business.

There are also instances of top loan sharks who are not recognized syndicate members. However, they cannot operate unless they have a direct connection with the syndicate. This usually comes in the form of a syndicate "partner" who supplies "prestige and brawn."

Syndicate Discipline—"The Sit-Down"

One significant aspect of underworld control of the loan-shark racket is the tendency to operate in a discreet and cautious manner. Syndicate moneylenders have generally recognized the need for good "public relations" which will allow them to function with a minimum of police attention and public clamor. Rather than solve internal disputes by gang warfare or resort to unnecessary violence, the syndicates now tend to arbitrate their differences using a more "civilized" approach known as the "sit-down." The full power of the underworld's absolute authority, iron discipline, and enforcement machinery is behind such arbitration.

When disputes arise in connection with any aspect of the underworld lending business, the opposing parties will arrange for a sit-down with a mediator. There the matter will be peaceably settled as quickly as possible rather than engaging in "open shooting wars which bring the hue and cry of the public and prosecutors on top of them." A high-ranking member of the underworld presides over every sit-down and his decision is final.

The sit-down is also used to adjudicate a claim against a borrower whose interest and penalty assessments have increased his indebtedness to a point where it is no longer collectible. In such cases, an amount will be decided upon in full settlement of the obligation.* This type of kangaroo court never requires a loan shark to accept a sum less than the original loan. Invariably the arbitrated figure is three or four times that amount.

The Relationship between Loan Sharking and Other Rackets

The close connection between loan sharking, on the one hand, and bookmaking and narcotics distribution on the other is also evident. The bookmaker who sustained high losses as a result of the unforeseen shutout of the Yankees in the 1963 World Series, for example, obtained refinancing through the loan shark. The narcotics importer who needs instant credit to meet an exceptionally large drug shipment also goes to the syndicate usurer. In another situation, the New York City Police Department arrested a narcotics pusher and found records on this person indicating that he was "not only pushing these doses of junk, but also shylocking them [the addicts] when they were unable to make their payments [for drugs]."

Instances were found in which a racket union in the construction field actually used loan sharking as a concession at construction sites. These concessions were sold or granted to others and operated by criminal underlings as a continuing source of revenue.

---

*Fixing a final figure by arbitration or a "sit-down" is known in the loan-shark racket as "stopping the clock," connoting the cessation of the accumulation of weekly vigorish and penalties. This only happens when the borrower has convinced the loan shark that he cannot continue paying weekly vigorish. The loan shark will stop the weekly accumulation of interest and penalties and will settle upon a lump-sum payment at a specific time.

The Profit Incentive

Of all the factors that led to the popularity of loan sharking as a principal crime syndicate activity, its fantastic profit was undoubtedly the most compelling. Just how much profit is involved in loan sharking was illustrated at a public hearing conducted by Sergeant of Detectives Ralph Salerno of the Criminal Intelligence Bureau of the New York City Police Department and summarized by the New York Commission of Investigation (1965, pp. 22–23):

> MR. SALERNO: A big racket boss could have a Christmas party in his home, to which he invites ten trusted lieutenants. He doesn't have to write their names down. He knows their names. They are friends of his. They can come to his home.
>
> MR. VERGARI: They are part of the underworld, and in the underworld parlance, they belong to him.
>
> MR. SALERNO: Yes. He can take one million dollars, which is not an inconceivable amount in cash, and distribute that $100,000 per man to these ten men. All he has to tell them is, I want 1 percent per week. I don't care what you get for it. But I want 1 percent per week.
>
> He does not have to record their names. He doesn't have to record the amount. These are easy enough to remember. And if you stop and think that 365 days later, at the next year's Christmas party, the only problem this gang leader has is where is he going to find five more men to hand out half-a-million dollars that he earned in the last year on the same terms.
>
> MR. VERGARI: In other words, he is making $10,000 a week on his million dollars. Is that right?
>
> MR. SALERNO: Yes, $520,000 a year.

Carrying this illustration out along the succeeding echelons of the racket, a matter of simple mathematics further underscores the tremendous profit-making potential of this type of syndicate activity. The third-echelon lender charges, on the average, 5 percent weekly vigorish. Therefore, a million-dollar "investment" at this level can produce as much as $50,000 a week or $2,600,000 a year. Of this amount, $15,000 to $25,000 a week or up to $1.3 million a year in vigorish alone is returned to underworld superiors.

Loan sharking has also become a convenient vehicle for turning so-called black money into "white money," or legitimate funds. Major racketeers have great fortunes available to them, namely, the proceeds of their illicit trade in narcotics and gambling. These underworld leaders have found that by lending money out to their chief lieutenants for further distribution in loan sharking, they can gain control of many legitimate businesses. A business take-over gives the hoodlum not only a corporate cover but a new source of money—this time, a legitimate one.

Loan sharks have constantly used corporate borrowers as a cover, or concealing device, to protect themselves and other hoodlums. A typical instance of this practice was one in which a loan shark took his weekly vigorish payment in the form of a salary check from an automobile dealer to whom he had lent money. The gangster appeared on the corporate books as an outside salesman; yet he had never sold a car. When questioned, he was able to claim legitimate employment, at least insofar as a weekly paycheck would indicate.

Opportunity to realize unusual profit in loan sharking was also disclosed in the case of an heir to a large sum of money in trust, who attempted to sell his inheritance rights for a loan-shark loan at one-third the actual value of the trust fund.

The hoodlum also acquires prestige in the eyes of fellow criminals by making loans to members of the legitimate business or professional community. Not only has the loan shark made a profit on his transaction, but there is "an additional profit in the sense of loyalty from this man (the borrower) to a racketeer (the lender)." The unique position of the loan shark in the underworld has been summarized by the New York State Commission of Investigation (1965, p. 22):

> It [loan sharking] is a demonstration of power. You have something which I think is unique in criminal fields in loan sharking. They have raised the status of loan sharking to a height and to a degree in their own criminal circles that I have never seen duplicated anywhere. It seems to be an unwritten law that even if you are a criminal, even if you are a top guy, you always pay the shylock.*
>
> The Gallo gang, for example. . . . I know that this very same group which challenged the criminal empire still very diligently paid the shylocks. Certainly not out of a sense of fear, but this is the status that it has achieved in their circles. You borrow money; you pay it back. They weren't afraid of the shylock. But they didn't know when they might need him again. So they very diligently paid the shylock. To enforce a debt, they will go very far. . . . I have known them to go as far as hanging a man out of a window by his feet, fifteen stories . . . he got the money up in one hour . . . after you are frightened, you will come up with it . . . the only time a man gets killed is when he has defied their law completely . . . when he has it and just doesn't pay it . . . then it pays to make an example of him.

This sworn testimony, quoted by the New York Committee of Investigation (1965, p. 32), was given by an individual who had been inside the underworld as a friend, confidant, and sometime employee of well-known racket figures. That it was stated in a calm, matter-of-fact way made it no less frightening. Investigation clearly indicates that to enforce a debt they will indeed "go very far." The measures used to extract money from a debtor sometimes have tragic consequences. Through intimidation and harsh, unyielding pressure, borrowers are virtually forced to commit criminal acts in order to come up with the money to meet their vigorish payments. Ever ingenious, loan sharks devise criminal ventures that fit the borrower's particular situation and capabilities.

---

*The term *shylock* or its derivations "shy" and "shell" are generally used in the underworld to refer to anyone in the moneylending business.

Sergeant of Detectives Salerno of the Criminal Investigation Bureau, New York City Police Department, testified about a hairdresser who operated a beauty salon in a fashionable area of New York City. His clients included wealthy women who possessed jewelry of great value, a fact which did not escape the loan shark. When it became apparent that the hairdresser could not meet his substantial vigorish payments, he was pressed into service as a "fingerman" for a burglary ring.

The hairdresser was able to identify those clients who owned gems, ascertain their value, and obtain addresses and apartment numbers. Casual conversation during a coiffing session would elicit such information as a husband's working hours, the maid's day off, and other facts vital to the planning of a burglary. After each successful jewel theft, the hairdresser's share of the proceeds from the crime was given to the loan shark as a vigorish payment.

Another case which also demonstrates the loan shark's ingenuity involved a prominent sports announcer. This individual had become so hopelessly in debt to several racket lenders that a sit-down had to be held. The indebtedness was consolidated, and two of the loan sharks were entrusted with devising a means of collection. A crooked dice game was set up. The broadcaster, who had numerous friends and contacts among affluent and "sporting" people, was required to act as a "steerer" for the game. A percentage of the proceeds from this "razzle-dazzle" affair was applied to satisfy his indebtedness.

Investigation by the commission disclosed many such instances. The following story about a trucker who was forced to ship and store stolen property in order to repay a debt to a loan shark is a case in point: Witness *J* is the secretary and vice president of a small trucking and warehouse corporation in the Bronx, New York. This corporation is family owned, and *J* and her eldest brother operate the business. Serious illness in the family adversely affected management efficiency. This problem, coupled with high medical costs, had completely drained cash resources. The usual sad pattern of events developed. Credit with legitimate lending sources was exhausted.

In 1957, the firm started borrowing from loan shark Frank Sacco. Over a period of four years through 1961, the firm borrowed a total of $40,000, paying and receiving loans averaging about $10,000 a year. These loans were ostensibly obtained from other Sacco "cover" firms, Hub Factors and Certified Discount Corporation. Most transactions were negotiated with Simon Geller and *J's* direct dealings with Sacco during the early years of their relationship were limited. *J* claimed that she did not at first fully realize who and what Sacco was. This may have very well been so, but she eventually learned.

On Election Day, 1961, *J's* brother was arrested on a charge of receiving stolen property. New York City police found a truck, belonging to *J's* firm and parked in *J's* garage, loaded with stolen transistor radios. *J* and her brother, who had handled the shipment, claimed innocence of any knowledge of the nature of the truck's cargo, although the brother eventually entered a plea of guilty to the charge. They would not implicate Sacco or his men and as late as the hearing in 1964, both continued to insist that Sacco had nothing to do with the stolen property. Information from reliable sources indicated that quite the opposite was true. Principals of *J's* firm were coerced into transporting and storing the stolen property out of fear of Sacco.

Loan Sharks in the Securities Business

Ever since the underworld realized that loan sharking was a relatively safe and highly lucrative enterprise, it has devised increasingly sophisticated ways of using loan sharking to invade the business world. The loan shark may no longer be stereotyped as an unshaven thug who stands on a street corner dispensing money by the traditional "six for five" formula.

With the development of our free-enterprise system, we have become a nation of stockholders. Millions of Americans own countless shares of stock in business corporations. The "board" rooms of brokerage houses across the country are filled daily with anxious customers who carefully watch the progress or decline of their favorite securities. Our expanding economy has brought on a corresponding expansion of the securities business, especially in the organization of many new over-the-counter firms.* Occasionally, some of these brokerage houses are undercapitalized and find it difficult to meet the strictly enforced monetary ratio requirements of the federal government. Here once again the loan shark finds a perfect opening.

The commission's investigation revealed several instances in which loan sharks were able to gain control of the operations of brokerage houses through usurious loans. Stockbrokers who became deeply indebted to underworld moneylenders were forced into high pressure schemes involving the sale of thousands of shares of worthless stock resulting in great losses to the investing public.

The Bank—A Base for Loan-Shark Operations

To the average citizen, public banking institutions present an indestructible image of well-regulated reliability and conservatism in financial matters—the last place in the world one would expect to find the corrupting and destructive handiwork of the loan shark. Nevertheless, the commission's investigation and hearings revealed the shocking fact that in certain instances bank funds were being used to finance usurious moneylending operations. This was accomplished through indiscriminate and improper lending practices and the systematic discounting of unsecured and often worthless third-party notes.

---

*The term *over-the-counter* is generally used to designate a brokerage firm which specializes in unlisted issues—that is, the stock of companies not appearing on the boards of the New York, American, or other major stock exchanges.

Also disturbing was the revelation that one New York City bank was used by loan sharks as a base of operations and as a source of borrowers. These serious abuses were made possible through the corruption of bank employees.

"Immediate Credit"

The seasonal nature of garment manufacturing and the rapid turnover of cash and merchandise, as well as the sudden demands of style changes, often create situations in which immediate cash financing becomes necessary—financing that is over and above ordinary credit limits in the garment industry. Due to its unique character, this industry is a fertile field for the usurer. Legitimate garment manufacturers often turn to loan sharks for ready cash to tide them over during a transition period. Some law-enforcement officials have stated that many garment firms in New York City are financially controlled by members of the criminal syndicate who engage in loan sharking.

Another direct result of this condition is the development of what has been described as the "immediate credit" department in certain garment area banks. According to a witness designated here as O, who ran such a department in an area bank, "immediate credit" service is designed primarily to permit depositors to draw against uncollected checks upon approval of a bank officer and payment of certain specified charges. Astounding as it seems, this bank-instituted service encourages a practice which plagues the banking business—that is, the "kiting" of checks. O so testified and gave his own quite accurate definition of "kiting":

> Kiting of checks, there are several forms. The best form I know is drawing a check on one bank to cover a check on another bank, for which neither account has money. That is the best way I can describe it.

Since the "immediate credit" department served bank customers who were habitually running short of funds, O's daily duties as head of that department made him familiar with the financial problems of depositors. His busiest time came between the hours of one-thirty and two-thirty in the afternoon. This period was characterized by the witness, and is apparently known in the garment district, as the "panic hour." It is at this time of day that previously issued checks are presented for collection. Thus operators who had insufficient cash on deposit to meet such obligations queued up at the "immediate credit" counter, desperate for help. This was the "panic hour"—the hour at which the loan sharks appeared at the bank. There, with the aid of bank employees, they operated their own version of an "immediate credit" department.

O became friendly with a number of loan sharks who kept accounts at the bank, transacted business during the day, and who always attended the "panic hour."

Bank Funds Finance Loan-Shark Operations

One facet of loan-shark operations uncovered by the investigation presented the gravest potential threat to the financial security of banking institutions. It was found that through various means, loan sharks were able to obtain and use bank funds as part of their capital for usurious moneylending ventures. Simple mathematics make obvious the extreme attractiveness of such an arrangement. The vast spread between legal bank rates of interest and the 260 percent (or more) annual vigorish charges that the loan shark imposes is much too enticing for him to resist. Here again, the loan shark accomplishes his purpose by corrupting bank officials.

The Note-Discounting Racket

One large-scale, usurious moneylending operation, using bank funds as capital, was conducted by loan shark John Massiello. This individual, convicted in 1956 of the crime of conspiracy, is believed by law-enforcement authorities to be a member of the crime syndicate headed by Vito Genovese. Massiello was called as a witness at the commission's hearing. Richly tailored and elegantly bejeweled and groomed, he looked every inch the top underworld figure. The nickname "Gentleman Johnny," by which he is known, seemed most fitting indeed. His performance also ran to form. He politely refused to answer some forty questions concerning his activities, asserting his privilege against self-incrimination.

Other witnesses were not so reticent. Their testimonies revealed the existence of a racket which put at least $1.5 million of the funds of a single bank branch to work for this loan shark. A substantial part of the money will never be recovered. Evidence indicated that the operation was much larger. An essential ingredient in this scheme was the corruption of the bank's loan officer.

The following case illustrates how this note-discounting racket operated. A businessman-borrower, unable to obtain credit, applied to the underworld moneylender for a $6,000 loan. The loan shark required the borrower to execute a promissory note payable to him for $8,000. This note was taken to the bank where it was discounted, with the approval of the corrupt loan officer at the bank rate of 6 percent. As in the case of most loans arranged by Massiello, the paper was worthless and was accepted without collateral. But proper banking procedure relating to the credit investigation and evaluation of collateral was never followed.

The person who was liable to the bank was the maker of the note, who had obligated himself to pay the 6 percent rate on the $8,000 and eventually to satisfy the note. The loan shark pocketed $2,000 of the $8,000 and gave $6,000 to the borrower. In effect, the $2,000 retained by the loan shark from the proceeds of the loan constituted his vigorish.

This was the basic scheme, but it had much broader and more serious ramifications. In addition to the discounting of third-party notes, Massiello himself borrowed substantial amounts from this same bank. These loans, obtained through the connivance of the corrupt bank official, were taken in the names of various dummy corporations. In each instance, Massiello paid the usual 6 percent rate. The operation was kept going by the continual pyramiding or broadening of the base amount of the bank loans. Prior obligations were kept current by the loan shark with proceeds obtained by the discounting of new notes or by obtaining new loans in the name of a dummy corporation. The loan shark had the continuing use of the ever-increasing sum lent by the bank, in addition to the constant turnover of the exorbitant vigorish that this money was earning.

In 1962, the bank discovered that the loan officer had been exceeding his authority in granting loans to Massiello and others. He was discharged immediately and is presently under indictment in a federal court. In May 1962, an assistant vice-president of the bank was assigned to investigate the extent of the note-pyramiding scheme and to seek recovery wherever possible. He found that between May 1959 and January 1962, the loan shark had obtained bank loans totaling close to $1.5 million. At one point when the pyramid hit its peak, he noted that this one branch had nearly $800,000 out on loan to the Massiello group. Up to the time of the hearing in December 1964, the bank had been able to recover only half that amount. The loss to the bank has been estimated at close to $400,000. The bank official stated that "several" other groups had conducted similar note-discounting operations at the bank and indicated that they too were connected with Massiello. Although he declined to estimate the total amount of bad loans issued in connection with the other pyramiding operations, he characterized them as "substantial."

A typical borrower from Massiello was one R. Simon Rosenthal, the owner of two garment manufacturing companies. A large number of the notes, which were discounted by Massiello, had been issued to him by Rosenthal. Rosenthal was asked why he involved himself in this scheme and explained that he owed Massiello between $70,000 and $80,000 and had no choice but to go along. Rosenthal and his firms were stripped by the loan shark and are now out of business and totally bankrupt. Rosenthal is but one example of the many issuers of paper held by the bank on which never a penny will be recovered.

"The Finder's Fee"

Further investigation disclosed another device through which bank capital was used to the great profit of unscrupulous moneylenders. An actual situation clearly illustrates how such operators obtain what in reality are unconscionable vigorish payments on bank loans to high-risk borrowers.

In 1962, the president of a light-bulb manufacturing concern, in debt to loan shark Julie Peters Gazia and in need of cash, was referred to one Peter D'Agostino. This individual headed a moneylending business known as Norwalk Investors, Inc., whose offices were located in Mineola, Long Island. D'Agostino, negotiating on behalf of the manufacturer, was able to obtain two loans for that firm. One loan from a bank located in Nassau County, Long Island, was made to the borrower in the amount of $50,000. Another $30,000 loan made to him from the Crown Savings Bank of Newport News, Virginia, was also arranged by D'Agostino. D'Agostino took approximately $10,000 from the borrower as a "finder's fee." Both loans were unsecured and given without investigation into the borrower's extremely fragile credit position. The so-called finder's fee was actually another form of vigorish earned by a moneylender on capital improperly advanced by a bank.

The gross disregard for proper banking procedures that marked such transactions was clearly demonstrated by the loan this bank made to First National Service and Discount Corporation, the firm used by Julie Peters Gazia as a front for his loan-shark operation. First National had lent large amounts of money to one Joseph La Monica. In May 1962, La Monica was convicted for his participation in a scheme to defraud the government by submitting false statements in loan applications under the Title I program of the Federal Housing Authority. Gazia, concerned about the pending sentence and likely incarceration of his borrower, pressed La Monica for full payment of vigorish and principal of the loan. Notwithstanding La Monica's difficulties with the law, D'Agostino had employed him as a "finder" for other Norwalk "deals." D'Agostino agreed to help La Monica settle his outstanding obligations to the loan shark by arranging for a $25,000 loan to Gazia's firm from the bank in Nassau County. Naturally, the arrangement was most attractive to Gazia. Also available was an additional sum of $25,000 to lend at 260 percent a year.

In this case, the loan investigation by the bank might have been considered farcical. Witness B, as an officer of First National, was interviewed by the bank president. This interview was described as completely superficial. He was not asked even rudimentary questions about the earnings, business activities, officers, or directors of the corporation, or any questions about the corporation's ability to repay the loan.

A Bank Goes Under

In addition to arranging deals involving "finder's fees," loan sharks do a brisk business in discounting third-party notes. Note discounting constituted the substantial part of the operations of the Norwalk Investors. The money that the loan shark acquired through discounting was typically used in financing his own moneylending activities. The notes were discounted chiefly through the institution in Nassau County and the Crown Savings Bank of Newport News.

In December 1964, the cashier of Crown Savings was indicted by a grand jury sitting in Fulton County, Atlanta, Georgia, together with five officers of money order firms based in Atlanta. These defendants were charged with defrauding hundreds of people in Georgia, Tennessee, and South Carolina who had purchased one million dollars' worth of money orders drawn on the Newport News bank. The cashier was accused of making false entries in accounts maintained by the money order firm, which in turn allowed the codefendants to drain off funds which should have been used to cash outstanding money orders.

In September 1964, just three months prior to the filing of the federal indictment, inspectors of the Federal Deposit Insurance Corporation found that extensive kiting operations had been practiced at Crown and that the bank was carrying more than $1.5 million worth of high-risk loans on its books. These revelations led to a prompt closing of the bank by the federal government and subsequently to the institution's bankruptcy. This same bank had accommodated Peter D'Agostino in the discounting of notes of the following companies: Nine Gee Lanes, Inc., of Red Hook, New York; Arm Truck Leasing Corporation of Maspeth, New York; and South Eastern Technicals, Inc. of Norfolk, Virginia.

The quality of the shark's clients is well summarized in a letter from the president of a New Jersey banking institution, who appeared to have much more discretion than did Crown Savings Bank officials. The letter, dated December 13, 1962, declined to make a $35,000 loan to a company referred to it by D'Agostino because of the company's financial condition. The letter also stated that the bank was "anxious to build deposits, but it appears that the companies and concerns which work through you are problem cases, which our bank cannot approve. . . ."

The irregularities in the various banks which were uncovered during the commission's investigation of loan sharking have come to the attention of the Committee on Banking and Currency of the House of Representatives, as well as the United States Senate Permanent Subcommittee on Investigations. At the request of both committees, information developed in this area has been furnished to them. At the date of this writing, the Senate subcommittee is engaged in public hearings on the infiltration of racketeers into the banking field.

Loan Sharking on the Waterfront

For many years, loan sharking has been a serious problem among the approximately twenty thousand longshoremen who work on the vast piers and docking facilities of New York Harbor. As in other areas, the loan-shark racket on the piers is financed and controlled by the underworld. Thomas F. Jones, chief investigator of the Waterfront Commission, testified at the public hearing about waterfront loan-shark operations. Jones' testimony can be summarized as follows:

Underworld money movers work through individuals whose employment provides them with credentials to go directly onto the piers. These individuals may be pier guards, hiring agents, checkers, or other longshoremen. The underworld financier provides the pier loan shark with what is called a "book." This is an advance of lending capital ranging from $1,000 to $10,000. The loan shark operating on the pier, also known as a money "pusher," is responsible for the "book" he receives and the vigorish it produces. Each week, the "pusher" must give his money supplier an accounting of his profits, which are determined by the current value of the "book." The profits from the enterprise are shared according to the terms of special arrangements made between them. As in other loan-shark ventures, the financiers are not concerned with the identity or reliability of their borrowers. This is entirely the pusher's responsibility. The pusher also is held accountable for all loans which remain uncollected.

Although the amounts of the loans made to longshoremen are relatively small, the volume is large owing to the great number of pushers. According to Mr. Jones, the "standard" vigorish charges on the waterfront are about 15 percent a week. As in other loan-shark operations, penalties for late payments are imposed.

Where the delinquency in payment continues, threats and even force are employed by "strong-arm" men to ensure collection. Not only is the borrower subjected to threats and physical violence, but his immediate family may be exposed to such tactics as well. These threats often drive the borrower to another loan shark for money to pay off his overdue loan. If the second loan shark knows of the borrower's difficulties, he will charge whatever the traffic will bear. At times, the borrower has to pay double the amount of the loan, plus vigorish.

In addition to employing threats and violence as means of ensuring collection, loan sharks have developed other effective means of extracting timely payments. One such technique was explained at the Senate subcommittee hearing:

> Because of the vast number of longshoremen working in the Port, and the transient nature of many of them, moving from pier to pier, the longshoreman is known to his employers almost exclusively as a social security number. So that when he is employed on the first day of the working week, he is given what they call a chit, or an identification card, a payroll identification card by the company that hires him.
>
> At the end of the payroll period, the monies that are earned by that particular individual are credited to him, and upon presentation of the payroll identification card, the salary due to that social security number is paid.
>
> Now, the man who possesses the identification card, or the brass chit, can pick up the salary, and as far as the employer is concerned, then it becomes his property. He can do with it what he will. Because they are, in effect, paying on the card, so that the loan-shark, if he has possession of this chit, or this payroll card, he can go and collect the man's salary. If it is in cash, he can extract from the payroll envelope what is due him, and he gives back to the victim what remains; if

it is a check we have found in some instances where the loan shark has endorsed it himself, forged the man's name and cashed the check, and others where he has taken it back to the individual, had him endorse it and then the loan shark will cash it and give the man back what is due out of the payroll check.

Loan sharks have also been known to station themselves outside of the banks and stores where the pier workers cash their paychecks. As these men leave the bank or check-cashier, they are dunned by the waiting loan shark for their weekly payments.

Also attributed to loan sharking—at least in part—is the serious problem of cargo pilferage on the piers. This was pointed out in the following testimony quoted by the New York State Commission on Investigation (1965, p. 32):

> Well, the loan sharking in and of itself is a very vicious crime because . . . these men thrive on the adversity of their fellow workers, but primarily on the waterfront we have the aftermath of the crime itself. The victim is so hard pressed many times for money that he turns to pilferage of cargo, theft of cargo, in order to meet his payments to the loan shark.
>
> We have uncovered instances in our investigation where pier guards have fallen victims to a loan shark, and in order to meet the payments, have entered into agreements with thieves to turn their backs and not to do their duty. And, of course, as I pointed out at the beginning, longshoremen or checkers, or other waterfront workers, have from time to time, been forced to engage in thefts of cargo in order to meet their loan shark payments.

A specific case is provided as an illustration. A hiring agent at one of the piers was operating as a loan shark. Being in a position to hire men, he gave preference in employment to his borrowers to ensure that they had enough work during the week to meet their obligation to him. Upon the arrest of this individual, and in searching his home pursuant to a search warrant, approximately $70,000 in cash was found hidden. The attic of his home was described "as being something similar to a discount store." Many of the items found in his possession were traced back to cargo at the piers. It was subsequently learned that this merchandise had been turned over to him by longshoremen for agreed credit amounts—usually only a fraction of the true value of the merchandise— that were applied toward payment on the outstanding indebtedness of each borrower.

There are undoubtedly many cases in which borrowers freely lend themselves to such thievery. Nevertheless, loan sharking remains the fundamental cause of much pilferage. Such conditions exist primarily because borrowers are afraid to complain to law-enforcement authorities. The Waterfront Commission of New York Harbor and local law-enforcement authorities have been exerting every effort to rid the waterfront of loan sharks. It is hoped that increased public awareness and legislation resulting from the commission's hearing will help in attaining this goal.

GLOSSARY OF LOAN-SHARKING TERMS

AMORTIZATION. The act of paying off the loan to a loan shark, usually by performing a criminal or semicriminal act.

CLASSICS. Large loans, usually in the $20,000 to $100,000 range.

COLLECTOR. An employee of the loan shark who has the responsibility of collecting weekly loan payments.

ENFORCER. An employee of the loan shark who has the responsibility of convincing a reluctant borrower that he should do everything in his power to pay the vigorish. Uses force to intimidate the borrower.

FIVE-PERCENTER. A loan shark.

JUICE RACKET. The business of lending money at exorbitant and usurious rates of interest.

LOAN SHARK. One who lends money at usurious rates of interest.

ON-THE-SHEET. The total amount of money that a given loan shark has lent out. The total of his outstanding loans.

SHY. A loan shark.

SHYLOCKING. The loan-sharking racket.

SIT-DOWN. A meeting that is held under the chairmanship of a powerful organized figure to arbitrate differences between the loan shark and large borrowers.

SIX FOR FIVE. In loan sharking, the amount of interest on small loans.

STEERER. One who finds customers for the loan shark.

STOPPING THE CLOCK. The agreement reached at a sit-down in which all parties agree that no more interest will be charged. Usually resorted to when the loan shark is convinced that the borrower cannot raise any more money.

VIGORISH. The interest charged by a loan shark for a loan.

VIG. Vigorish.

REFERENCES

Chamber of Commerce of the United States. *White Collar Crime*. Washington, D.C.: U.S. Government Printing Office, 1974.

DeFranco, Edward. *Anatomy of a Scam: A Case Study of a Planned Bankruptcy by Organized Crime*. Washington, D.C.: U.S. Department of Justice, Law Enforcement Assistance Administration, 1973.

New York State Commission of Investigation. *The Loan Shark Racket*. New York, 1965.

President's Commission on Law Enforcement and the Administration of Justice. *Task Force Report: Organized Crime*. Washington, D.C.: U.S. Government Printing Office, 1967.

Chapter 4

Prostitution

To be a successful prostitute, you've got to have at least one of three things; either outstanding good looks and figure—and many of us are really beautiful; or the personality and individuality to make a man look at you twice, and then come back again and again; or the ability to talk or scare your clients, once you've got them back in your flat, into paying more than the original sum stipulated for extra attentions, or less ordinary functions—you must persuade them into something new, or roll them, steal from them. . . . Most of us, however, are endowed with only one of these qualities, and quite a large number have none at all. (Anonymous 1962, p. 1)

This statement, perhaps better than any other passage in the literature of prostitution, expresses the emotional, psychological, sociological, and criminal problems inherent in the age-old practice of offering one's body as a sexual commodity. In and between those lines one can discern the doubts and anxieties of the street woman about her looks, her figure, her femininity; one begins to understand that implicit in the prostitute's self-concept is the notion that she is no more than an object, one who is capable of mechanically performing almost any type of sexual function—from the ordinary to the more esoteric varieties —in exchange for a mere fee of money. And finally, one can see that the correlation between prostitution and a number of other peripheral crimes, such as robbery, blackmail, and assault, is in fact much greater than it might appear on the surface.

The above words, spoken by a modern-day streetwalker, might suggest that the profession of prostitution, which began in the shrouded mists of history and evolved to its present state, has finally reached some sort of culmination, yet if we examine its historical development, we find that these same sentiments have been repeatedly expressed throughout the history of the profession. François Villon (1431–1463) in his *Lament of Belle Heauliumire* has one of his characters give the following advice to a young prostitute: "Make your money while you can, spare no man, for an aged prostitute has no more value than a worn-out coin."

Historical Background

In the earliest recorded history of mankind—particularly in the religious writings of the ancients—we find countless references to prostitution. The Hammurabic Code, our earliest example of a written code of law, contained sections pertaining to the status of women—especially that of widows and unwed girls—and made provisions for "temporary" marriages for those who were without the means to support themselves. Most ancient societies placed no particular value on virginity, and many anthropological studies indicate that, in fact, promiscuity among the young was sometimes even encouraged. In many societies, marriages did not take place until the woman had "proved" her fertility by becoming pregnant.

In the older religions of Western Asia, temple prostitutes were not uncommon and were expected to provide sexual services to the priests and male affiliates of the temples. This practice was particularly prevalent in temples devoted to the worship of Aphrodite and Astarte. The association between sex and religion can perhaps be traced back to early man's awe at the origins of life, and thus to his recognition of the relationship between the sex act and the "miracle" of birth. Some historians have postulated that ancient religions venerated the human sex organs for precisely this reason.

The goddesses depicted in ancient statues were invariably endowed with prominent breasts and exaggerated sex organs. Likewise, worship of the male sex organ was equally prevalent, as evidenced by the number of phallic statues discovered in archeological digs. Some authorities have gone so far as to equate our modern church steeples with the symbols of ancient phallic worship.

In Babylon, it was common practice for women of both the upper and lower social classes to sit in the doorway of the temple and offer their virginity to the goddesses. This custom required that the women remain at the doorway of the temple until any passing male threw a silver coin into her lap. The sacrifice thus made, she was admitted to full participation in the life of the temple. Bullough (1965) speculated on the fate of the unattractive woman who, not being chosen immediately, was forced to remain at the portal until a passing stranger took pity on her.

Although the ancient Jews were forbidden to sell their daughters into prostitution, there was no punishment for girls who willingly entered the profession. And prostitutes were present in abundance in most of the cities of Judea, with the exception of the holy city of Jerusalem. Jewish religious law condemned an adulterous wife to death but relegated the unwed prostitute to live by the walls of the city. Though originally intended to be a form of punishment, this edict eventually led streetwalkers to congregate at the fringes of the city, a custom that may in part account for the fact that prostitution is traditionally practiced in areas in which large numbers of strangers are continually passing by.

The Christian church accorded veneration to a number of reformed prostitutes who, in repenting their former way of life, demonstrated such unusual rectitude—even to the point of becoming martyrs for their faith—that they were eventually elevated to positions of sainthood. Perhaps the best known of these women is St. Mary Magdalene, the confidante of Jesus who was the first to discover that He had risen and was the first to speak to Him following His resurrection. Some church historians believe that Mary Magdalene was the same harlot whom, according to the Bible, Jesus saved from a stoning with the words "Let him among you who is without sin cast the first stone." Other converted prostitutes who were eventually martyred for their faith include St. Mary the Egyptian, St. Afra, St. Pelagia, and St. Theodota.

It was not uncommon in many of the ancient societies for girls of marriageable age to be expected to provide their new husbands with a dowry as part of the marriage contract. Women belonging to poor families and thus unable to provide the dowry were encouraged to enter the temples as prostitutes to earn the dowry. In North Africa, girls from poor, rural families would travel many miles to the large cities in order to work as prostitutes until they had earned enough money to be able to afford marriage. The more money earned in this way, the more honor to the intended bridegroom, for no self-respecting man could accept a bride without a dowry.

In Athens, Solon (638?–559? B.C.) the lawgiver promulgated laws for public decency and order which included the establishment of houses of prostitution called *dicteriades*. Here, slave girls were housed by their masters to provide sexual services to the men of Athens. These prostitutes, known as *pornoi,* represented the lowest class of prostitutes in ancient Greece. Young, handsome male slaves were also used in this fashion to cater to the whims of those who preferred boys to girls. Just one notch above the *pornoi* was the class of streetwalkers who peddled their services in the streets. Streetwalkers were regulated by a law which permitted them to work only in the lower-class districts of the city and forced them to wear distinctive clothing so that they might be easily identified. Often, these streetwalkers were free citizens who for one reason or another were forced into prostitution as a means of survival.

Another class of prostitutes, known as the *auletrides,* was composed of entertainers, cymbal and flute players who were hired to perform at dinners and parties. Following their musical performances, they would provide sexual services for the guests. The *auletrides* were paid a flat fee that covered all services for the evening, regardless of the number of sexual partners they had to engage. Among the *auletrides* were erotic dancers who performed in the nude. (This practice was not considered out of the ordinary, since the ancient Greeks appreciated the well-formed human body, and in fact many of their athletic events were regularly performed in the nude.) Following a performance of these erotic dances, members of the audience would be invited to relieve the tensions and sexual desires that had been aroused by the dance.

The highest class of prostitutes in the Greek city-states was the *hetairae,* a group of women who were renowned for their extraordinary beauty and sophistication and their ability to converse about art, culture, politics, and business.

They were well educated and in many instances were themselves members of the patrician class. The *hetairae* served as courtesans and mistresses to the rich and powerful of Greece. They were envied by women of all social classes because they were allowed into the conventions of power from which ordinary women—even the wives of the politically powerful—were excluded.

In ancient Rome, prostitution was severely regulated. Practitioners were required to dye their hair or wear blonde wigs. They were also forced to dress in distinctive clothing so that they stood apart from the general populace. Their places of operation were strictly limited, and they were relegated to the least desirable sections of the city. Although the lives led by the various empresses would seem to belie it, feminine virtue was highly prized. The state allowed prostitution to flourish only as a protection for the decent women of Rome. Prostitutes were required to register with the police, and a special officer was designated to inspect the prostitutes and their places of business. In the streets leading to and from the Coloseum, many prostitutes plied their trade. Historians tell us that trade was unusually brisk immediately following the orgies of killing and the gladitorial bouts held in the Coloseum.

During the Middle Ages, which were dominated by the Holy Roman Empire and the Christian religion, prostitution was tolerated as a necessary evil in order to protect the chaste members of the female population. Nonetheless, a number of regulations were imposed on prostitutes, most of them promulgated by the ecclesiastical courts. As the church grew in strength, increasing emphasis was placed on virtue, chastity, and the celibate life. Many efforts were made to rehabilitate prostitutes, and several church fathers believed that marrying a prostitute and saving her soul was an act of supreme Christian charity and benevolence. On the other side of the coin, however, we find that the vow of celibacy was widely abused in the early church. And public scandals involving the clergy prompted many people to either leave the church or to join puritan groups dedicated to a purging of the existing establishment.

During this same period, the laws of France allowed prostitution but regulated the prostitutes by requiring them to wear identification badges and forbidding them to wear jewelry. In Paris, the prostitutes of the city formed their own guild, naming St. Mary Magdalene as their patron saint. The guild of prostitutes operated much like any other occupational guild, establishing classes of prostitutes, designating certain areas of the city in which its members could work, and training apprentices. By 1097, prostitution had been banned throughout the country, but owing to the increasing number of sexual assaults, many of which directly involved the chaste wives of prominent French officials, the ban was lifted several years later. Eventually, the whores of Paris were relegated to a section of the city called Clapier, from whence the word "clap," a slang expression for gonorrhea, is derived.

By the thirteenth century, prostitutes were so numerous in England that it was almost impossible for any man to walk along a public street without being propositioned. In 1252, the statutes of Winchester attempted to regulate prostitution by restricting its practitioners to the Soho district of London. It is said that the boundaries of this section of the city were marked by red lanterns, thus giving us our term "red-light district." In any event, bordellos marked their location by hanging red lanterns on their doorposts as guides for prospective customers.

For several hundred years, the prostitution laws in England vacillated between tolerance and repression until, during the fifteenth and sixteenth centuries, it became increasingly apparent that the high incidence of venereal disease was directly related to the prevalence of prostitution. In a matter of only a short time, a veritable war of blame broke out between the countries of Europe and Asia, each blaming the other for the spread of the dreaded disease. The Italians called it the French disease; the Turks called it the Chinese disease; the Chinese called it the Portuguese disease; and the French called it the English disease. Although the term *venereal disease*—which is derived from the word *venery,* meaning the pursuit of the goddess of love—did not come into vogue until the sixteenth century, it was the fear and loathing of this frightful disease that ultimately led to the strict repression of the practice of prostitution.

Up until the sixteenth century, prostitution was tried and punished in the ecclesiastical courts, and was then tried in the courts of common law. Although prostitution was never a crime in itself, prostitutes were nonetheless charged with being a public nuisance and brothel keepers were charged with maintaining houses that were also public nuisances. Yet prostitution did not legally become a crime in England until 1908.

After that time a variety of laws was passed in every country of the world to control prostitution. Some were extremely severe and others were extremely permissive—for example, the British law which carefully differentiated between the professional prostitute and the housewife who occasionally dabbled in prostitution to supplement her allowance. As might have been expected, the uprooting of thousands of people during the industrial revolution, the existence of child labor in the factories, and the miserable poverty that prevailed throughout England had a tremendous impact on the amount of prostitution taking place in the country's crowded cities. This in turn motivated the governments to become more and more stringent in their attempts to suppress the trade. During the seventeenth and eighteenth centuries, the British Parliament enacted a number of laws designed to suppress prostitution, rehabilitate prostitutes, and punish pimps and madams. Yet despite these measures, the profession of prostitution continued to flourish. Even in Victorian England efforts made by authorities to bring prostitution under control merely succeeded in forcing it underground, which produced one of the most licentious periods in British history.

The colonization of America, initiated as it was by those seeking religious freedom, produced very little prostitution. Religious scruples, strict laws, and swift punishment for adultery discouraged any who might otherwise have entered the field of prostitution. This is not to say that our puritan forefathers renounced sex. On the contrary, they often had large families, and some of their early customs were designed to heat the blood of their daughters' young suitors to the point that marriage was inevitable. One of the most common of these practices was "bundling." This quaint custom allowed the young swain who came a-courtin' to spend the night with his heart's desire, in her bed. The only problem was that their sexual congress was impeded by a "bundling board," which was placed down the middle of the bed by the girl's father. Thus the young lovers were expected to sleep side by side but without touching one another. Needless to say, this kind of emotional torture soon brought the young man to heel and a quick proposal was forthcoming.

Those who dared to break the rules were often severely punished if caught. Nathaniel Hawthorne, in a famous novel written in 1850, describes the fate of one such offender, who was condemned to wear the scarlet letter A embroidered on her outer garmet as a punishment for her adultery. Another common form of punishment—used in dealing with both male and female offenders—involved branding the "sinner" on the cheek so that the entire population of a village might be reminded of the consequences of such wrongdoings. Those who violated the sexual mores of a community might be sentenced to sit in the stocks or might be marked with an outward sign that indicated their particular misdeeds. And women offenders were sometimes required to sit astride a sharp board as a poignant reminder that their sexual organs were only to be exercised within the bounds of holy matrimony.

Probably another reason for the notable absence of prostitution in early America was the presence of the bond servant in the North and the slave in the South. The bond servant was a member of the community who had either been deported to the colonies as a form of punishment or who had bound him- or herself to indentured servitude in exchange for transportation to the New World. The presence of female bond servants, who were often easy prey for the male members of a household, may have contributed in part to the visible absence of prostitution in early America. Likewise, the slave in the South served much the same function, and many viewed sexual relations with slaves as a means of producing more slaves for the plantation on which they lived.

Because prostitution is mainly an urban phenomenon, it is not surprising that as the cities grew in the United States, so grew the incidence of prostitution. This is not to say that prostitution does not exist in the rural areas as well. In fact, there is hardly a rural community in the country that does not have at least one "lady of the night," who is a town institution in herself, and who has initiated the youth of the community into the mysteries of sex.

The Laws Governing Prostitution Today

Although the laws governing prostitution vary throughout the United States, every state prohibits certain types of activities associated with prostitution. All states have statutes prohibiting soliciting (commonly called hustling) whereby the prostitute approaches and propositions a potential customer. Most states prohibit houses of prostitution, although in the state of Nevada they are legal, provided they are approved by local county referendum. Two houses of prostitution are operating in the state of Nevada at this writing, the Mustang Ranch in Storey County just outside of Reno and the One M Ranch in Lyon County south of Reno. A Reno cabdriver explains that the eight-mile trip to Mustang Ranch will cost the customer $12. The prostitute charges $15. Most drivers wait for the return fare (waiting time usually does not exceed twenty minutes). Sometimes coffee is provided for the waiting cabbies and occasionally they are treated to the "courtesy of the house."

Most states have laws which prohibit promiscuous sexual intercourse for hire; others define prostitution simply as promiscuous sexual intercourse and make no mention of money. Still others prohibit any kind of sexual conduct for hire. Every state has laws against compelling prostitution, inducing minors to engage in prostitution, promoting prostitution—that is, maintaining or operating a brothel—procuring (pimping), and soliciting.

In some states, offenders can be tried and convicted on the basis of only one act of soliciting or one act of prostitution. In other states, prostitution is treated as an ongoing crime, and in order to bring charges it must be shown that between one date and another the defendant has regularly engaged in the business of prostitution. In these cases, vice officers must keep detailed records of a suspect's infractions over a sufficient period of time to warrant bringing charges against her. Needless to say, such laws almost seem to be designed to thwart police efforts to bring prostitution under control. In the majority of states, prostitution is treated as a misdemeanor, punished by short sentences and minimal fines. And in the few states that do treat prostitution as a felony, judges usually mete out probation and small fines. Because the courts throughout the land do not seem to regard prostitution as a serious problem, any police effort to clean up the situation is doomed from the outset. This has resulted in a type of enforcement, most commonly seen in the larger cities, called "the pros patrol" in which officers assigned to a patrol merely sweep the streets, picking up the prostitutes and taking them to jail. Although this action may alleviate the problem for a few hours, the girls are free to go back to work as soon as they have made bail.

Types of Prostitutes and Their Operations

In the United States, as in ancient Greece and Rome, prostitution may be divided into a hierarchy or caste system which classifies prostitutes according to method of operation, price, number of girls working in that class, and the socioeconomic group served. A comparison of these caste systems is shown below:

United States	*Ancient Greece*	*Ancient Rome*
Call Girl	Hetairae	Courtesan
House Girl	Auletrides	Streetwalker
Streetwalker	Streetwalker	Brothel Prostitute
B-Girl	Pornoi (slave)	(slave)

The Call Girl

Call girls represent the highest class of prostitutes in the American hierarchy of prostitution. They are usually younger, prettier, and better educated (though not always) than their lower-class sisters. The majority of independent prostitutes—that is, those who do not share their earnings with a pimp—are found in this class. Their prices are high, ranging from $100 to $200 per night or higher, depending on the customer and the type of services provided. Many call girls are part-time prostitutes, holding down "straight" jobs during the day and selling sex at night. Many schoolteachers, nurses, secretaries, models, and so forth take this route into prostitution.

The call girl depends on word-of-mouth advertising and business cards listing her phone number for making her contacts. She may answer the phone herself or use an answering service to screen her calls. She is selective in her choice of clientele, a luxury not afforded prostitutes in the lower classes. Talking with customers over the phone, she discusses money arrangements and decides on the meeting place and means of identification. This allows her to scrutinize the prospect before committing herself for the evening. She will either take him back to her place or go to his apartment or to a hotel or motel. She collects her fee in advance to avoid any unpleasantness later.

Some types of call girls are employed by an agency which provides clientele and shares in the profits. These agencies advertise themselves as model agencies or escort services, but their main business is to provide girls for well-heeled customers. They keep files on their clients, noting their preferences for particular types of girls, price range, and any other idiosyncrasies. Prices may range up to $1,000 per night.

Another type of operation, which is similar to a brothel, requires customers to call in for an appointment with a particular girl and to arrive at the apartment at a designated time. The apartment may house three or four girls working for a pimp or working on a straight commission basis. The operator pays for the apartment, provides transportation to the apartment for the girls, and takes 60 percent of the fees. An operation of this type was recently broken up in an Ohio city. The operator, a local accountant, had rented a luxury apartment, installed four girls whom he had obtained by advertising for secretarial help in the accounting firm, and installed a telephone-answering device. He made contacts in local bars and motels and provided "steerers" with nude photos of the girls.

Prices ranged from \$25 to \$50, depending on the type of sexual services provided. One of the girls was a seventeen-year-old high school senior. When she was beaten by a customer, her parents questioned her, learned the story, and complained to the police. On the basis of the complaint and the girl's story, police were able to get a search warrant. They found the incriminating tapes from the telephone-answering device, as well as the "John list," a list of regular customers, also known as a "trick book." They picked up the girls and were able to convict both them and the accountant.

This kind of luck on the part of the police is unusual. Ordinarily there is no complainant, and probable cause for obtaining a search warrant does not exist. Consequently, it is highly unusual for a call girl to be arrested. Working entirely over the telephone, she is extremely elusive. In most states, in order to prove soliciting or prostitution, the police must be able to show that it was the prostitute who initiated the business deal. This is especially difficult to prove in the case of the call girl because it is typically the customer who makes the first call. Therefore, if the police call the number, most courts will rule entrapment. The call girl arranges the meeting in such a way that she can size up the customer before she approaches him. If she suspects that the customer is a police officer, she merely walks away.

Several years ago, an interview with a part-time call girl produced the following taped conversation:

Q. Good evening. Our mutual friend tells me that you are a prostitute. Is that true?
A. [With a smile] I prefer to be called a personal service consultant.
Q. Do you mean call girl?
A. I've been called that.
Q. How long have you been a personal service consultant?
A. About six years.
Q. You don't look old enough to have been in the business that long.
A. I'm 26. I take good care of myself.
Q. How did you get into the business?
A. I was a senior in college and I needed the money for tuition. I had been sleeping with a few casual friends and decided to stop giving it away.
Q. Then you're a college graduate?
A. I'm a law school graduate.
Q. Have you passed the bar?
A. No, I've never taken the bar exam . . . besides, I make more than most attorneys.
Q. Are you a full-time call girl?
A. No, I have a regular job.
Q. Where do you work?
A. In the legal department of [a large multi-national firm].
Q. How much do you earn there?
A. About \$12,000 a year.

Q. With an income like that, I don't understand why you have to be a call girl.

A. I don't have to do anything. I provide a service strictly for the money.

Q. What is your income from providing your service?

A. Last year I made $57,000.

Q. Isn't that high for a part-time occupation?

A. My fees are high and I'm consultant to several large companies who keep me on retainer.

Q. You mean that they actually pay you to be available?

A. Yes.

Q. Would you explain how that system operates?

A. Sure. I'm listed on the payrolls of four companies as a consultant. They pay me from four to five thousand dollars a year to be on call. Whenever an important client is in town, they call me, tell me where to meet the client, and I meet him. My job is to keep him happy and, if possible, to convince him to buy from or sell to my employer.

Q. What kind of services do you provide?

A. Sexual services, naturally . . . mostly straight sex. Occasionally the customer wants something out of the ordinary, and I provide that, too.

Q. Where do you provide these services?

A. Usually at the client's hotel.

Q. How often do these companies call on you to provide your services?

A. Once or twice a month, sometimes not that often.

Q. That explains about $20,000 of your income. Where does the rest of it come from?

A. I have about thirty private clients who call whenever they are in town. They buy my services two or three nights a week.

Q. What fees do you charge your private clients?

A. Usually $200.

Q. Is that for one act of intercourse, or for an hour, a night?

A. That's for the whole night.

Q. Any other source of income?

A. Occasionally one of my contacts will call me to work a convention, usually on a weekend.

Q. How much are you paid in a situation like that?

A. It varies . . . sometimes a thousand dollars, sometimes more.

Q. What is required of you at a convention?

A. Sexual services to prospective clients of the company who hired me.

Q. How many sexual partners would you deal with on one of these weekends?

A. Around six or seven.

Q. Would you be the only girl present during a convention?

A. Heavens no! Most of the time there may be five or six of us.

Q. Are you all paid the same fee?

A. I don't know. I value my privacy and don't usually mix with the other girls.

Q. How would the company account for your services?

A. I was told once that I was listed under business expenses—hospitality.

Q. Is there anything else you would like to tell me about yourself?

A. No, I don't think so. I've told you enough already.

The House Girl

Next in line after the call girl is the house girl, a prostitute who works in a brothel or whorehouse. These girls share their earnings with one or two people. In some operations, the madam of the house serves as both madam and pimp. In this role, she provides a place to do business and takes a cut of the profits. Were she acting only as a madam she would provide these same services but take a smaller cut. When the girl has been placed in a brothel by a pimp, he takes the lion's share of her earnings.

In the house operation, the inmates are expected to be at the house during business hours. When customers arrive, the girls line up in their working clothes, usually a revealing dress that has a zipper down the front. The customer takes his pick and pays the madam. The girl carries a card which is punched once for each customer. When the card is completely punched she has satisfied her quota for the week. On the average, a popular girl may service five or six clients a night at $20 to $50 per trick. If the girl is working for the madam, they will split the profits 50–50. If she is working for a pimp, she will not see much of the money she has earned.

A variation of the brothel operation is the recently revived "massage parlor." These parlors are openly advertised as health-giving, tension-relieving spas. In the Los Angeles area, billboard advertising is used showing a staff of beautiful, well-endowed women dressed in bikini outfits. Swedish massage is advertised, but word of mouth soon lets prospective customers know that other services are available for a fee. The usual fee is $20 for a complete or localized massage, in the nude. The localized massage refers to masturbation of the customer by the masseuse. For an additional $30, the masseuse will perform fellatio on the customer. Ordinarily, services are limited to these two forms of sexual activity.

In a current Midwest operation, the owner of a massage parlor openly advertises in the newspapers and with the state unemployment agency for masseuses. When the girls apply, he explains in veiled terms what is expected of them, suggesting that localized massage, in its several forms, is extremely healthful and is, in fact, a contribution to society. He offers the applicants a salary of $150 per week plus tips and assures them that their tips can be as plentiful as they wish, depending on their willingness to fulfill the customers' whims.

Although it is difficult for police to control brothels and massage parlors, it is not impossible. Proper surveillance of the premises plus questioning of customers can often produce sufficient evidence to obtain a search warrant, and the subsequent raid can close the operation. Because the location of houses and parlors is stationary and because they operate publicly, they are relatively susceptible to control. The most important factor in investigating such establishments is to avoid entrapment. If an officer poses as a customer by going to a house or massage parlor, a court may rule entrapment on grounds that the officer sought out the service. An officer who participates in the sex act or who pays money for a massage would be declared in violation of the law along with the operator and the girl, and the case would be dismissed. One approach would be to have an informer pose as a customer and then use his statement in court. A house or a massage parlor cannot operate for very long without the knowledge of the police. Should such an establishment manage to stay in business for a long time, the public has a right to question the honesty of the police force.

The Streetwalker

The most common type of prostitute in this country is the streetwalker, the girl who walks the streets and prowls the bars in search of customers. The streetwalker ranks lower on the prostitution scale than the call girl and the house girl because her prices are much lower and she generally takes on all but the most obnoxious customers. However, Bryan (1965; cited in Cressey and Ward 1969, p. 514) quotes a pimp who managed both call girls and "high-class" streetwalkers as saying,

> The girl that goes out into the street is the sharper of the two, because she is capable of handling herself in the streets, getting around the law, picking out the trick that is not absolutely psycho. . . . The streetwalker, as you term her, is really a prima donna of the prostitutes . . . her field is unlimited, she goes to all of the top places so she meets the top people.

The pimp's high-class streetwalker may be a soul mate to the run-of-the-mill streetwalker since both must develop certain skills in observation and approach, but the average girl who works the streets has a tough life, hardly glamorized by "going to the top places or meeting top people." She must be able to size up the prospects, assess their ability to pay, and determine that they are not "kinky" enough to get their kicks by beating her up. Her method of operating is solicitation. She approaches the "John" on the street and makes her pitch. "Whadda ya say? How about a good time? Twenty and ten?" She has offered her wares for twenty dollars plus ten for the room. If the John accepts, she takes him to a hotel which caters to whores and their customers. The activity is simply one of relieving sexual tension, devoid of any semblance of emotion . . . a purely mechanical joining of two bodies for a few minutes. Kissing, fondling, and other time-consuming erotic play is not allowed. Within fifteen minutes she is back on the street looking for another customer. Adler (1953, p. 9) says,

> A prostitute can count on no more than ten money-making years. Then she is through—if not dead or diseased, so broken by drugs, alcohol and the steady abuse of her body that no one will hire her again.

Adler, who herself was the most famous madam in American history until the advent of Xaviera Hollander, also quotes the rich, well-bred girl who, working as a prostitute, offered the following reply when asked what a girl like herself was doing in the business: "Oh, I don't know. I'm just lucky, I guess."

As noted earlier, the streetwalker must develop observational skills. Through experience she learns to identify "the man." She usually will not approach men in their early twenties because she has learned to equate youth with police officers. Besides she also knows that college-aged men seldom have enough money to afford her. She avoids men wearing black shoes or other vestiges of a uniform because she suspects they might be police officers. When she is working a beat several blocks from her pad, it is expected that she and the John will go there in his car. Upon entering the car she will first ask to see his money. Once satisfied, she will throw her arms around him and rub his entire body. Love? Emotion? Anticipation? Hardly. She is merely making sure that he is not the law. She is frisking for the gun and badge. Ordinarily, on her beat she will seek out the working-class types on the street or in the bars. In a bar, she will size up the customers and pick a likely prospect. She stares until she gets an interested response and then saunters over to the prospective John. "Buy a girl a drink?" If she gets an affirmative response she might suggest a party or a good time. In reply to the question "How much?" she states her price and if asked what the price will buy she spells it out. Once the bargain has been struck, they leave together. She is usually back on the street again within thirty minutes.

The average streetwalker, who is dedicated and hardworking, can service an average of sixty to seventy-five Johns a week. At the going rate of $20, this amounts to $1500 per week or $75,000 per year. One would expect that she lives high on the hog with this type of income, but in reality, she sees little of the money. A very small number of all streetwalkers are independents. Invariably there is a pimp in the background. He takes all of the money earned and she is enraptured if he buys her a present. It is difficult to understand why a girl would be willing to engage in the sordid business of prostitution and then turn practically all her proceeds over to a pimp. Most researchers contend that she does it out of love and concern for the pimp. He flatters her in the beginning and convinces her that she is something special to him. Her relationship with him becomes sexual and gradually he convinces her that he needs her to help him get some money. Finally he "turns her out" to prostitute for him. He in turn takes the money she earns and she lives for his infrequent caresses. She takes pride in the fact that he is the best-dressed man in town or that he drives a brand-new car. Even though she learns that he is running several other girls, her "sisters-in-law," she continues to work diligently for him, competing with the others for his approval.

In return for her work, the pimp provides a number of services for the working girl. If she is not working out of a hotel, he provides a place for her to take her tricks; he provides bail when she is arrested; and he or one of his flunkies provides protection from the occasional John who gets his kicks by beating her up. In some cities, the pimp acts as procurer, bringing her customers. But most of all he provides her with what she considers true affection. He makes her feel wanted and loved while at the same time beating her if she doesn't make enough money or if she tries to hold out money on him. Ironically, most prostitutes consider their relationship to the pimp a natural one and feel that they are beaten because they deserve it and because he loves them.

Control of the streetwalker is best carried out by the undercover vice officer. Dressed as the men who frequent the area where the streetwalker works, he makes himself available as a prospective John. When she approaches and makes her pitch he asks, "How much?" Given the price, he agrees or haggles depending on the figure and then gets her to say what he will get for the money. He tries to get her into his car and once this is accomplished, he drives toward her room, or the hotel. Once out of sight of the beat he drives past a pickup car containing two vice-team officers. They pull alongside, and the girl is transferred to their custody for booking on a charge of soliciting. This leaves the officer free for the remainder of his shift to maintain his cover and make more arrests. If the girl returns, the undercover man moves to another beat and repeats the procedure. In a large city, the vice officer can move around until he becomes so well known that he is of no further use as an undercover agent. Sometimes by altering his appearance or wearing a disguise, he can go back to the original neighborhood and begin the operation all over again. If the vice officer pays in advance, he will do so with bills whose numbers have been recorded so that later he can prove that money actually changed hands. The most common charge brought against prostitutes is soliciting. A charge of prostitution requires proof of a sexual act, and such evidence is impossible for the officer to obtain without ruining the case. In order to gain the necessary evidence, the officer would have to participate in the crime, and this is frowned on by the courts.

It is rare that a pimp is arrested and charged with procuring or pandering. Unless he actually does the soliciting for his girl (and he seldom does), there is little opportunity to arrest him. He usually makes his appearance near the end of the evening when he contacts his girls to collect their earnings. The only time we get a chance at the pimp is when he makes the mistake of beating one of his women to the point that she is willing to talk to the police in order to protect herself, or as an act of revenge. On the basis of her testimony we can arrest and try him. Otherwise the same situation prevails—the prostitute takes all the risks and does all the work. She is the one who is arrested. The pimp takes most of the money, the hotels and motels which cater to prostitution make their profit, and the prostitute supports them all.

The B-Girl

At the lowest end of the prostitution caste system is the B-girl. This lady works in a bar, serving as a drinking companion and supplementing her earnings as a prostitute. The B-girl approaches her John with a smile and a welcome to the establishment and offers to sit with him. If the invitation is accepted, the

John is in for an expensive night. He orders drinks for himself and the lady. He will usually get the cheapest brands of liquor at inflated prices. The B-girl will order the most expensive drinks in the house, also at inflated prices, but in most cases, she is not being served alcohol at all: her champagne cocktail is a mixture of ginger ale and white wine, and her whiskey is tea. Yet the customer pays for high-priced drinks. If he declines to buy her drinks, she moves close to him, rubs herself against him and promises him a party at her place when she gets off work. He continues to buy the drinks until she gets through work or until his money runs out, whichever comes first. If his money holds out, he takes her home, and for the usual $20 to $50 she takes him to bed. The bar pays the B-girl a commission on the drinks bought by the John. Each time he buys a drink, she receives a chit. At the end of the evening, she presents her chits to the bartender, who redeems them for cash.

Although most states have laws prohibiting employees of bars, cafés, and nightclubs from sitting with customers, in many places these laws are not enforced. For example, along Savannah's riverfront there are a group of small topless bars. The topless dancers take turns dancing behind the bar, and, after each has taken her turn, she mingles with the audience on the floor, still topless, encouraging the customers to buy drinks. Ohio does not have such a law, and in that state a chain of drinking places is being developed in the more populous cities. In a recent interview, one of the local managers explained that the chain employs bikini-clad girls to act as companions to the customers. He frankly admits that the purpose of using the girls is to encourage the customers to buy drinks. Appropriately enough, this chain of bars is called "The Hustler," although the manager claims that the girls are not allowed to socialize with customers outside the premises.

Enforcing the laws against B-girl operations is not difficult. Officers merely have to visit the bars to see what is going on. Since the activity is so open, the local police departments in cities which have ordinances against such activity must be suspect.

Enforcement Techniques

In our discussion of each type of prostitute, we have outlined some of the approved methods of control. There are several other methods of enforcement which might be termed general control of prostitution. The laws of many states prohibit soliciting or participating in an act of prostitution and as such can be enforced not only against the prostitute but against her customer as well. However, most states do not arrest the John, despite the provisions in the law. In Portland, Oregon, officers are enforcing the law against the John as well as against the girl and are publicizing the arrests. This type of approach should deter all but the most callous customers. Many men would never patronize a prostitute if they thought that they would be arrested and exposed. Such publication could lead to a breakup of one's marriage, the loss of a job, and great embarrassment in the community. It still remains to be seen how effective the Portland plan will be.

Large numbers of prostitutes work out of bars, hotels, motels, and restaurants. Many steerers are bartenders, cabdrivers, and waiters. Each of these places is licensed by a number of city and state agencies. Each of the steerers is employed by a licensed employer. Most of these licensing agencies have established regulations prohibiting, among other violations, using the premises for immoral purposes. Continual complaints by the police to the licensing agencies can result in suspension or removal of the license. After the proprietors of these places have been hit in the pocketbook several times, they will soon take steps to keep the prostitutes out of their establishments.

Legalized Prostitution

The most radical solution to the problem of prostitution, and the one which generates the most controversy, is legalization and control. In recent years, there have been a number of proposals advocating the legalization of prostitution, and in every case, both the proponents and the opponents of these proposals have marshaled impressive arguments to bolster their positions. The proponents of legalized prostitution put forth the following arguments:

The function of criminal law is not to coerce citizens toward virtue by imposing public standards on private morality.

The resources of the criminal justice system are limited while the incidence of serious crime is high. We cannot justify the hundreds of thousands of police man-hours used in the abortive efforts to eliminate prostitution.

For centuries we have been trying to eliminate prostitution and have failed. Legalization and control will at last put society in control.

Legalization and control will eliminate the pimp and the middlemen who live off the earnings of the prostitute.

Legalization and control will eliminate the peripheral crimes which attach to prostitution. Drunk rolling, robbery, and extortion will become things of the past in relation to prostitution.

Legalized houses of prostitution would provide weekly medical examinations of prostitutes, thus reducing the incidence of venereal disease.

Most prostitutes enter the business voluntarily and so legalization will merely be the recognition of this fact.

The effort and the subsequent failure to enforce laws against prostitution breed disrespect for the law and cynicism for all law enforcement.

The opponents of legalized prostitution present the following arguments:

Prostitution exploits women unconscionably.

Licensed houses of prostitution are disseminators of VD to as full an extent as an unregulated system of prostitution.

No system of prostitution has been able to eliminate the pimps, who take so much of the prostitutes' earnings.

Legalization would require an elaborate retirement system to take care of the prostitute as she got older and unable to work.

Many prostitutes are members of minority groups. Licensing black, Puerto Rican, and Chicano women as prostitutes for white customers would only increase racial tensions.

Wherever prostitution has been legalized there have always been a greater number of unlicensed, illegal prostitutes.

We have no experience with decriminalization and cannot tell in advance if it would work.

Perhaps we should take the point of view of Mrs. Patrick Campbell, who stated in a letter to George Bernard Shaw that she did not care what people did so long as they did not do it in the streets and frighten the horses.

Crimes Peripheral to Prostitution

The existence of prostitution in our cities presents problems that go beyond the questions of morality, disease, exploitation, and violation of the laws governing public chastity and decency. We are also faced with the commission of a number of peripheral crimes which are fostered and abetted by those who engage in prostitution, and others who seek to profit by its existence. There are prostitutes and their pimps who rob their customers once they have them out of the public view. And sex is frequently used as the bait to lure a victim to an apartment or motel room where he is robbed. Others prey upon the vulnerability of their customers to extort money on the threat of exposing them to their wives or bosses. Bunco schemes are also practiced in which the pimp breaks into the bedroom and accuses the John of "fooling around with my wife." A customer who can be successfully intimidated by these tactics will hand over money to avoid exposure of his peccadillo.

Often, while the John is preoccupied with the whore in a motel room, the pimp breaks into his car and steals anything that is not nailed down, including his luggage, his stereo, and his radio. In most cases, the victim does not report these thefts to the police for fear that his association with the prostitute will become known. If he does report the thefts he usually changes the location of the incident and thus his report is useless from an enforcement point of view. However, the false report does satisfy his insurance company and he is usually paid for his loss.

In the major cities, most prostitutes will arm themselves as protection against the overly aggressive customers. Often they are guilty of assault on a customer either as a prelude to robbery or to enforce payment of a higher fee. Not all prostitutes engage in these other crimes, but enough of them do to make the problem a serious one. Those who do not participate in this additional illegal activity take pride in the fact and refer to themselves as "dedicated women," meaning that the John gets what he pays for and is in no danger of being rolled, mugged, or robbed.

Another type of criminal circulates around the fringes of prostitution victimizing the John whenever possible. He is called the "murphy-man." He operates by posing as a pimp or procurer. When he spots a likely prospect, he will offer him a girl for a modest fee. If the John accepts, the murphy-man offers to drive him to the apartment. On the way, he drives down a deserted street, stops the car, and pulls a gun on the John and robs him. Another version of the murphy scam occurs when the murphy-man insists on payment in advance and sends the John to a fictitious address. By the time the John returns to the bar, the murphy-man is gone. In still another variation, the murphy-man will approach the John, point out a particularly attractive girl sitting alone at the bar, and offer the John a trick with the girl. If the John agrees, the murphy-man will approach the girl and talk to her for a few minutes about the weather, the time of day—anything. He will then return to the John and say that the date is all arranged, and ask for payment. He tells the John that the girl will meet him outside. After the John leaves, the murphy-man leaves by the back door. After waiting for the girl, who does not appear, the John returns to the bar, accosts the innocent girl, and learns to his chagrin that he has been taken.

In a final variation of the scheme, the murphy-man accompanies the John, who is preferably drunk, to a walk-up apartment. In the lobby he gives the John the name of the girl and explains to him that he should be careful because the girl has been known to roll customers who have been drinking. Because he is such a nice guy, the murphy-man offers to hold the John's wallet, watch, and car keys while he is upstairs. If the John is drunk enough, he agrees. Of course, both the girl and the apartment are fictitious and if the John happens to knock on the wrong door he is liable to encounter additional trouble. When he returns to the lobby, he finds that the murphy-man has escaped with his wallet, his watch, and his car, proving of course that Phineas T. Barnum was right when he said, "There's a sucker born every minute."

GLOSSARY OF PROSTITUTION TERMS

B-GIRL. A prostitute who works in a bar in the dual capacity of "companion for customers" and prostitute. She is paid a commission for each drink her customer buys. She also provides sexual service for a fee.

CALL GIRL. A prostitute who makes arrangements with her customers by telephone. She is more selective than other prostitutes and her prices are higher. By far the most difficult prostitute to arrest and prosecute.

DEDICATED WOMAN. A prostitute who does not engage in robbing, rolling, or mugging her customers. One who provides the John with everything he has paid for.

HOOKER. A prostitute.

HOUSE GIRL. A prostitute who works in a stationary establishment.

HUSTLER. A prostitute, usually a streetwalker.

JOHN. The prostitute's customer.

JOHN LIST. A list of steady customers kept by a call girl.

MADAM. A panderer or procurer who manages a house of prostitution.

MAN (THE). The police.

MASSAGE PARLOR. A front for prostitution which usually provides "local massage," masturbation, or fellatio.

MURPHY-MAN. A criminal who poses as a pimp or procurer and then steals from the John either by robbery or fraud.

MURPHY SCAM. The act of defrauding the John by setting him up with a nonexistent prostitute and demanding payment in advance.

PANDERER. One who supplies a prostitute to the John. One who convinces a woman to become a prostitute.

PIMP. One who derives his living from the earnings of a prostitute.

PROCURING. The act of soliciting for a prostitute. Supplying a prostitute for a customer.

PROS PATROL. In some police departments, a patrol which has the duty of sweeping the streets and arresting any prostitute found in public areas.

PROSTITUTE. A woman or man who engages in sexual conduct or sexual intercourse for a fee of money.

SOLICITING. The act of offering to engage in sexual conduct or sexual intercourse for a fee.

STREETWALKER. A prostitute who solicits her customers on the public streets or in other public places.

TRICK. One act of sexual intercourse. Sometimes, a customer.

TURN OUT. The act of a pimp as he sends a woman out on the street to work as a prostitute.

VENEREAL DISEASE. Those diseases, usually syphilis and gonorrhea, associated with or arising from sexual intercourse.

REFERENCES

Adler, Polly. *A House Is Not a Home.* New York: Holt, Rinehart and Winston, 1953.

Anonymous. *The Streetwalker*. New York: Gramercy Publishing Co., 1962.

Bryan, James H. "Apprenticeships in Prostitution," *Social Problems* 12 (1965): 287–297.

Bullough, Vern L. *The History of Prostitution*. New Hyde Park, N.Y.: University Books, 1965.

Cressey, Donald R., and Ward, David A. *Delinquency, Crime, and Social Process*. New York: Harper and Row, 1969.

Chapter 5

Sex Crimes*

The question of how to deal with sex offenders is, for a number of reasons, one of the most difficult enforcement problems faced by police today. One difficulty stems from the fact that the majority of these crimes are committed by abnormal persons, whose motivations and behavior frequently elude the understanding of the average police officer. The typical officer, whose attitudes toward sex are relatively normal, may experience unusual emotional reactions to the sex criminal and his crimes, thus reducing his ability to handle those cases in an objective, rational manner. Second, the vicious and revolting nature of some of these crimes creates fear and panic among members of the community, placing additional strain on the police. This panic and fear is often compounded by the sensational news coverage given such crimes by the media. Finally, lurid sex crimes invariably stimulate a morbid interest on the part of the public, forcing the police to conduct their investigation in the harsh glare of heightened publicity and public interest. For obvious reasons, these conditions are hardly conducive to a rational, objective police investigation, and if they occasionally produce failure on the part of the police, public confidence in the department is lessened and the general morale of the officers suffers.

In addition to the immediate sex crime, police are often faced with a secondary crime "fallout." The sex offender may be involved in other crimes as well, either as the perpetrator or as the victim. Because he is shunned by society he is often unable to earn a normal living or hold a job for more than a short time, which may force him into robbery, burglary, mugging, or similar crimes. As a victim, he is frequently subjected to blackmail (extortion), robbery, or assault, and those who prey on him assume that he will not report their crimes to the police for fear of revealing his own activities (Lentini and France 1972).

The Role of the Police

While the responsibilities of the police in dealing with sex crimes do not differ markedly from their responsibilities in dealing with other types of crime,

---

*Some of the material in this chapter was developed for use in the FBI National Academy by Special Agents Frank Sass and Walter McLaughlin and is used here with the special permission of the late Director J. Edgar Hoover.

the very nature of these crimes and their offenders makes their job much more difficult.

The first responsibility of the police in carrying out their mission is in the area of prevention. In dealing with most crimes, plans can be made, task forces established, and the incidence of the crimes reduced. However, in dealing with sex crimes such strategies usually do not work. Moreover, the law does not permit the police to take any form of direct preventive action against sex crimes. Rather they must wait until the crime is committed before taking action, even though their records and the conditions of the community may indicate that a sex crime by a particular offender is imminent. These crimes are very private in nature and are committed against one individual at a time. Since they are committed by psychopathic personalities, it is extremely difficult to predict exactly how or when they will be committed and by whom. Sexual perversion or mental deficiencies are not readily apparent to an observer.

The police also have the responsibility of recognizing sex crimes when they occur, but these offenses are not always easily identified since in many cases no sexual element is apparent to the investigator. For example, the sex pyro-maniac, the accidental masochistic suicide, and the lust-mutilation offender may achieve sexual satisfaction without resorting to actual sexual contact with the victim or victims. By recognizing a particular act or set of cir-cumstances as having a sexual motivation, police are sometimes able to make a timely arrest by simply checking their sex offender files for known offenders and their *modus operandi* (M.O.).

It is imperative that police departments maintain adequate records of known sex offenders in the community. These files should contain names, addresses, descriptions, pictures, and M.O.s. In many states, laws exist which require that administrators of jails, prisons, and mental institutions notify police any time a committed or convicted sex offender is released back into the community. This allows the police to maintain an up-to-date system of records on all sex offend-ers within their jurisdiction. In many cases these records allow for quick iden-tification and apprehension and do much to relieve panic and fear in the com-munity following a sex offense.

The investigation of a sex crime must be thorough. At best, sex offenses are extremely difficult to prove. In most cases the victim, if still alive, is in shock. Often the victim is a child who does not really comprehend the nature of the crime. Investigators must always be sensitive to the feelings of the victim and must do everything in their power to reduce the trauma which results from the often shocking atrocities committed by the offender. At the same time, the investigator must get all the facts, more often than not in clinical detail, and must prepare a case for court which will stand up under intensive and often embarrassing cross-examination by the defense counsel. The investigator will find that often the victim of the crime becomes the accused as the defense counsel defend their client by conducting an intense scrutiny of the victim's past life and sexual history.

The sex-crime investigator must not only keep in mind the sensitivity of the victim; he must also be an expert interviewer when he questions the suspect. Probing the mind of a mentally ill person is difficult. The investigator must know when to be tough and when to be sympathetic. He must understand that the psychotic offender may be ridden with improbable fantasies and may offer elaborate rationalizations to justify his actions.

The Human Sex Drive

Psychologist Abraham Maslow (1943; quoted in Kalish 1970, p. 28) outlined a hierarchy of human needs which, according to his theory, are inherent in all human beings. Among the basic needs are hunger, security, affection, and the need for stimulation, and sex is one of the activities which falls into this latter category.

> The desire for sex in humans results from biochemical changes within the body, but these changes are set off by information sent through the sense organs to the brain or by thinking which began in the brain. Thinking of something with sexual meanings can lead to stirring up the sex need; seeing, touching, or hearing something with sexual meanings will also lead to sexual arousal.
>
> How to satisfy the hunger, thirst, activity and other physiological motives is very easy to learn. The satisfying of some needs, as the need for air or sleep, requires no learning—we breathe and sleep without any help or learning at all. Sex is quite different. Human beings must learn how to satisfy their sexual needs.

Although sex, or gender, is determined at birth, personality differences associated with sex roles begin to appear very early in life and are largely the product of learning. A small boy, for example, learns to adopt the male sex role by interacting with and imitating his father and by associating with his male peers. Likewise, a little girl learns the female role by interacting with her mother and other females. If these sex-role models somehow fail to impart the appropriate sex-role behavior, the child may develop attitudes toward sex that later result in a deviate sex personality. By the time a person has reached adolescence or young adulthood, his attitudes toward sex have been fairly well established. Generally speaking, individuals can be classified according to their sexual role and preference, and fall into one of three basic categories.

The first of these sexual categories is the heterosexual, the person who prefers to have sexual relations only with members of the opposite sex. The majority of the human race falls into this category. The second classification is the bisexual—that is, the person who practices sexual relations with members of both sexes. Here we have an individual who is both heterosexual and homosexual. He or she represents only a small percentage of the population. The third category is the homosexual, the person who is inclined to engage in sexual relations with members of the same sex. In the majority of cases this individual lacks the ability to enjoy sexual relations with members of the opposite sex.

In this chapter we will discuss a variety of sex crimes involving criminal acts committed by members of, or containing elements of, all three sexual categories. As stated above, no individual is born with a particular sexual preference. Rather, sex roles develop as a result of learning.

Types of Sexual Deviation

Kalish (1970), quoted above, tells us that sexual feelings are caused by biochemical changes which are experienced through the senses and transmitted to the brain. These feelings vary from individual to individual and therefore sexual satisfaction is achieved by different people in different ways. Although no one has been able to define what is "normal" in regard to sexual practice, there are a number of activities which society has deemed "abnormal" and thus fit for criminal legislation. Among the "abnormal" elements which motivate sex crimes are sadism, masochism, or a combination of both—sadomasochism. These elements are the motivating factors in the commission of the majority of sex crimes.

A sadist is one who derives his sexual satisfaction through cruelty, torture, or the suffering of others. This person is mentally unstable and presents a constant threat to society. He may indulge himself by beating, slashing, cutting, or otherwise torturing his victim or sexual partner. These activities are carried out for the sole purpose of achieving sexual gratification. In many cases, the crimes committed by the sadist contain no element of normal sex, but for him they represent the epitome of sexual gratification. The sadist often experiences orgasm while inflicting these cruelties on his victims.

The masochist, on the other hand, is an individual who derives his sexual satisfaction by being tortured or humiliated. Gratification, up to and including orgasm, is attained by experiencing pain and suffering. He enjoys being tortured and will often solicit sadistic partners by advertising in sex-oriented publications. He describes himself in these ads as one who appreciates "discipline." Both the sadist and the masochist are often unable to achieve complete sexual gratification through normal sexual intercourse and must resort to inflicting torture or being tortured in order to be completely satisfied.

The sadomasochist is an individual who is afflicted with a dual deviation and who seeks his sexual gratification by playing either the aggressive (sadistic) or the passive (masochistic) role. The criminal sadomasochist is a dangerous individual whose crimes may include rape, murder, and assault. Generally, the aggressive, sadistic side of his nature is predominant and in some instances he will commit a crime and then confess to it in order to be punished. Police in every city have encountered individuals who confess to widely publicized crimes which in fact they did not commit. The sadomasochist harbors strong feelings of guilt and feels a need to be punished in order to expiate that guilt. For this reason, he confesses to crimes which he did not commit. The police, of course, must carefully check out these admissions since in many instances they turn out to be fraudulent.

There are several masochistic practices in particular with which police should be familiar because they figure as the cause of a number of deaths in the United States each year. The first of these practices is bondage, which in recent years has been widely publicized by those who manufacture and sell pornography. Pictures showing individuals tied up or being dominated by a woman dressed in black leather and holding a whip seem to appeal to the twisted senses of the masochist. In the personal-ad columns of the sex magazines this practice is referred to as "domination."

Another dangerous practice is infibulation, or self-torture, of the sex organs. A recent case in a midwestern city involved a woman who had fainted on a city street. Upon closer examination at a hospital, it was discovered that the woman had sewn the lips of her vagina together. Among males this type of self-torture is practiced by tying a length of piano wire around the penis and attaching weights to the end of the wire. As one can imagine, the pain caused by such self-inflicted tortures must be excruciating.

A recent article, which appeared in an Ohio paper, described the "accidental hanging" of a sixteen-year-old boy, who was found hanging by the neck from the top of a door. The age of the boy rules out the usual children's games. An interview with one of the investigating officers revealed that when the police arrived, they found the body in a nude state. The boy had apparently placed the rope around his neck and tied the other end to a box which he had suspended over the top of the door. The victim had positioned a large mirror in front of the door so that he could watch himself.

This type of hanging is a common masochistic practice which, when coupled with abnormal sexual fantasy, produces sexual gratification. In the case described above, as in many similar cases, the victim became so sexually aroused that he passed out (owing to an insufficient supply of blood to the brain) and inadvertently hanged himself. The majority of the victims in this type of case are adolescent boys.

Exhibitionism or Indecent Exposure

Exhibitionism is the most common of the sex crimes and the one that is most frequently encountered by the police. An act of exhibitionism occurs when an individual (typically a man) exposes his sex organs or his nude body in a public place. His victims are generally women or young girls. This individual derives his sexual satisfaction from the look of shock or fear on the faces of his victims as he exposes himself. Many exhibitionists go to great lengths to practice their deviation. Some will cut out the front or crotch area of their trousers, and then cover themselves with a topcoat. Thus attired for action, they go into a public area to await their unwitting victim. As a woman approaches, her attention is attracted by whistling or calling out and then the coat is opened, thus revealing the sex organs. Gratification is achieved when she screams, runs away, or blushes.

Other exhibitionists have been known to cut off nine inches or so from the legs of a pair of pants and then sew them onto the hem of a topcoat. Then, wearing only a shirt and tie underneath, they don this costume and go off in search of a victim. To even the shrewdest observer, the exhibitionist outwardly appears to be fully dressed. But by merely opening his coat he reveals all, and the telephones in the police station start to ring.

Another type of exhibitionist is the adamist. This individual exhibits his entire nude body in public. In police jargon he is referred to as a "Tarzan." It might be well to add a word of caution at this point. Do not confuse the adamist with the current faddist streaker. Psychiatrists tell us that the streaker is merely a prankster carrying out an antiestablishment joke designed to shock "uptight" members of the community. To arrest the average streaker and charge him with indecent exposure could brand him as a sex deviate for life. Fortunately, most police departments are using discretion in this area and are booking these individuals only for disorderly conduct.

Psychiatrists have been able to identify four types of exhibitionists on the basis of their underlying motivations. From a police point of view, a person who engages in these practices is an exhibitionist regardless of his motivation, but investigating officers should be aware of the types of individuals they are dealing with. The four types of exhibitionists are classified as follows:

1. The compulsive—an individual who is compelled by his inner tensions to expose himself. Typically, he has no desire for normal sexual activity but derives complete satisfaction from the act of exposure itself. Individuals belonging to this category usually have no control over their actions and behave almost entirely on impulse.

2. The intentional—a type of deviate who is in control of his actions and who is under no compulsion to expose himself. He has found that the exposure of his sex organs alone can often lead to further sexual activity. He uses exposure to incite curiosity in his victims and to stimulate their interest. Because children respond most readily to this type of practice, it is a favorite tactic of the child molester.

3. The incompetent—a type of exhibitionist who exposes himself because of his mental condition and whose actions may be prompted by such irrational stimuli as certain phases of the moon, weather conditions, and drunkenness. Others belonging to this category have been found to have recently experienced a severe shock or trauma. One such case involved a thirty-two-year-old married man who, at the time of his arrest for indecent exposure, was awaiting the burial of his eight-year-old daughter. Obviously, the shock of her death had created sufficient imbalance in him to cause his deviate activity.

4. The unfortunate—the use of this particular term is somewhat unclear since it could easily apply to all types of exhibitionists. Offenders belonging to this category are typically respected members of the community—people whom one would never associate with sexual deviation—such as doctors, lawyers, teachers, clergymen, businessmen, and other professionals. For one reason or another, these people are led to expose themselves, and when arrested and taken into custody, they find themselves faced with disgrace and ruin. This type of individual can be extremely dangerous to himself, and many try to commit suicide when the gravity of their situation becomes fully apparent to them. Thus they should be carefully watched while in police custody.

Officers should be on the alert for the exhibitionist. He is usually found in public places, such as bus or railway stations, public parks, beaches or places of amusement, outside playgrounds or schoolyards, or on the public street. Individuals who loiter in such places and who are dressed unseasonably should be watched carefully. A person wearing a topcoat in warm weather or a raincoat in dry weather or at the beach on a sunny day should at least arouse suspicion.

Voyeurism—Peeping Toms

This type of crime is committed by persons who obtain sexual gratification by viewing the naked or near-naked bodies of others, or who derive gratification by watching others perform sex acts. Of course, to a certain extent, even sexually healthy individuals have some voyeuristic tendencies—this is evidenced by the current popularity of such publications as *Playboy* and *Playgirl* and X-rated movies. This desire to look at the nude body is quite normal and, in fact, plays a very important role in human sexual activity. The voyeur, however, gains his sexual satisfaction through the sense of sight and the invasion of another's privacy. He requires no physical contact with the victim and will often achieve orgasm by merely "looking." Others combine peeping and masturbation to achieve orgasm.

Although the Peeping Tom is generally regarded as a relatively harmless type of deviate, this is not always true. In some cases, the Peeping Tom can be extremely dangerous, and his actions can lead to rape, assault, and sometimes even murder. As the voyeur peeps through a bedroom window watching his unknowing victim prepare for bed, he often convinces himself that she knows he is watching and is putting on a show for his benefit. With a little rationalization he can convince himself that she would welcome his advances, and he goes through the window and commits rape. Such assaults often result in the death of the victim.

Some states do not have laws prohibiting peeping, but rather rely on laws against trespassing to prosecute this type of offense. In other states, the laws apply only to those who use binoculars or who peep from their own homes. The difficulty of proving a case in situations such as these makes the law practically unenforceable.

Frottage

The frotteur, also known as a "rubber" or a "hugger," derives his sexual satisfaction by hugging, feeling, or rubbing against the clothed buttocks, breasts, or legs of a woman and sometimes a man. The act of frottage is usually committed in congested, public places, such as buses, elevators, bus stops, and crowded sporting events. The offender is often attracted to his victim by the color or material of the clothing he or she is wearing. He may be attracted to silk, satin, velvet, or leather in various bright hues. A person in such a situation is usually at a loss to prevent being exploited. If the victim attempts to move away, the offender simply follows and continues his activity. The victim is often too embarrassed to scream or to turn and face the deviate and thus suffers in silence while the offender achieves his sexual gratification, protected by the anonymity of the crowd.

Again this is a difficult crime to prove either because the victim is embarrassed or because the activity is passed off as an accidental touching caused by the crowded conditions. If the frotteur is persistent and there are witnesses, it may be possible to obtain a conviction for indecent assault and battery or sexual imposition. In one recorded instance, a victim stabbed an offender through his erect penis using a hatpin, an action which the court trying the case deemed to be poetic justice.

Troilism

Troilism is a combination of exhibitionism and voyeurism. Individuals who practice this form of deviation receive their sexual gratification by watching others perform sexual acts or by knowing that others are watching them. The crime usually comes to the attention of the police when complaints are made of group sex parties or mate-swapping among several couples. A recent case in Long Island, New York, involved a group of adults who hired children to perform sex acts while the adults watched.

A common form of this activity occurs when a husband encourages a friend to have sexual intercourse with his wife while the husband watches. The husband then has relations with his wife in the presence of the friend. A certain amount of latent homosexuality is present in this type of activity. It may be theorized that the husband really wishes to relate to the other man but is unable to bring himself to openly engage in a homosexual act. Thus he uses his wife to effect the desired relationship.

Sex researchers tell us that the most common form of sexual fantasy entertained by men involves imagining oneself having sexual relations with two women at the same time. Of course, fantasies are not criminal, and most sexually normal people are subject to them. However, acting out one's fantasy in this case would constitute an act of troilism.

Kleptomania

Kleptomania is characterized by an abnormal, persistent desire to steal. The person who is afflicted with this condition receives sexual gratification from the anticipation, tension, and fear which accompany the act of stealing. This individual typically steals articles that are of little value. In most cases, he or she has no use for the stolen articles and loses interest in them after the theft. Kleptomania is compulsive. Many kleptomaniacs are menopausal or middle-aged women who feel they are no longer sexually attractive to their husbands. Males who are psychologically impotent are often subject to kleptomania. Complete sexual satisfaction may be derived from the feelings experienced, although no orgasm takes place. These individuals should not be confused with the thief or shoplifter, although kleptomaniacs are often arrested and charged with shoplifting. In several lower-court decisions, judges have ruled that kleptomania is a valid defense to the charges, especially in cases in which the individual is under the care of a physician or psychiatrist.

Bestiality

Bestiality is defined as sexual relations between a human being and an animal. This is a rare deviation. Recent studies reveal that less than 1 percent of females and slightly over 2 percent of males have ever had sexual contact with animals. When bestiality does occur, it is usually in isolated, rural areas; it is also practiced among prostitutes who participate in "smokers" and stag parties.

Zoophilia

Zoophilia, though not a crime, is a condition which is characterized by an unnatural fondness for certain types of animals, and those who are prone to this affliction achieve sexual gratification by stroking, petting, and fondling the animal. The presence of this condition can lead to bestiality. Zoophilia often comes to the attention of the police through complaints by neighbors that an individual is keeping large numbers of cats, dogs, or other animals in the house. Such problems are handled by referring the case to the health authorities, who will usually decree the animals a health hazard and order their removal.

Transvestism

Transvestism is characterized by a compulsive desire on the part of a person to dress in the clothing of the opposite sex and thereby to obtain sexual gratification. In many instances, persons who practice this aberration realize that their psychological orientation is closer to that of the opposite sex than to their own and consider themselves to be trapped in a body that, in fact, does not suit them at all. This type of individual often has the desire to match his physical appearance to his psychological orientation and requests the so-called sex-change operation. Psychiatric studies have indicated that many of these people have made accurate self-assessments and have concluded that some transvestites would indeed be better-adjusted human beings if their requests for surgery were granted. This operation, which is called transsexual surgery, has been most successful on males who have a strong female orientation. To become eligible for surgery, a patient must undergo a thorough psychiatric evaluation. Males who have had the emotional and psychological makeup of females since childhood are the most viable candidates. Most of these individuals dress, behave, and have the physical appearance of a woman, often holding down jobs as models, secretaries, or entertainers. For many months prior to surgery, transsexual patients are given injections of female hormones, which develop their breasts and hips. (In some cases silastic rubber implants are used to facilitate this process.) The male sex organs are removed and an artificial vagina, which has the normal appearance of the external female genitalia, is inserted by plastic surgeons. Following the operation these patients can engage in sexual intercourse, and many report that they are even able to achieve orgasm. They are, however, unable to reproduce. In the United States, twelve medical centers perform this operation, although, to date, there have been no successful operations to change females to males.

Most police officers assume that a man found wearing women's clothing must be a homosexual, but this assumption is not always correct. Not all transvestites are necessarily homosexuals. Generally speaking, transvestites may be divided into four categories, only one of which is definitely homosexual:

1. The homosexual transvestite is an individual who dresses in women's clothing, uses cosmetics, and acts as feminine as possible in order to make himself attractive as the "wife" or feminine partner in a homosexual relationship. Among members of this category can be found the "Nelly Queen," as well as homosexual prostitutes.

2. Male or female impersonators are persons who make their living in show business by impersonating members of the opposite sex. Many of these people are sexually normal and thus cannot be considered true transvestites. They are simply good at impersonation and capitalize on this talent. Among well-known show-business personalities who have used female impersonation as part of their acts are Milton Berle, Flip Wilson (Geraldine), and the late Billy DeWolfe (Mrs. Murgatroyd). Charlie Weaver's "Mrs. Butterworth" television commercial is another example of female impersonation.

3. The periodic transvestite is a person who normally conducts himself according to the boundaries of his own sex (and sexual) role. Most of the time he is a normal husband and father who represents himself as a male in his work as well. However, at certain periods of the month, roughly corresponding to the female menstrual cycle, he is overcome with a compulsion to alter his sexual identity by posing as a woman. He may return home from work, help his wife feed and

prepare the children for bed, and then prepare himself for an evening as a woman. He will bathe, powder, and perfume his body and dress in very feminine clothing (including a wig), and he and his wife will spend the evening as "girl friends." He achieves a certain amount of sexual satisfaction from this activity. Most periodics are troubled people who may be under the care of a psychiatrist. Their wives, although they don't really understand the aberration, make an attempt to understand and assist them in resolving their problems. In one midwestern city, a group of periodics ("in drag") and their wives meet regularly each month for group sessions with a psychologist.

4. The true transvestite is an individual who has a desire to be what by nature he is not—for example, a male who wishes to be female or a female who wishes to be male. These individuals dress as women—or men—and work at typically female or male occupations. Neither has any desire for sexual relations with members of either sex (they are not homosexuals), their sexual gratification being derived solely from cross-dressing.

Many states have enacted laws which make it a crime for a person to dress in the clothing of the opposite sex. These laws are enforced mainly against males since feminine fashions are often unisex and therefore are open to interpretation.

Pygmalionism

Pygmalionism is a condition wherein a person exhibits a sexual desire for a statue or some other nonsexual article. Although not a crime in itself, pygmalionism includes a great deal of fetishism and symbolism in which nonsexual objects arouse sexual desire. This condition can lead to such crimes as petty theft—for example, the common complaint received by police is that underclothing has been stolen from a neighborhood clothesline or laundromat.

Gerontophilia

Gerontophilia is a condition which manifests itself as a desire for sexual relations with a much older person of the opposite sex. It is not a crime in itself. Recent studies of robbery/rape and burglary/rape indicate that a large percentage of sex crimes in which elderly persons are victimized are committed by adolescents and teen-agers. It has been theorized that these older victims are not as sexually threatening to their young assailants as a person closer to their own age might be. The assaultive-type sex crime is usually the only time the gerontophile comes to the attention of the police.

Sex Pyromania

Sex pyromania, also known as the fire-water complex, is associated with arson and the malicious setting of fires as a means of obtaining sexual gratification. As with the kleptomaniac, gratification often is achieved from the feelings of tension, excitement, and danger associated with fires. Satisfaction may also be triggered by the smell of smoke, the sight of dancing flames, the sounds of fire sirens and people shouting, and the general air of excitement surrounding the scene of the fire. The "firebug" who sets a fire and then stays to watch the burning structure may even attempt to put the fire out. His proximity to the fire produces in him such an intense sexual gratification that he often experiences orgasm. The sex pyromaniac is an extremely dangerous criminal because he gives no thought to the lives or property he might be endangering. His only concern is for his own immediate sexual gratification.

Officers responding to an alarm of fire should be particularly observant of the onlookers at the fire. It is difficult for the firebug to hide his excitement and he can sometimes be identified by his actions and responses to the fire. If, during the early stages of the fire, consultations with the fire chief lead police officers to believe that arson has taken place, pictures should be taken of members of the crowd watching the fire. The firebug is usually a repeater, having set fires on previous occasions. A careful examination of pictures taken at various fires may turn up the same face at different times. Very often a suspected arsonist can be conclusively identified in this manner.

Pedophilia—Child Molesting

The child molester is an extremely dangerous sex criminal. In most instances, the individual who sexually molests children is a male who is unable to relate normally to mature women. He is a potential killer because his victim, the frightened and desperate child, will often cry out or threaten to tell his parents about the assault. The molester panics and kills the child to protect himself.

This crime, because of its nature, produces a high degree of adverse emotional reaction, not only within the general public but among police officers themselves. Several years ago, a study group of police officers was asked to rank ten felonies in order of their repugnancy. The officers ranked child molesting as the most repugnant crime, even before murder and rape.

The child molester may be found in any place where children congregate —movie houses, playgrounds, schoolyards—or he may simply cruise the streets hoping to lure a child into his car.

It is interesting to note that approximately 70 percent of all child molestation crimes are committed by persons who are previously known to the child—a neighbor, a friend of the child's parents, a relative, or a baby-sitter. This closeness contributes to the fact that the child molester is often a potential killer. Being known to the child, he fears that the child will expose him to the parents and he will be caught. In an effort to avoid being discovered, he may resort to killing the child.

For years, police agencies, in cooperation with schools, have been trying to educate children to stay away from "strangers." "Don't get into a car with a stranger. Don't take candy from a stranger. Don't go for a walk with a stranger.'' Schools have been provided with coloring books to teach these lessons to the youngsters, showing the stranger as a sinister-looking individual with a slouch hat and an upturned coat collar. These attempts at education have by and large been unsuccessful for several reasons. First, the concept of ''stranger'' is relatively meaningless to the young child, who views everyone as a potential friend; second, these attempts ignore the 70 percent figure cited above; and third, most children are naturally friendly, even to people they don't know.

Educational programs geared to protect the child from the molester should be designed to impress on the child that he or she should not go for rides or walks with or take candy or other gifts from *anyone* without first getting permission from the parent.

Piquerism—Lust Mutilation

The piquerist, or lust mutilator, is an extremely dangerous sex criminal. He derives his most intense sexual satisfaction from cutting, slashing, or mutilating his victim, usually before, during, or immediately after a rape or other sexual assault. In many instances, the piquerist will cut off parts of the body. Newspaper accounts of various murders will often describe these heinous crimes by stating, ''The body was horribly mutilated.'' Some piquerists will cut the body in such a way that patterns emerge. This symbolic cutting can often be an indication that will lead to the identification of the criminal. The symbol often has some particular meaning to the sick mind of the perpetrator.

Necrophilia

''Sexual assault took place after death.'' A line such as this one appearing in a newspaper story is often indicative that a necrophiliac is at large in the community. The necrophiliac is a sex criminal who achieves his sexual satisfaction by having sexual intercourse with corpses. In many instances, of course, a rapist who believes he has subdued his victim engages in necrophilia without actually realizing that his victim has died. In other instances, persons who, by the nature of their work, have access to the newly dead may practice this perversion. Necrophiliacs become dangerous when no body is available to them and, in order to satisfy their desires, they resort to murder. There are a number of recorded instances of grave-robbing in order to satisfy necrophiliac desires.

Rape

Rape is probably the best known and most publicized of the sex crimes. It has been estimated that only 10 percent of all rapes committed are reported to the police. In recent years the incidence of rape has risen alarmingly. The 90 percent unreported rapes should be of major concern to both the police and the community. Rape is defined as "sexual intercourse with a woman against her will and despite her resistance." In a prosecution for rape, the police must present evidence of force or constructive force, lack of consent, and penetration in order to convict the suspect.

Rapists can be divided into three generic types: first, the "true sex offender"—typically a psychopathic personality who finds it impossible to control his sexual impulses. The sight of a woman who stimulates his desires triggers his impulses and he commits rape. The victim is usually a victim of opportunity. The true sex offender is probably responsible for the largest number of stranger/stranger rapes committed in this country.

The second category of rapist is the "sadistic rapist," the person who rapes because the force, violence, and cruelty of the act provide him with his greatest sexual satisfaction. Unlike the true sex offender he can control his desires and impulses but finds rape more satisfying than sex with a willing partner.

Finally, the third type of rapist has been described as the "aggressive criminal." He is the individual who, while committing another crime such as burglary or robbery, rapes a female whom he finds alone in a house or with her boyfriend in a lovers' lane. He has no compulsion to rape but merely seizes the opportunity when it presents itself.

In the past two years, a great deal of publicity has been given to the crime of rape and the victims of rape. Newspaper stories, television programs, and national women's organizations have centered in on the problem and have proposed a number of programs designed to teach women how to protect themselves from rape and, failing that, how to remain alive.

Police handling of rape and rape victims has been the focus of a great deal of criticism. Male officers, in many cases, have approached the rape victim in an insensitive manner, and some have even appeared to "get their kicks" by forcing the victim to recount over and over the most personal and clinical details of the crime. This reported insensitivity on the part of male officers has led to many demands that female officers be assigned to question rape victims. The Sex Crimes Analysis Unit of the New York City Police Department is headed by a female officer and is composed of a staff of women officers whose primary function is to question victims and to protect them from as much embarrassment as possible. The theory that only another woman can possibly understand the trauma produced by the forcible invasion of the body experienced by the rape victim is a good and valid reason for assigning female officers to this task.

The large number of unreported rapes has been attributed to two main causes: the insensitivity of the police officers handling the investigation and the tactics used by defense attorneys during the trial. Rape is one of the few crimes in which the victim is put on trial. It has become almost standard procedure for defense attorneys to probe into the sexual history of rape victims, intimating to the jury that since the victim was not a virgin she could hardly have been raped.

The California Legislature recently passed a rape reform measure which should alleviate such practices. Under the law a woman's previous sexual conduct is no longer permissible as evidence in rape trials. The law provides that only when it can be established that the victim has had previous sexual contact with the accused rapist will such evidence be admitted into court.

With the advent of special training programs for males acting as sex-crime investigators, the inclusion of women officers on investigating teams, and the passage of laws such as that described above, we can expect more rape victims to report these crimes to the police in the future.

Another aspect of the attempt to increase reporting and reduce the number of rapes has been the formation of a women's organization called Women Against Rape (WAR). This organization seeks to provide volunteer women to work with local police departments by providing solace and counseling services to rape victims. The volunteers would give support to the victim during the ordeal of questioning and hospital examination and during the period of psychological trauma following the rape. WAR also provides counseling to the husband and family of the rape victim who, in many instances, shun the victim and treat her as the guilty party.

The investigator assigned to the rape case should conduct the investigation in the following manner:

1. Obtain all the necessary facts from the victim, keeping in mind the personal nature of the crime and the embarrassment of the victim.

2. During the interview never assume a demeanor that could be interpreted as enjoyment of the recital of the clinical details.

3. Don't ask such questions as "Did you enjoy it?"

4. Whenever possible have a female officer present at all times during the interview.

5. Take the victim to the hospital for medical examination. Whenever possible she should be accompanied by another woman.

6. Prior to the examination, inform the examining physician about the types of evidence you are looking for. The following types of evidence are needed from the victim:

   a. Any loose pubic hair from the clothing or body of the victim.

   b. A sample of the victim's pubic hair should be obtained for comparison. This hair should be plucked (about ten strands) rather than cut so that the hair follicle can be matched microscopically.

   c. A vaginal smear should be taken from the victim to determine whether semen is present. (Semen may be typed just like blood and will indicate the blood type of the rapist.)

   d. A complete report should be made of any physical trauma (cuts, bruises) in the vaginal area, thighs, abdomen, or on any other part of the body which may indicate a struggle.

   e. If the victim claims she struggled with or fought her assailant, scrapings from her fingernails should be taken. These can help determine the skin color, hair color, and often the age of her assailant.

Each item of physical evidence provided by the examining physician should be identified according to the location on the body where it was found. Each item should be placed in a separate envelope or container and marked by the investigator as to its source or probable source, the name of the victim, the date, and the investigator's personal identifying mark.

Anthropophagy

There are two categories of anthropophagist—the cannibal and the vampire. The cannibal is an individual who eats human flesh in order to achieve sexual satisfaction. The vampire drinks human blood for the same reason. Many murder victims are found with bites on the breasts, thighs, arms, and so forth. The two most recent cases of this nature occurred in California. In 1973, Edmund Emil Kemper III confessed that he had acted out homicidal, cannibalistic, and sexual fantasies in the killing of eight women. He was found sane and convicted of first-degree murder in Santa Cruz, California.

In another California case, a suspect was arrested after the victim's family reported him missing. The suspect was found driving the victim's car, which contained the partially eaten body of the victim. The suspect confessed that he had killed his victim (a man) in northern California and had driven south along the coast for three weeks, during which time he had eaten the body. He admitted to psychiatrists that he had derived a great deal of sexual satisfaction from these acts.

Incest

For thousands of years incest has been prohibited by all the civilizations of the world. In the Western world incest was originally treated as an ecclesiastical crime. It was included in the old English common law, but trial for the crime was conducted by the ecclesiastical court. It was not until 1908 that incest was written into the criminal law of England. Its earliest prohibition was designed to lessen quarrels between family members who might lust after one another's wives. In modern times the prohibition of sexual intercourse with near relatives is justified on genetic grounds. Following the discovery of genetic traits by Mendel, it was learned that intercourse between persons having similar genetic makeups tended to produce offspring who were afflicted with a variety of mental and physical weaknesses. Such illnesses as hemophilia, which was prevalent among the royal families of Europe who practiced intermarriage for political reasons, and Tay-Sachs disease among Jews, whose Hasidic ancestors in ghettos of old Warsaw practiced intermarriage as an alternative to forced segregation during the pogroms, are examples which support the need for prohibiting sexual relations between close relatives.

In the United States incest has always been prohibited between persons who are closely related by blood. Marriages between such close blood relations are declared by law to be incestuous and void. This prohibition includes sexual relationships between fathers and daughters, mothers and sons, and sisters and brothers. The prohibition laws in some states extend to aunts, uncles, grandparents, step-parents, daughters- and sons-in-law, and first cousins. Incest is a relatively rare crime which occurs predominantly in rural and ghetto areas. The crime seldom comes to the attention of police, and when it does it is usually as a result of a domestic disturbance. The most common instances of incest are between brothers and sisters and forced relations between fathers and daughters. The wife generally knows about the practice but, for obvious reasons, is reluctant to turn her husband in. Clergymen handle more cases of incest than do the police. A clergyman who receives a complaint—usually from a wife—orders the father to stop the practice by threatening to expose his activities to the police.

Sodomy

In its original definition, the term sodomy referred to anal intercourse between males. Over the years, various states in this country have expanded their sodomy statutes to include bestiality, necrophilia, buggery, pederasty, fellatio, cunnilingus, annilingus, and mutual masturbation in which one of the participants is a child. These terms are defined below:

Bestiality   Sexual intercourse with an animal or bird.

Necrophilia   Sexual intercourse with the dead.

Buggery   Anal intercourse with a man or a woman.

Pederasty   Anal intercourse with a boy or girl.

Fellatio   Oral copulation with a male.

Cunnilingus   Oral copulation with a female.

Annilingus   Oral/anal contact with a male or female.

Mutual masturbation   Manual stimulation of the genitals in which one of the participants is a child.

Police students should note that the activities defined above are not typically performed in public places. With the exception of the two activities that involve children—pederasty and mutual masturbation—these activities very seldom come to the attention of the police. This fact, coupled with the sexual liberation movement, which began in the 1960s and early 1970s, has led eight states to adopt the Model Penal Code advocated by the American Law Institute in 1962 and to revise their sex laws by dropping from the list of crimes most or all private sex acts between consenting adults. Illinois, Connecticut, Colorado, Oregon, Ohio, North Dakota, Delaware, and Hawaii have eradicated their long-standing penalties against private consensual sodomy, both heterosexual and homosexual. In most states the old laws against fornication, cohabitation, adultery, and sodomy still stand, but with a few notable exceptions, such laws are now rarely enforced (Hunt 1973).

Hunt (1973) also reports on the results of a study conducted by The Research Guild, Inc., a behavioral research organization. This study, titled "Sexual Behavior in the 1970's," reports that the following percentages of Americans have participated in various legally proscribed sexual activities:

Fellatio (heterosexual, in the past year)—over 50 percent of the population.

Anal intercourse (on at least one occasion)—30 percent of the population.

Cunnilingus (heterosexual)—over 50 percent of married couples.*

Although much of the activity reported above takes place between married couples in the privacy of their own homes, from a legal standpoint those who reside in the forty-two states which have not yet adopted the Model Penal Code must technically be considered criminals. Because of the private nature of these activities, the laws pertaining to them are practically unenforceable. Fortunately, we have not yet reached a point in this country where the public condones police invasion of the most intimate areas of their private lives. Nevertheless, laws which are on the books but are not being enforced, or which are unenforceable, breed disrespect for all law. Sex acts between consenting adults, in private, should not be the subject of criminal sanctions in the opinion of this author.

Sex-Crime Investigations

The officer who is assigned to investigate sex crimes must keep a number of points in mind as he attempts to bring sex criminals to justice. First, he must remember that the sex crime is different from all other types of crime. The sex offender is driven by a basic urge and is often subject to compulsions which he cannot control; therefore, his behavior is almost impossible to predict. Second, sexual gratification may be obtained in a number of bizarre ways which have nothing whatsoever to do with the elements of normal sex. In many abnormal sexual practices, the offender need not achieve orgasm in order to derive satisfaction.

Fetishism and Symbolism

Some sex criminals are "turned on" by nonsexual objects and these objects often figure prominently in his crimes. Nonsexual objects which arouse sexual feelings in some people are called fetishes, which may be classified into several categories:

A. A fetish may be some part of the human body, such as the eyes, mouth, hair, legs, or buttocks. Even normal people exhibit a mild degree of fetishism. How often have you heard a man describe himself as a "breast man" or a "leg man"?

---

*These statistics are based on a randomly selected population sample of 2,026 subjects.

B. A fetish may be an article of clothing, such as lingerie, shoes, stockings, or gloves. The manufacturers of diaphanous nightgowns clearly recognize the fetishistic tendencies present in the normal man. The abnormal individual will often steal lingerie or some other article of clothing from clotheslines and laundromats for the purpose of achieving sexual satisfaction. The fetishist is capable of achieving orgasm by merely fondling the garment or by masturbating into it. This is a common occurrence and accounts for many of the complaints that are made to police departments.

C. A fetish may consist of a particular type of material, such as silk, satin, velvet, fur, or leather. Color may also play an important role in the mind of the fetishist.

D. A fetish may be related to certain acts or attitudes, such as the way a woman undresses or arranges her hair. Many sex criminals force their victims to cater to their particular fetish by disrobing in a certain manner, or the victim may be forced to perform certain acts or to assume various positions to satisfy the fetishist's whims.

The investigator at the scene of a sex crime should look around for any signs suggesting that a fetish may have been involved in the crime. Particular fetishes fit certain M.O.s adopted by habitual sex criminals and can often lead to the identification of the offender.

Symbolism also plays a large part in many sex crimes. A symbol is something that represents something else in much the same way that a four-leaf clover represents good luck or a black cat represents bad luck. Everyone has certain sex symbols to which he or she is responsive. In America a large bustline is considered a symbol of sexuality. Other such symbols include black stockings (the *Playboy* symbol), tight skirts, and so forth. Generally, objects that symbolize sexuality are relatively harmless, especially in the "normal" individual. It is only when the symbol becomes an obsession in the mind of the psychopath and produces in him some violent reaction that it becomes really dangerous.

Ritualism and *Modus Operandi*

Like most habitual criminals, the sex criminal develops his own special *modus operandi*, which usually involves a certain amount of ritualism. Sex offenders tend to commit each of their crimes in basically the same manner. They develop a ritual from which they will not deviate. In fact, any deviation from the ritual usually prevents the offender from achieving the optimum satisfaction he desires. Because the deviate is compelled to repeat the same ritual in each of his crimes, he inadvertently provides the alert investigator with a handle on his crime and on himself. He conducts each crime in exactly the same manner, entering the building at the same point, and usually at the same time of day or night. He may choose victims who are similar in appearance or life-style. Or he may force each of his victims to engage in certain ritualistic acts which are part of his perverse design. He may himself wear types of clothing or insist that his victims dress a certain way. He may even have his victims engage in an elaborate ritualistic dialogue, or he may force them to utter certain ritualistic phrases. When investigating a series of sex crimes, evidence of such ritualistic acts can sometimes prove as valuable as a fingerprint as a means of identification. Moreover, this evidence allows investigators to determine whether a series of crimes is being committed by the same person or whether several different criminals are involved.

The best example of a ritualistic sex criminal and killer was the late Albert DeSalvo, also known as "The Boston Strangler." The Strangler left his trademark at the scene of eleven rape-murders. In each case he posed as a handyman or utilityman, wearing white overalls. In almost all the cases he used the same story to gain entry into his victims' apartments. All of his victims were connected in one way or another with hospitals or the field of medicine. All lived alone. All were raped and strangled. All the stranglings were accomplished with a piece of lingerie or nylon stocking. The knots used to tie the clothing around the victims' necks were all tied in the same manner. Even when the Strangler deviated from his ritual, he did so in a ritualistic manner. In the cases where he did not rape or kill, he forced the victim to perform fellatio on him. Those among his victims who lived reported that he said the same things to them and behaved in the same manner.

Role of Sexual Fantasies

The sex criminal, like the normal individual, is subject to sexual fantasies. Each of us probably has a favorite sexual fantasy which assists us in our normal sex lives. The fantasies of the deviate, however, take the form of sadistic and masochistic practices, which may include cutting, bloodletting, hanging, and so on. The difference between the normal individual and the sex deviate is that the normal individual realizes that his fantasies are just that. The sex criminal has difficulty distinguishing between fantasy and reality and thus he attempts and often succeeds in turning his fantasy into the real thing.

Ensconced in his unreal world of sexual fantasy, the sex criminal carefully plans the details of his next crime. He might spend many hours and achieve much sexual gratification writing out his plan—complete with dates, time, and victim—and he may describe in full detail just how he will go about committing his crime. Frequently, such plans are discovered in an offender's pocket at the time of apprehension. When the police have a viable suspect and probable cause for arrest, they should obtain a search warrant in order to enter his apartment or house. One of the items to be searched for is the plan. If such a plan can be found—and in many cases it can be—it will serve as excellent evidence in court.

Interrogating the Suspect

The efficient sex-crime investigator must make every effort to perceive the crime through the eyes of the deviate. This is often difficult for the investigator who is a sexually normal person. The investigator must not ignore items or circumstances simply because they do not appear to fit a preconceived notion of criminal motivation or method. Sex crimes are committed by abnormal persons and what has meaning for them may not mean anything to the investigator. This same approach should be taken during the interrogation of a sex-crime suspect. The interrogator must appear to be sympathetic and understanding when dealing with the psychopathic individual. Often merely giving the impression that he understands the reasons for the crime and sympathizes with the offender's rationalizations will serve to elicit a confession and produce supportive evidence necessary for a conviction.

Often the investigator will find that even though the evidence against a suspect is strong, he cannot elicit a confession because the offender is hiding behind another identity, a second, imaginary individual who, in the mind of the offender, is the one who is really responsible for committing the crime. In this way, the deviate is absolved of all guilt. This type of depersonalization is common among sex offenders.

Homosexuality as a Police Problem

Homosexuality, proscribed in the old English common law as "abominable and detestable carnal copulation, against nature, with mankind," is a controversial problem in modern American society. The traditional condemnation of sexual activity between persons of the same sex—by both ancient and modern religious institutions—has carried over into the criminal law of our modern-day Judeo-Christian society. Consensual sodomy is a violation of the criminal laws of forty-two states, and although these laws are not enforced to any great extent in most of these states, such acts as buggery, fellatio, cunnilingus, and annilingus still constitute felonies in the majority of states which have not adopted the Model Penal Code of the American Law Institute. According to Hunt (1973, p. 54):

Sexual liberation has considerably moderated public antipathy toward homosexuality. The gay world is discussed and portrayed openly—often sympathetically—in fiction, nonfiction and drama; many gays have "come out" and today live openly and without shame as homosexuals; gay liberationists fight publicly for equal rights. In late 1973, in fact, the American Psychiatric Association voted to drop its classification of homosexuality as a "mental disorder" and to reclassify it in some cases as a "sexual orientation disturbance," and in other cases not even that.

In the "straight" world, homosexuality is considered to be an unpleasant topic and is one that is little understood by the general public or the average police officer. A limited amount of training on the subject of homosexuality is offered in police training academies, with the result that police officers often approach investigations involving homosexuals with an attitude of disgust and repugnance. Naturally, this attitude can interfere with efficient, objective police work, a problem that is particularly serious in light of the fact that homosexuals are becoming more and more visible in today's society.

If we can accept the statement made by the American Psychiatric Association (quoted above), as well as the fact that the laws against consensual sodomy are rarely enforced, we can take a more objective approach in dealing with the problems that arise from homosexuality in the community.

The homosexual world, like the "straight" world, has its own share of sex criminals who are as abhorrent to the average homosexual as are sex criminals to the average "straight" citizen. But the existence of homosexual sex criminals within the gay community only brings additional condemnation and discrimination to all homosexuals.

Crimes Peripheral to Homosexuality

Homosexuality does not constitute a major police problem in itself, but the many crimes that are committed in connection with it are of serious concern. Homosexuality is looked upon as shameful, antisocial, and abnormal. It is perhaps for this reason primarily that criminals tend to follow those who practice it—either to indulge their own sexual desires or simply to victimize the homosexual. In police jargon these criminals are known as "fairy hawks," "fairy hustlers," "queer shakers," "fag workers," and "toilet workers." Members of the gay community refer to these criminals as "rough trade." They make their living through trapping, swindling, robbing, and blackmailing those who are known or suspected homosexuals. In the days when homosexuality was much more taboo, these criminals enjoyed great success because their victims would not report their crimes to the police for fear of exposing themselves. As more and more homosexuals "come out," this type of crime will undoubtedly diminish.

In those states which still enforce consensual sodomy laws, the homosexual is faced with a dilemma. He or she is not only involved in a crime for which he can be sent to prison, but also faces disgrace, loss of job, public ridicule, and ostracism by friends and family. This often produces tension, fear, and desperation, which, when coupled with the depredations of the "fairy hawks," produces a situation which can result in serious crime. The crimes most commonly committed in connection with homosexuality are:

1. Blackmail—Many homosexuals are persons in recognized walks of life. They have good jobs, respectable families, and excellent reputations. Often, were their

homosexuality exposed their entire livelihood would be destroyed. Obviously, such conditions are ideal for blackmail.

2. Robbery, larceny, and burglary—In many instances, a man who is picked up by a homosexual will take his money, jewelry, clothing, and automobile. These criminals rely on the fact that the homosexual will be reluctant to report the crime to the police and that even if he does, they believe that police antipathy to the homosexual will result in no action and little likelihood of arrest.

3. Assault and battery and mayhem—The homosexual who resists robbery may be assaulted, or an assault may ensue from an act of solicitation by the homosexual. In other instances, jealousy among homosexuals may result in assault and mayhem upon a sexual partner who has decided to end the liaison.

4. Murder—Murder among homosexuals arises from the same causes as murder in the "straight" world—resistance to a sexual approach, jealousy, revenge, panic, fear, or, in rare cases, it may occur as the culmination of a sadistic sex orgy. This type of crime is most prevalent among homosexuals who have not been able to achieve an acceptance of their homosexuality and therefore are subject to more highly emotional states and tensions produced by their conflicting life-styles.

5. Arson and vandalism—Among some homosexuals, fire has always been a favorite weapon for revenge against an unfaithful lover. Overcome with jealousy they have set fire to the homes, apartments, or automobiles of former lovers. Destruction of property for the same reasons is also common.

6. Suicide—Suicide is common among those who cannot accept the fact of their own homosexuality. As in the "straight" world, those of unstable or highly emotional temperaments are more likely to commit suicide than others.

The Homo-Criminal

The type of homosexual who usually comes to the attention of the police is one who engages in practices which are equally proscribed by the "straight" world. Among these are the following:

1. Homo-prostitutes—These are usually boys or young men who actively solicit on the streets for the purpose of securing money for engaging in pederasty or fellatio. They can be divided into two specific groups: the "stud hustler," who simulates the virile he-man and makes himself available as the male partner in a homosexual sex act; and the "nelly queen," who tries to be as feminine as possible, wearing elaborate hair styles, exotic clothes, and cosmetics in order to make himself available as the "female" partner in a homosexual sex act. Homo-prostitutes operate in much the same way as "straight" prostitutes. Their approach is one of solicitation. Many are transvestites.

2. Pederasts (child molesters)—These are adult male homosexuals who desire sexual relations with a young boy who will act as the passive partner. They, as well as the homo-prostitutes, are looked down upon by the vast majority of the homosexual community because their activities bring police action and perpetrate a false image of the average male homosexual.

3. Wolves and prowlers—This type of male homosexual is definitely dangerous. Because of their appearance or age, they are unwelcome in traditional homosexual circles. They are forced to prowl or "cruise" because of their strong, neurotic sex drive. These are the individuals who loiter in public rest rooms and back streets in search of sexual contacts.

In almost every major city certain bars, restaurants, hotels, and other locations can be identified as gathering places for homosexuals. In these establishments homosexuals can be certain of meeting others whose life-styles are similar to their own and of receiving assurance and support. Generally speaking, the average homosexual wishes to live a quiet, orderly existence. As with "straights," if there is jealousy, distrust, or infidelity, violence is apt to occur.

The homo-criminal, on the other hand, pursues his activities just as aggressively and diligently as does his heterosexual counterpart. The homo-criminal typically operates in the following manner. Public rest rooms (known in the gay world as "tearooms"), subways, railroad stations, theatres, parks, and other public places are centers of operation for wolves and prowlers. These places are usually well known to the police and in many cities are kept under constant surveillance (a particularly distasteful police assignment). Surveillance is maintained to protect the general public, especially children, from solicitation and molestation, and to prevent violent reaction on the part of "straight" citizens when accosted.

Wolves and prowlers who operate in theatres move from seat to seat until they find a willing partner. Saturday and Sunday matinees are the favorite operating times for pederasts, or child molesters. Railroad and bus-station rest rooms are a constant source of aggravation to the railroad police throughout the country. In many rest rooms, prowlers have cut holes in the partitions between the stalls in order to facilitate their activities. Most of the major public parks in the nation are known meeting places for male homosexuals. Often prowlers will cruise the streets looking for "trade," although this is not a safe practice in that it can result in assault or possibly arrest in the event that the person solicited happens to be a vice-squad officer.

Another method of operation is the use of automobiles to make contact with young boys who are hitchhiking. In many instances arrests have resulted when the person solicited has provided police with license numbers from which the identity of the offender can be traced. Occasionally, younger homosexuals and homo-prostitutes will hitchhike and then solicit the driver of the car who picks them up. In these cases there is always the danger that the prostitute will make a demand for money, which if refused will prompt him to threaten to inform the police that an indecent proposal has been made to him by the driver.

Homosexual crime can become a major problem, and police cannot afford to operate solely on the basis of information that may be spiced with contempt. Police must be aware of the seriousness of the situation and act in an intelligent, objective, and effective manner. If police understand the problem, it is more likely that they will handle their investigations and interviews in a professional manner that will inspire respect and confidence among the general public.

GLOSSARY OF SEX-CRIME TERMS

ADAMISM. An act of exhibitionism in which a person exposes his entire, nude body to an innocent onlooker.

AGGRESSIVE CRIMINAL. A type of rapist who commits rape as a secondary act while committing another crime.

ANNILINGUS. The sexual use of the mouth on the anus of another. Usually included in the sodomy statutes.

ANTHROPOPHAGY. The act of eating human flesh in order to derive sexual gratification.

ANUS. The opening at the lower end of the digestive tract through which solid waste is excreted.

BESTIALITY. Sexual intercourse between man and animal. Usually included in sodomy statutes.

BISEXUAL. The ability, the desire, and the inclination to have sexual relations with members of both sexes.

BUGGERY. Anal intercourse. Buggery is the act which is the subject of the common-law definition of sodomy.

CHILD MOLESTER. An adult who gains his sexual satisfaction from sexually molesting children. Usually is impotent in the presence of a mature female sex partner. A pedophile.

CROSS-DRESSING. In transvestism, a deviation in which sexual gratification is achieved by dressing in the clothing of the opposite sex.

CUNNILINGUS. The sexual use of the mouth on the genitalia of a female.

DISCIPLINE. The act of bondage or flagellation imposed by a sadist on a masochist.

DOMINATION. *See* DISCIPLINE.

DOUBLE-GAITED. A slang term for bisexual.

EJACULATION. A discharge of seminal fluid. An emission. Male orgasm.

EXHIBITIONISM. The act of exposing one's sex organs in public for the purpose of obtaining sexual gratification. Usually by a male.

FELLATIO. The sexual use of the mouth on the sex organs of a male.

FETISHISM. The arousal of sexual desire by a nonsexual object. A fetish can be a piece of clothing, a body part, an act, or an attitude.

FIRE-WATER COMPLEX. A synonym for sex pyromania in which a deviate sets fires and then gains sexual gratification, including orgasm, from the sight of the fire and the sounds of the excitement surrounding the fire.

FLASHER. An exhibitionist.

FORNICATION. Sexual intercourse between two unmarried persons.

FROTTAGE. From the French word *frotteur,* which means "to rub." The act of achieving sexual gratification by rubbing against the clothed buttocks or bodies of women and sometimes men. Sexual imposition. Indecent assault and battery.

GERONTOPHILIA. A condition whereby a person chooses or prefers an elderly person of the opposite sex as a sex partner.

HETEROSEXUAL. A person who desires to have sexual intercourse only with persons of the opposite sex.

HOMOSEXUAL. A person who desires to have sexual intercourse only with persons of the same sex. Invert.

HUGGER. A person who derives his sexual gratification by practicing frottage. *See* FROTTAGE.

IMPOTENCE. The inability of the male to engage in sexual intercourse.

INCEST. Sexual intercourse between persons who are so closely related (by consanguinity [blood], affinity [marriage], or adoption) that the law forbids them to marry.

INFIBULATION. Self-torture of the sex organs. This is a masochistic act.

KLEPTOMANIA. An uncontrollable compulsion to steal which produces sexual gratification.

LUST MUTILATION. Piquerism. The achieving of sexual gratification by mutilating the body of the victim.

MASOCHISM. A condition whereby sexual gratification is obtained by being tortured, beaten, or bound.

MASOCHIST. A person who derives sexual gratification from being tortured, beaten, or bound.

MENOPAUSE. The period in a woman's life when her menstrual cycle becomes irregular just prior to the complete cessation of the cycle.

MUTUAL MASTURBATION. A sex crime, usually included in the sodomy statutes, defined as mutual excitation of the sex organs in which one of the participants is a child.

NECROPHILIA. Sexual intercourse with a dead body.

ORGASM. A complex series of responses of the sex organs which occurs at the end of the sex act. Includes ejaculation in the male and strong contractions in the female.

PEDERASTY. Anal intercourse in which a child is the passive partner.

PEDOPHILIA. Child molesting. Obtaining sexual gratification by molesting or having sexual intercourse with a child.

PEEPING TOM. One who gains sexual gratification by peeking at the nude or semi-nude bodies of those who are unaware of his presence. Also peeks at others who are having sexual intercourse. A voyeur.

PENIS. The male sex organ.

PIQUERISM. Lust mutilation. The act of obtaining sexual gratification by cutting or slashing the body of the victim.

PYGMALIONISM. The act of obtaining sexual gratification by association with a statue or other nonsexual object. Fetishism.

RAPE. Carnal knowledge with a female by force or against her will. Penetration, no matter how slight, is necessary to complete the act. Males may also be the victims of rape.

RITUALISM. The modus operandi in sex crimes. Habitual sex criminals will repeat their crimes in the same fashion over and over again.

RUBBER. See HUGGER, FROTTAGE.

SADISM. A motivating element in sex crimes in which the criminal derives his sexual satisfaction from beating, torturing, or humiliating his victim.

SADIST. One who derives sexual satisfaction by beating, slashing, or torturing others.

SADISTIC RAPIST. A type of rapist who rapes in order to vent his aggressive feelings. The violence and force of the rape produce his sexual satisfaction.

SADOMASOCHISM. A condition in which the offender achieves sexual satisfaction by beating or by being beaten. He can assume either the sadistic or the masochistic role.

SEX FANTASY. A condition in which the individual imagines himself in a variety of sexual episodes. The difference between normal and abnormal fantasy is that the normal person realizes that his imaginings are fantasy. The abnormal person attempts to convert his fantasies into reality.

SEX PYROMANIA. A condition whereby a sex criminal achieves sexual satisfaction by setting fires. Gratification comes from watching the flames and listening to the sounds of the excitement surrounding the fire.

SODOMY. Historically, the term applied to anal intercourse, but in modern usage the term is applied to a number of crimes and sex acts—for example, buggery, necrophilia, bestiality, pederasty, fellatio, cunnilingus, annilingus, and mutual masturbation.

SWITCH HITTER. A bisexual.

SYMBOLISM. A condition in which an object represents something else. Examples of sex symbols may include a large bust, black lace nightgowns, and so forth.

TRANSSEXUAL SURGERY. A surgical operation in which a person of one sex is surgically transformed into the opposite sex. Usually performed only after extensive psychological investigation and preparation.

TRANSVESTISM. Cross-dressing. A condition wherein a person achieves sexual satisfaction by wearing the clothing of the opposite sex.

TRANSVESTITE. A person who gains sexual satisfaction by wearing the clothing of the opposite sex. There are four distinct types of transvestites: the homosexual transvestite; the female impersonator; the periodic transvestite; and the true transvestite.

TROILISM. A sexual deviation which includes both exhibitionism and voyeurism. Sexual gratification is achieved when three or more persons are present and engage in sexual acts. Practitioners are sexually gratified by watching others perform sexual acts and by having others watch them perform sexual acts.

TRUE SEX OFFENDER. A type of rapist who is psychotic and who finds it impossible to control his sexual desires. He is the most frequent offender in "stranger to stranger" rapes.

VAGINA. The passage leading from the vulva to the uterus in females. Also the point of entry during sexual intercourse.

VAGINAL SMEAR. A sample of the fluid found in the vaginal passage of rape victims. The smear is taken for analysis to affirm the presence of semen as an indication of recent sexual activity.

VOYEUR. A Peeping Tom. One who achieves sexual satisfaction by peeking at the nude or semi-nude bodies of others.

VOYEURISM. The act of peeking at others as they prepare for bed or engage in sexual intercourse for the purpose of obtaining sexual gratification.

ZOOPHILIA. A condition wherein the deviate obtains sexual satisfaction by associating with animals, and obtains sexual satisfaction by stroking, petting, or fondling animals. May lead to bestiality.

GLOSSARY OF HOMOSEXUALITY TERMS

TO CRUISE. The act of loitering in the streets in search of homosexual partners.

FAG. A slang term denoting a male homosexual whose actions are blatantly effeminate.

FAIRY HAWK. A criminal who chooses homosexuals as his victims on the assumption that they will not report him to the police for fear of revealing their homosexuality.

FAIRY HUSTLER. *See* FAIRY HAWK.

GAY. A contemporary term preferred by homosexuals. It denotes homosexuals of either sex.

HOMO-PROSTITUTE. A homosexual person, usually a male, who offers himself for sexual intercourse or sexual conduct to homosexuals for a fee.

NELLY QUEEN. A homo-prostitute who offers himself as the ''feminine'' partner in a homosexual act for a fee.

PROWLER. An older male homosexual who ''cruises'' the streets in search of homosexual partners.

QUEER SHAKER. *See* FAIRY HAWK.

QUEEN. An extremely effeminate homosexual who flaunts his condition by the use of makeup and exaggerated gestures.

ROUGH TRADE. *See* FAIRY HAWK.

STUD HUSTLER. A homo-prostitute who offers himself as the ''male'' partner in a homosexual act, for a fee.

TEAROOM. A public rest room.

TOILET WORKER. A homosexual male who solicits homosexual acts in public rest rooms.

TRADE. Usually one homosexual act with a stranger.

WOLF. *See* PROWLER.

REFERENCES

''At a Glance.'' *Akron Beacon Journal* (January 12, 1973).

Hunt, Morton. ''Sexual Behavior in the 1970's.'' Playboy 20 (March 1974).

Kalish, Richard A. *The Psychology of Human Behavior*. (Belmont, Calif.: Brooks-Cole Publishing Co., 1970.)

Lentini, Joseph R., and France, James G. *Ohio Peace Officer's Manual*. Cincinnati: W. H. Anderson Co., 1972.

McLaughlin, Walter V. *F.B.I. Training Material*. Washington, D.C.: U.S. Department of Justice, Federal Bureau of Investigation, undated.

Chapter 6

Narcotics and Drug Abuse

Thirty years ago, when police departments had occasion to handle drug problems, they were usually faced with "dope"—that is, hard narcotics that were almost exclusively derivatives of opium. Also confronting police was the problem of marijuana, which at that time was considered to be an addictive drug. Marijuana was a relatively small problem when considered by today's standards, its use being largely confined to the ghettos and to members of certain subcultures, such as artists and musicians. A well-known drummer made national headlines during the "big-band era" of the 1940s when he was caught smoking marijuana. Today, such a violation would go virtually unnoticed.

The advent of synthetic drugs following World War II played a significant role in the growth of the drug problem in this country. And because both drugs and money were more plentiful than ever before, the problem gradually became national—even international in scope. The original opiate problem was suddenly compounded by the availability of barbiturates, amphetamines, hallucinogens, cocaine, and the myriad of other compounds which have come to be known as "drugs of abuse." In this chapter we will explore the most commonly abused drugs, the effects of these drugs, and the methods by which they are used and abused. We will also take a close look at the various strategies that are employed by police to combat the problem.

Terms Relating to Narcotics and Drug Addiction

Before we can formulate a perspective on the narcotics problem, we must be able to communicate about it in terms that are mutually acceptable to all concerned. When the World Health Organization (WHO) of the United Nations finally recognized the international implications of the drug problem, its Expert Committee on Drugs Liable to Produce Addiction formulated a number of definitions which are now accepted by most authorities on the subject.

According to the WHO definition, *narcotics addiction* is a periodic or chronic state of intoxication which is produced by the repeated consumption of a drug (natural or synthetic) and which may be detrimental to the individual

106

and/or society. Its characteristics include: (1) an overpowering desire or need (compulsion) to continue taking the drug and to obtain it by any means; (2) a tendency to increase the dose; (3) a psychic (psychological and sometimes physical) dependence on the effect of the drug.

Drug habituation (habit) is a condition resulting from the repeated administration of a drug. Its characteristics include: (1) a desire (but not a compulsion) to continue taking the drug for the sense of improved well-being that it engenders; (2) little or no tendency to increase the dose; (3) some degree of psychic dependence on the effect of the drug, but absence of physical dependence and hence absence of an abstinence syndrome; (4) a detrimental effect, if any, primarily to the individual.

Withdrawal and *abstinence syndrome* are used synonymously to indicate the physical and mental discomforts experienced on withdrawal of an addicting drug. Following is a description of heroin withdrawal symptoms: At first, there is despondency, irritability, apprehension, and restlessness; then the subject begins to yawn and stretch. Later, sneezing develops and the symptoms of a fresh cold appear, such as watering of the eyes and nose. The hands become shaky and the muscles of the body jerk. The subject feels cold in spite of added clothing. Acute sickness accompanied by a complete distaste for food develops. The skin is cold and covered with goose flesh, resembling the skin of a plucked turkey—this has given rise to the slang expression "cold turkey," which refers to the conditions observed in a person who is undergoing a complete and abrupt withdrawal from drugs. There may also be weakness, restlessness, and gnawing sensations in the stomach, which are followed by nausea and vomiting. Other symptoms may include fever, pains in the abdomen and back, diarrhea, muscle twitchings, convulsions, dilated pupils, and hot and cold flashes. In severe cases, the most acute symptoms may last from two to three days and will gradually subside until they have disappeared completely; this usually requires about a week or ten days, depending on the addiction of the individual.

Tolerance is a state in which the body's tissue cells adjust to the presence of the drug. However, the body must readjust virtually all of its normal functions to compensate for the presence of a narcotic or drug. As the body's tolerance grows, increased quantities of the drug are required to produce the desired effect. Tolerance to one drug may result in a cross-tolerance to other drugs in the same family. Tolerance, therefore, results in a tendency to increase the dose of the addicting drug.

Abstinence syndrome—a collection of symptoms induced by abrupt withdrawal of opiates or barbiturates in addicted persons. Synonymous with withdrawal syndrome.

Alkaloid—an organic substance of alkaline properties, especially one occurring naturally in plants.

Analgesic—a remedy that relieves or removes pain.

Anorexia—a state of diminished appetite for food; a characteristic symptom of opiate addiction.

Euphoria—a sense of well-being and buoyancy.

Intravenous—an injection into a vein; also known as "mainlining."

Subcutaneous—under the skin; also known as "skin popping."

With these few definitions as a base we can now begin our study of the most commonly abused drugs, and those who abuse them.

Recognizing the Addict

There was a time when we believed that it took three things to make an addict: a psychologically maladjusted individual; an available drug; and a means of bringing the two together. However, during the 1960s it became increasingly apparent that a number of additional factors were involved in drug experimentation, drug abuse, and drug addiction. The most important of these was—and still is today—peer group pressure, particularly among the thirteen-to twenty-year-old segment of the population. If we must single out one characteristic that is common to people in this age group, it is the desire *not* to be different. This is evidenced by clothing styles, hair styles, and the popularity of certain fads. When the ingroup at the junior high school, high school, or college level is "doing" drugs, it takes an extremely strong-willed individual to resist the pressure and temptation to go along with the crowd.

Adolescence, which represents a time of physical change, tension, fear, and uncertainty, is characterized by a striving for independence, a rebellion against authority, and a strong dependence on the support of the peer group. Each of these factors can potentially lead to drug abuse. At the college level, we often find that intellectual curiosity leads to experimentation with drugs. Add to these variables individuals who are psychologically maladjusted and thus unable to face reality, and those who are merely seeking *"kicks,"* and we have a broad spectrum of persons who are using and abusing drugs.

Many times, even those closest to the abuser are unable to detect that drugs are being used. However, there are a number of symptoms which, if recognized, may indicate drug abuse. Parents and teachers, for example, may notice an abrupt change in a person's behavior patterns and life-style—a sudden withdrawal from the company of parents or siblings, changes in grades, inability to concentrate, abrupt loss of appetite, personality changes, an abnormal desire for privacy—all of these may lead to the suspicion that a person is using drugs. From the police point of view, these changes can be brought to light by talking with the parents and teachers of suspected users. During drug investigations, especially during interviews, officers can frequently elicit an admission from the suspect that he is using drugs. The presence of tracks or needle marks on the arms or legs or the appearance of withdrawal syndrome after being jailed for a few hours can also confirm suspicions that drugs are being used. Often, the suspect's manner of dress can be suggestive of drug abuse—long-sleeved shirts and sweaters during hot weather, sunglasses at night, inappropriately heavy clothing during warm weather. Of course, none of these activities alone is proof of drug use or addiction, but they can be signposts for the narcotics investigator.

Classification of Drugs

There are a number of drug classification systems in use today: systems defined by law (both federal and state), systems defined by symptoms, and systems defined by the action of the drugs on the body. Perhaps the simplest method of classification is the legal system, coupled with a description of the effects of the various drugs on the body.

Over-the-Counter Drugs (OTC)

This is a group of drugs that is available without a prescription in any drugstore or supermarket—for example, aspirin, bromides, Contac cold pills, Dristan, and so forth. Drugs of this nature are frequently abused and can even lead to death. The police role in handling those who misuse OTC drugs is limited only to a first-aid function, since it is not illegal to possess them.

Prescription Drugs

These are drugs which bear the label "CAUTION: FEDERAL LAW PROHIBITS DISPENSING WITHOUT A PRESCRIPTION." Possession of these drugs with a prescription is not illegal. However, many of these drugs are being sold illegally on the street and their possession without a prescription is illegal. Among the most commonly abused prescription drugs are Librium, Equanil, and Orinase (tranquilizers); Achromycin and penicillin (antibiotics); and a number of other harmful drugs including barbiturates, amphetamines, ergot, hypnotics, somnifacients, and legal narcotic preparations. (See figure 6.1.) This latter group will be discussed in detail in other sections of this chapter.

Exempt Narcotics

An exempt narcotic is a preparation which usually contains less than one grain of a narcotic per fluid ounce of preparation. Drugs belonging to this group are called "exempt" because they can be purchased without a prescription. The law of most states requires that the purchaser be twenty-one years of age and sign the narcotics book at the pharmacy when purchasing such drugs. Typical examples of exempt narcotics are Cheracol, Robitussin A.A., Histadyl E.C., Elixir Terpin Hydrate, and codeine. These are the so-called cough suppressants. All contain about 40 percent alcohol, plus one grain of codeine. They are never sold in quantities greater than four ounces.

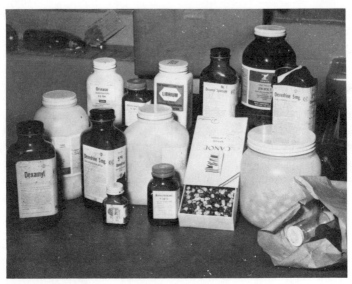

Photo by William Bickett.
Figure 6.1 Large amounts of prescription drugs seized in a raid. On the street these drugs are sold for up to ten times their legal value.

Exempt narcotics appeal to two types of abusers. Individuals who are addicted to more dangerous drugs may resort to exempt narcotics when other types of narcotics are in short supply on the street. Such a person might make the rounds of the drugstores, buying one four-ounce bottle in each store. He then boils down the liquid until all that remains is a white, powdery residue. This is the narcotic which is then injected into the vein. From the addict's point of view this is most unsatisfactory but it "keeps the monkey in check" until the "good stuff" becomes available.

The second and most common abuser of exempt narcotics is the high-school student. This individual purchases the cough syrup and then drinks it straight, mostly for its alcoholic content. It produces a slight narcotic reaction and the user experiences a drunken-like glow. Patrol officers often find empty cough syrup bottles in schoolyards on Sunday nights or Monday mornings.

Most exempt narcotics come in liquid form; in fact, the only exempt narcotic that comes in solid form is the old army and navy cure-all, APC tablets with codeine.

Hypnotic Drugs

Hypnotic drugs are drugs which produce a sedative or sleep-producing effect. They are generally manufactured in several forms—gelatin capsules with semiliquid centers, tablets, syrups, or white, crystalline powder. Common examples of the hypnotics are chloral hydrate, Playcydyl, and Noludar. Chloral hydrate, commonly known as "Mickey Finn," "Mickey," "Peter," or "Knockout Drops," comes in three forms—red, black, or yellow gelatin capsules, white crystals, or red syrup. Placydyl is manufactured as red gelatin capsules, and Noludar comes in the form of two-toned white capsules, or white tablets with the name ROCHE imprinted on them. It is illegal to possess a hypnotic drug without a prescription.

Somnifacient Drugs

Somnifacient drugs are nonbarbituric, depressant drugs which induce sleep in the normal individual. The most common example is Doriden (glutethimide), a white tablet about the size of an aspirin tablet with the name CIBA imprinted on it. It is illegal to possess a somnifacient without a prescription.

Barbiturates

Barbiturates are a group of sedative and sleep-producing drugs. These drugs are derived from barbituric acid and act on the central nervous system. They are usually taken orally but recently there has been a trend toward "shooting" the drug. Barbiturates produce drowsiness, staggering, slurred speech, nausea, and tremor of the hands. The user is prone to stumbling and dropping objects. He is often bruised, and if he smokes nonfilter cigarettes, may have burned fingers. His reactions are sluggish and he is emotionally erratic. Often he is irritable and antagonistic. The barbiturate user exhibits all the symptoms of drunkenness with one important exception: there is no odor of alcohol on his breath.

When a constant user of barbiturates is suddenly deprived of the drugs he goes into a state of withdrawal, which may be accompanied by convulsions. When under arrest, the barbiturate user should be watched carefully. Barbiturate withdrawal is extremely dangerous and sometimes even results in death. Be prepared to provide medical assistance if necessary.

Barbiturates are manufactured in various forms: tablets, capsules, suppositories, and liquid. They are the second most commonly used agent for suicide and are often used to offset the "jag" caused by amphetamine abuse. Among the street names for the drug are "barbs," "goofballs," "sleeping pills," and "peanuts." Specific types of barbiturates are often named after their color or shape. Among the more commonly used barbiturates are the following:

Pentobarbital sodium (in solid-yellow-capsule form) is known by abusers as "yellows," "yellow jackets," or "nimbies" (after the trade name Nembutal).

Secobarbital sodium (in red-capsule form) is called "reds," "pinks," "red birds," "red devils," and "seggy" (after the trade name Seconal).

Amobarbital sodium combined with secobarbital sodium (in red-and-blue-capsule form) is known as "rainbows," "red and blues," or "double trouble."

Amobarbital sodium (in solid-blue-capsule form) is known by abusers as "blues," "blue birds," "blue devils," or "blue heavens."

The variety of colors, color combinations, and shapes is due to the fact that these drugs are manufactured by several different drug companies, each of which has its own means of identifying its products.

Amphetamines

Amphetamines are drugs which directly stimulate the central nervous system, producing excitation, alertness, and wakefulness. The amphetamine abuser experiences dryness of the mouth and lips. He constantly licks his lips, causing chapping and reddening. His lips are often cracked and raw. This dryness also extends to the mucous membranes of the nose, which causes itching. The abuser rubs and scratches his nose to relieve the itching sensation.

The abuser will become talkative, excitable, and restless. He experiences a "high," suffers insomnia, perspires a great deal, and urinates frequently. He may exhibit a tremor of the hands. Ordinarily the user will take amphetamines orally, but some forms of the drug are injected by means of a needle and syringe or eye dropper.

Amphetamines, like the other synthetic drugs, are manufactured in a number of different forms—capsules, tablets, spansules, and liquids. Capsules are usually two-toned in color but some are solid colored. "Speed" (methamphetamine), which appears as a white or grayish-white powder, is usually sold in small tinfoil packets ⅜ inch by 1¼ inches, in small plastic bags 1 inch by 2 inches, or in clear gelatin capsules. It is usually injected into the veins, in much the same manner as heroin. When taken in this way, its effects are felt almost immediately. A so-called speed-freak may often stay "high" for four or five days without sleep. He will not eat during his high and because of this will often suffer from malnutrition; after a prolonged period of time he may become completely debilitated.

Known to abusers as "pep pills," "wake-ups," "eye-openers," "co-pilots," "truck drivers," or "bennies," the slang names for the drug are derived from the shapes and colors of the various amphetamine capsules and tablets. Following is a description of some of the most commonly abused amphetamines:

Amphetamine sulfate—rose-colored, heart-shaped tablets known as "peaches," "roses," or "bennies."

Amphetamine sulfate—round, white, double-scored tablets called "cartwheels," "whites," or "bennies."

Long-acting amphetamine sulfate capsules—found in many colors and known as "coast-to-coasts," "L.A. turnabouts," "co-pilots," "browns," and "black beauties."

Amphetamine sulfate—oval-shaped tablets of various colors called "footballs," or "greenies."

Injectable amphetamine—available in small glass vials and called "bombido," "jugs," or "bottles."

Dextroamphetamine sulfate—orange-colored, heart-shaped tablets known as "hearts," "oranges," or "dexies."

Hallucinogenic Drugs

Hallucinogenic, or psychedelic, drugs act on the central nervous system and affect the user's psychic and mental functions. Principal symptoms are distortion of sense perception and vision and hallucinations. Varying degrees of emotional reactions will occur depending upon the type and the dosage of the drug. However, the effect of the drug is not always euphoric. On occasion, users become fearful and experience a degree of terror which may cause them to want to escape, thereby causing injuries to themselves.

These drugs are usually taken orally and are available in tablet, capsule, and liquid form. Users put drops of the liquid in beverages or on sugar cubes or other carriers, such as animal crackers, chocolate bars, wintergreen mints, chewing gum, vitamin tablets, or the gummed label of an envelope. When in powder form, the drug may be dissolved in water, fruit juice, or a cola drink.

The most common of the true hallucinogenic drugs is LSD (D-lysergic acid diethylamide-25), otherwise known as "acid" or "the beast." (See figure 6.2.) An average dose of LSD is about 150 micrograms (just enough to fit on the head of a pin). One pound of LSD yields about 3,000,000 individual doses. LSD users tend to have visual, auditory, and even olfactory hallucinations, and experience a marked sense of depersonalization. Many have described the apparent ability to step out of their bodies and see themselves sitting against a wall. A "trip"

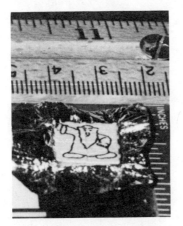

Photo by Pinson, courtesy of Mogadore Police Dept., Ohio.
Figure 6.2 "Mr. Natural," a form of LSD equal to four "hits" of "acid." Note the perforated lines. Each square is one "hit."

can last from six to sixteen hours, and users have been known to experience recurring effects of the drug days or even months after the original trip. This phenomenon is known as a "flashback."

STP (an amphetamine derivative also known as DOM) is a synthetic hallucinogen which is available in powder, tablet, and capsule form. Chemically it has been identified as 4-methyl 1-2-5 dimethoxyamphetamine. In small doses, it acts like an amphetamine. In large doses, it produces hallucinogenic effects said to be 200 times stronger than mescaline but only one-tenth as strong as LSD.

Peyote is made from buttons of the cactus plant *Lophophora*. These buttons are chopped or ground and put into capsules or rolled into small balls. Peyote is also available in liquid form (made by soaking the buttons in alcohol and then filtering) and sold in glass vials. It is usually taken orally. The buttons, whole or chopped, may be brewed with tea or chewed while drinking tea, coffee, or milk. A dose of 350 to 500 milligrams produces hallucinations for up to twelve hours. While not addictive, it can produce psychological dependence. (See figure 6.3.)

Psilocybin is available in three different forms: as a crystalline powder, a liquid, or a tablet, which is usually white and about the size of a baby aspirin. An extract of a Mexican mushroom, psilocybin produces the same types of

Photo by Richard McEvoy, courtesy of Georgia State Crime Laboratory, Atlanta.
Figure 6.3 Lophophora cactus from which peyote buttons are obtained.

hallucinations as those produced by mescaline, another commonly used hallucinogenic drug. The psilocybin trip lasts approximately six hours, and although the drug itself does not produce physical dependence, habitual users have been known to develop a tolerance for it.

Cannabis (Marijuana)

Although the laws of many states treat marijuana as a hallucinogen, this classification is actually misleading since only rarely does marijuana produce hallucinations. The active ingredient in marijuana is a complex molecule known as THC (tetrahydrocannabinol), which is found in the resin exuded from the leaves, flowers, stems, and seeds of the female plants of the common weed *Cannabis sativa*. (See figures 6.4 and 6.5.) Also called Indian hemp, this five-leafed plant is grown throughout Mexico, Canada, and the United States. Marijuana is made by drying the serrated leaves of the top of the plant—which then may be smoked. Once the plant has been harvested and dried, it resembles oregano. (See figure 6.6.) Marijuana is typically packaged for sale in manila envelopes, plastic bags (baggies), or heavy, plastic zip-lock bags (larger amounts).

Large lots of kilo bricks are smuggled into United States cities by every known means of transportation—car, plane, motorhome, boat, and so on. The importer may bring in as much as 500 pounds or more using "mules" (couriers) to do the actual transporting. The kilo bricks, which are wrapped in gray, brown, or light green paper resembling thin blotting paper, are broken up into

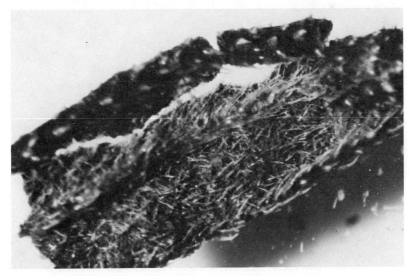

Photo by Richard McEvoy, courtesy of Georgia State Crime Laboratory, Atlanta.
Figure 6.4 Magnified view of marijuana.

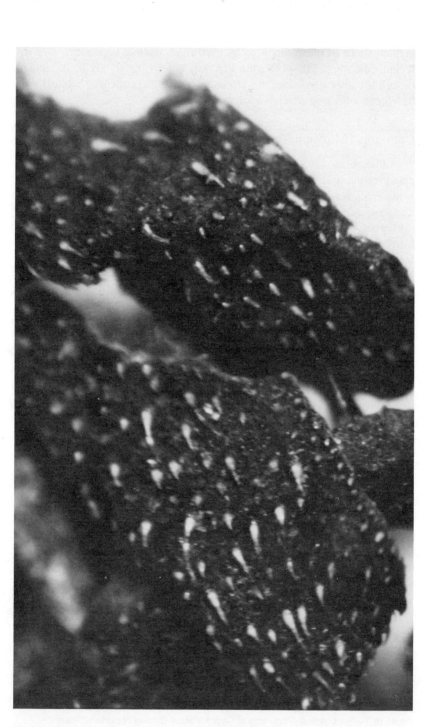

Photo by Richard McEvoy, courtesy of Georgia State Crime Laboratory, Atlanta.
Figure 6.5 Marijuana under extreme magnification.

Photo by William Bickett.
Figure 6.6 Poorly manicured marijuana.

pounds and packaged in zip-lock bags for sale to area dealers who in turn divide the "pot" into nickel ($5) and dime ($10) bags. These nickel and dime bags are sold to the users. At the present time, the average price of a pound on the street ranges from $110 to $130. (See figure 6.7.)

The user will smoke the pot in "joints" or "sticks" that are made by rolling the weed up in cigarette papers. He may also use regular smoking pipes, homemade pipes, or elaborate hookahs (bottles, either glass or metal, partially filled with water and having a bowl at the top and rubber or plastic tubing for smoking). (See figure 6.8.)

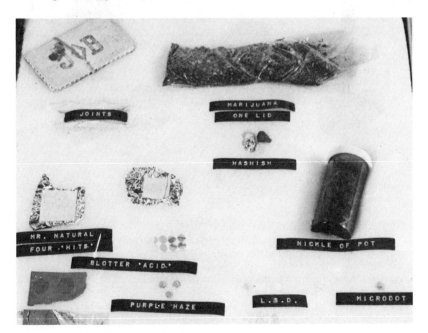

Photo by William Bickett.
Figure 6.7 Marijuana and hallucinogens.

Figure 6.8

    (a) A marijuana smoker's kit. This kit includes a pot pipe, a hash pipe, and a tobacco pouch for carrying equipment.

    (b) A cigarette holder used as a pot pipe.

    (c) An ingenious pot pipe which incorporates a small oxygen mask to insure that the smoker does not lose any of the smoke.

    (d) A lid of grass and a roach clip. The roach clip is used to hold a marijuana cigarette ("joint") when it burns down close to the fingers.

    (e) An ordinary telephone handset converted for pot smoking. After removing the speaker and receiver, the receiver is lined with aluminum foil and a pipe mouthpiece is attached to the wiring hole. A sharp-eyed officer spotted this device on a car seat during a routine traffic stop.

    (f) A hookah, used for smoking marijuana. Four persons may smoke at the same time.

Cannabis, when smoked, produces a sweet, pungent odor (similar to burning vegetation), which can be easily detected. The smoke, when held in the lungs for a long period before exhaling, produces a mild high and a floating sensation. There is some sense distortion although the effect may vary from user to user. Some people derive little or no feeling from marijuana, whereas others experience a real high and a sensation of euphoria. The effects of smoking also vary with the amount of THC found in the plant. The amount of THC varies depending on where the plant was grown. Turkish marijuana and some types of Mexican marijuana typically contain large amounts of THC and thus produce a stronger and longer-lasting effect. Marijuana grown in the midwestern part of the United States contains less THC and thus produces a weak, short-term high.

Hashish

Hashish is the unadulterated resin from the flowering tops of the cultivated female cannabis plant and it is the most refined form of cannabis. It is a brown powder, which when pressed into blocks resembles the sole of a shoe in shape and appearance. These ''soles'' are usually wrapped in foil or in red paper and cellophane. The user scrapes the block into a powder which can then be mixed with tobacco for smoking. Hashish can also be mixed with instant coffee and drunk as a beverage. It produces a mild hallucinatory effect. (See figure 6.9.)

Hashish is also available in a liquid form known as hash oil. Whereas most of the marijuana grown in the United States has a THC content of .5–2.0 percent, the THC content of hashish is approximately 10 percent. Liquid hashish has a THC content of 20–65 percent. Because of its high potency, hash oil produces special problems for the narcotics investigator. Its highly concentrated form allows it to be easily concealed, and thus thousands of doses can be smuggled into the country. In appearance, hash oil resembles extra-thick honey or molasses and is greenish-yellow or dark brown in color. One small drop can produce a high. The drop may be placed on a regular cigarette and smoked. It may be placed in an alcoholic beverage, smeared on bread, or used in cooking. When in a pipe, a special instrument is used. The drop is smeared on the inside of a pipe bowl which has one flat surface. The user exhales deeply, holds a match to the outside of the pipe bowl to melt the hash oil, and then inhales deeply. In one inhalation he draws the smoke into his lungs. He continues until the oil is burned up.

Hash oil can be made in a number of ways, but the most popular method is to percolate it as though percolating coffee. A perforated basket is filled with ground marijuana and suspended in a larger container. A solvent (alcohol or ether) is placed in the bottom of the larger container. A cover is placed on the larger container to which copper tubing is attached. Cold water is run through the tubing. The solvent is heated; it vaporizes and rises to the top of the container. When it reaches the cold-water tubing, it condenses, falls onto the ground marijuana, and filters back through the basket to be reheated. As the

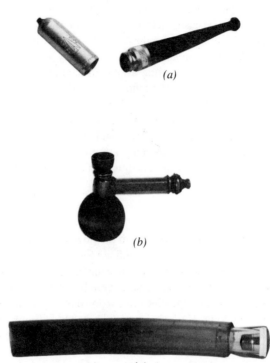

(a)

(b)

(c)

Photos by William Bickett.
Figure 6.9
  (a) A cigarette holder used for hash smoking. The cover is removed, hash is inserted and lighted, and the cover is replaced. The hole at the front of the cover allows a concentrated intake of smoke.
  (b) A hash pipe.
  (c) A hash pipe. Hashish is placed in the round bowl at the bottom of the pipe and in the pipe bowl. Suction draws hashish into the pipe bowl for burning.

solvent passes through the marijuana it dissolves the THC in the plant. As percolation continues the solution becomes stronger until all the THC has been brought into solution.

The equipment is very simple and can be improvised from easily obtainable components. A 55-gallon oil drum, a smaller drum, copper tubing, and a heat source are all that is necessary. (See figure 6.10.)

Hash oil may be dissolved in alcoholic beverages, shaving lotion, perfume, or any other type of commercial solvent, making it relatively easy to transport. Prior to use, the solvent is vaporized, leaving the hash oil behind. It is often transported in condoms and is sold in a variety of small containers, such as glass

Simple Percolator for Manufacturing Hash Oil

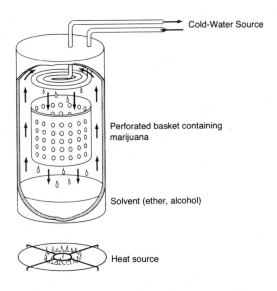

After drawing by James H. Johnston.

Figure 6.10 A simple percolator for manufacturing hash oil. The heated solvent vaporizes and rises. The vapor condenses on the cold-water coil and falls back through the perforated basket containing marijuana, removing the THC. Continued heating, vaporizing, and condensing produces a viscous liquid hashish in the bottom of the large container.

vials or sewing thimbles with aluminum foil tops. A thimbleful may range in price from $30 to $90 depending on the area of the country in which it is being sold.

The high THC content of hash oil presents problems for the user. Even at the 20 percent level, hash oil is from 10 to 100 times stronger than domestic marijuana. At the present time we do not know the effect of such high concentrations of THC. The user has no way of determining the strength of the drug and thus runs the risk of obtaining a highly potent substance.

The Opiates

Opium, the "mother drug," is produced from the opium poppy, a beautiful flower which is grown legally in Turkey and illegally in Mexico and Indochina. Turkish poppy is grown in a 55,000-square-mile area by over 175,000 farmers, and represents roughly 1 percent of Turkey's gross national product. Under

Turkish law and by international agreement, the Turkish government buys all of the plants produced. The entire plant is dried and baled and the government pays the farmer a set price for his crop. However, Turkey is flooded with illegal buyers who purchase gum opium at double the government price. Naturally, the temptation is great for native farmers to sell to the illegal buyers. The product sold is produced by slitting the poppy pod with a sharp finger knife. The plant is allowed to "bleed" overnight, and before the sun rises, the opium gum is wiped from the pod onto poppy leaves. The leaves are stuck together to form large balls of gum opium. This is sold to the illicit buyer, who smuggles it out of Turkey to an illegal lab where the gum opium is boiled with a hydrochloride solution. The leaves and twigs are skimmed off the boiling mixture and as the solution evaporates, a dark, gummy residue remains which is called morphine base. One hundred pounds of gum opium produce about ten pounds of morphine base. The morphine base is then smuggled into Marseilles to clandestine laboratories where it is converted into heroin by a process known as anhydrous acetylization. Ten pounds of morphine base produce ten pounds of heroin.

As the "mother drug," opium is the base for a number of derivative drugs which can be classified either as legal or illegal. The legal derivatives of opium include morphine, dionin, dilaudid, apomorphine, metopon, dromoran, and codeine. All of these drugs have valid medicinal purposes and properly used are a boon to mankind. In addition, there are a number of synthetic opiates which also have medicinal uses. These include demerol and dolophine. The major illegal narcotic is heroin.

Morphine and Its Derivatives

Morphine is the chief alkaloid of opium. It is medically used as a sedative and analgesic (painkiller) and has a bitter taste when taken orally. Morphine is manufactured in several forms—as white powder tablets (about the size of a saccharine tablet), as a thick liquid, and as a thin, colorless liquid which is stored in small vials. When abused, morphine produces a "high" followed by a euphoric feeling and a drowsy state. These effects are common to all of the opiates, both natural and synthetic.

Morphine has a number of recognized medical uses but it is sold on the streets as well. The drug is obtained for illegal purposes through theft, diverted shipments, and counterfeit prescriptions ("scripts"). Several recent cases in the Midwest revealed that a number of unscrupulous physicians were selling prescriptions for the drug for cash and, in the case of female addicts, for sexual favors. On the street, morphine is known as "Big M," "Miss Emma," "white stuff," "M," "emsel," "hocus," "unkie," "hard stuff," and "morpho."

Owing to inflation, shortages caused by police pressure, and higher penalties, the price of morphine has risen from $5 per tablet to as high as $10. A one-ounce vial (30 cc) which used to sell for about $30 now sells for $50.

Morphine is also the source of a number of other drugs, including the following:

Dionin, a white, crystalline powder whose effects closely resemble those of codeine but are weaker. Dionin causes intense irritation of the mucous membranes and for this reason it is not generally used by addicts.

Dilaudid, a fine, white, crystalline powder which has the same general actions and uses as dionin.

Apomorphine, prepared as a hydrochloride of morphine, is a dangerous drug, producing severe depression of the nervous system. It, too, is a white, crystalline powder.

Metopon, a white, crystalline powder, produced as a hydrochloride, is soluble in water. Its actions closely resemble those of morphine. It is actually derived from thebaine, another alkaloid of opium.

Dromoran is a synthetic drug of the morphine series which closely resembles morphine in its action, although it is somewhat more potent.

Codeine appears as white crystals or powder obtained from opium or prepared from morphine. Commercially, it is prepared in tablets for oral use or in liquid form for hypodermic injection.

Legal codeine is a relatively inexpensive drug, but when purchased on the street, one tablet may sell for as much as three to four dollars. It can be found in all sizes, shapes, and colors: a powder, tablet, liquid, or capsule. It is also used in combination with other drugs. Most popular in the illegal drug traffic are small white tablets (about the size of a saccharine tablet) and white tablets marked "Empirin" with the numbers 1, 2, 3, or 4 on them.

Small-size tablets of codeine, morphine, and dilaudid all look about the same, making it extremely difficult to differentiate between them.

Eukodal is a white crystalline powder derived from codeine. Its uses and actions are similar to morphine and codeine but it is much stronger.

Demerol is a synthetic opiate drug resembling morphine in its use and actions. It is sold under the names Meperidine and Isonipecaine. It is commercially prepared in two sizes of white tablets, one about the size of an aspirin tablet, the other about the size of a baby aspirin. It also appears as a white, crystalline powder and as a liquid.

Demerol is ordinarily taken by injection but it can be taken orally. Most Demerol being sold on the street is stolen from hospitals, doctors' offices, and pharmacies, or is obtained by forging prescriptions. Officers who have occasion to charge possession or sale of Demerol should identify it as isonipecaine (Demerol), a narcotic drug. Isonipecaine is the generic name for the drug. Use of trade names when filing complaints or affidavits can lose the case because the substance in evidence may be known by another trade name. However, the generic name includes all forms of the drug, no matter who the manufacturer is.

Dolophine is an effective antitussive (cough-control drug) and analgesic. It is a synthetic opium derivative which is usually taken orally as a white tablet or as a liquid. Also known as Methadone or by its generic name isoamidone, it is used extensively in narcotic addiction programs. Methadone has recently made its appearance on the street and is currently being purchased by heroin addicts. Abuse of this drug produces drowsiness, sweating, mental depression, hallucinations, circulatory collapse, and coma. At times the abuser will experience nausea, vomiting, dizziness, and dryness of the mouth. Officers who have occasion to file a complaint or affidavit should use the generic term isoamidone (dolophine or methadone), a narcotic drug.

All of these opium and morphine derivatives are manufactured legally and sold by prescription. All are physically addicting, and all are being sold illegally on the street. It is important to note that all of these drugs come in the form of a white powder. When taken orally all have a bitter taste. Quite often, television shows depict a dealer (or a narc) testing a white powder by wetting his finger and tasting the substance in order to determine its quality and character. In reality, however, no tongue is educated enough to be able to determine the nature or purity of a drug by merely tasting it. The only way to determine the type and quality of a drug is by field or lab testing using the proper equipment. Often, noxious and poisonous substances are used to cut illegal drugs to street strength, and thus an officer who makes a habit of tasting drugs could easily find himself the victim of strychnine or some other form of poisoning. *NEVER TASTE A DRUG OR ANY OTHER UNKNOWN SUBSTANCE!*

Heroin

Heroin is the most popular illegal derivative of opium. It has no known medical uses and is banned by international agreement from manufacture or sale throughout the world. Heroin is a white, crystalline powder, usually sold in glassine bags (stamp collector size), clear, gelatine capsules, or wrapped in aluminum foil. The bags and foil are called "decks" and the capsules are known as "caps." Heroin, produced by the process described earlier, is approximately 86 percent pure. Tracing the price structure of the heroin market best explains why heroin traffic is such a problem in the United States. The illegal buyer of raw opium in Turkey pays the farmer $35 per kilo or $350 for ten kilos of raw opium. The ten kilos is converted into one kilo of morphine base which can be sold in Syria or Lebanon for $700 to $800. One kilo of morphine base can be converted into one kilo of heroin valued at $6,000 on the Marseilles market.

Smuggled into a United States port, the one kilo of 86 percent pure heroin can be sold to an importer or wholesaler for $40,000. The wholesaler splits the kilo into quarter kilos, which he sells for $16,000 each, or $64,000 for the entire kilo. The dealers who purchase quarter-kilo lots from the wholesaler "step on the stuff" (dilute the heroin) with quinine, milk sugar, or baking powder seven times, to produce two kilos of 12.2 percent pure heroin. The original kilo of 86 percent pure heroin is thus transformed into eight kilos or seventeen and six-tenths pounds of adulterated heroin having a purity of 12.2 percent.

At sixteen ounces to the pound, the dealer sells 281.6 ounces of 12.2 percent heroin to the pushers at the going rate of $1,900 per ounce or $533,900 for the whole lot. The pushers, in turn, step on the stuff four times by adding twenty-four kilos of adulterates to produce thirty-two kilos or seventy and four-tenths pounds of 3 percent pure heroin. The pusher packages the heroin into ounces or capsules. He will produce a total of 1,126 ounces. Each ounce contains 437 grains. Packaged into the usual five-grain dose, the 1,126 ounces will produce 100,112 doses which sell for approximately $15 per dose. Thus by the time the original kilo of heroin reaches the street, it yields $1,501,680 in revenue. It has been estimated that over 1,000 kilos of 86 percent pure heroin is smuggled into the United States each year, producing revenue of over $1.5 billion and supplying some 200,000 addicts.

When the heroin addict purchases his "fix," he mixes the heroin with water in a bent spoon or bottle cap and heats the solution until the heroin is dissolved. He then draws the solution into his "spike" or syringe, using a small ball of cotton as a strainer. The syringe is usually made of an eyedropper or baby syringe to which a needle has been attached. He uses this type of syringe for two reasons. First, possession of a hypodermic syringe without a prescription is a felony in most states; second, a commercial hypodermic syringe produces a great deal of pressure on the veins. By using the eyedropper he can prolong the time before which his veins will collapse from repeated use of the needle. (See figure 6.11.)

The addict will then "mainline" his fix by injecting the solution directly into the vein. Often he will tease himself by shooting a little of the fix and then drawing it back. In this way he "builds his high." Several minutes after completing the shot, he will begin to feel a tingling sensation in the abdomen and gradually will be overcome with a sense of euphoria, a feeling that everything is fine. In the language of the addict, "he is fixed." Shortly thereafter, he will go "on the nod," a dreamlike state of semiconsciousness. He will remain "on the nod" for an hour or more and then gradually return to reality. Within

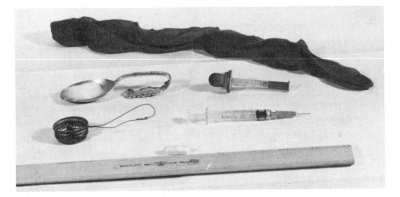

Photo by William Bickett.
Figure 6.11 "The works" —*the addict's equipment. Note the bent spoon, bottle cap, and eyedropper syringe. The nylon stocking at the top is used as a tourniquet.*

two to three hours he begins to feel a gnawing in the stomach and becomes nervous. Four hours later he needs another fix. The addict spends his life looking for his next fix, and there is nothing that he or she will not resort to in order to buy drugs. At $60 to $70 per day, the addict is always in need of money. Addicts generally cannot hold a job for long and are forced to turn to theft, prostitution (both male and female), and pushing in order to acquire enough money to support their habits. It has been estimated that a typical addict in New York City must steal goods worth $52,000 every year in order to support an average habit. Straight society pays for these theft losses in the 2 percent that most merchants add to the price of goods to cover "inventory shrinkage." Robbery and burglary are also common among addicts who need money for a fix.

Preoccupation with drugs causes most addicts to neglect their health. Many suffer from malnutrition because drug use kills their appetites. Failure to take hygienic precautions in the use of needles or using equipment belonging to other addicts causes many to contract hepatitis or syphilis, both of which can be spread through the bloodstream. The use of dirty needles often produces festering sores on the addict's arms and legs. These ulcers produce a scarring of the skin over the vein sites and the needle marks are plainly visible as "tracks" or "snakes." In order to hide the needle marks, many addicts shoot between the toes, behind the lower lip, and, in some rare instances, inside the eyelid.

An addict with visible "tracks" on his arms will wear long-sleeved shirts and sweaters, even in the hottest weather. Opiate use causes the pupils of the eyes to become as small as a pinpoint. For this reason addicts often wear sunglasses, even at night. Maurer and Vogel (1970, pp. 164–168) provide seventeen indications which may be used to recognize possible addicts:

1. A statement by the individual that he is an addict.

2. The possession of addicting drugs (either medical or contraband) without adequate medical explanation.

3. A tendency on the part of the suspect to hide or conceal these drugs.

4. The presence of needle-marks in the form of black or blue spots resembling tattooing; these may indicate skin-shooting, and will usually appear on the arms and legs, or even on the backs of the hands. Fresh needle punctures, sometimes topped by minute scabs or crusts, are especially significant.

5. The presence of elongated scars (frequently of tattooed appearance) over the veins, especially those of the forearms, the instep, or the lower legs; however, these may have a medical explanation unrelated to addiction.

6. The presence of boil-like abscesses over the veins or near the sites where veins approach the surface.

7. An appearance of drowsiness, sleepiness, or lethargy (on the nod), especially if accompanied by a tendency to scratch the body as if itching. This sometimes indicates a slight overdose of opiates or their synthetic equivalents.

8. The tendency to develop withdrawal symptoms if isolated completely and observed constantly for a period of 12 to 24 hours.

9. Wide fluctuations in the size of the pupils of the eyes, with the pupil reaching a maximum of constriction immediately after the suspect may have taken an injection.

10. The possession of equipment for opium unless, of course, this equipment has only a curiosity value, or is owned by a collector.

11. The possession of hypodermic equipment, excepting those persons with a legitimate need for such equipment, such as diabetics who must take regular injections of insulin, or medical addicts. However, the legitimate user will invariably possess a standard medical syringe and needle, while the addict usually (but not always) tends to prefer the home-made syringes.

12. A tendency for the individual to sit looking off into space, known to young addicts as "goofing," this may indicate the use of heroin or barbiturates, or both.

13. The possession of a cooking spoon with handle characteristically bent backwards, or a cooker made from a metal bottle cap with a wire handle; small glass vials are also sometimes used. They are all characteristically blackened from being over a lighted match.

14. A knowledge of the argot (slang) of the underworld narcotic addict. While some addicts who secure their drugs exclusively from medical sources never learn any of the argot, they are in the minority; most addicts will know or respond to terms from the argot of the underworld addict, and especially to terms employed predominately by users of the type of drug which the addict takes.

    Note: Much of the language of the drug culture has, since 1967, been adopted by modern youth and can no longer be considered as a strong indication that the speaker is a drug user.

15. A tendency for the suspect to isolate himself at regular intervals (about four or five hours apart) in order to take hypodermic injections.

16. An obvious discrepancy between the amount of money the suspect earns, and the amount he spends for the necessities of life. If he makes $100 ($200 today), and is always broke, with no obvious expenditures for necessities, he may be supporting a drug habit.

17. The tendency for a person who has previously been reliable to resort to thievery, embezzlement, forgery, prostitution, etc. This may indicate that he or she needs the large amounts of money necessary to support a drug habit.

From *Narcotics and Narcotic Addiction,* Fourth Edition, by David W. Maurer and Victor H. Vogel. Courtesy of Charles C. Thomas, Publisher, Springfield, Illinois 62717.

Cocaine

Cocaine is the active alkaloid obtained from the coca leaf, which is grown in South America. It is one of the stimulant drugs which produces no physical dependence (not addictive); however, it is capable of producing a psychological dependence. It is a white, odorless, crystalline powder having a bitter taste. In medicine, cocaine is used as a surface anesthetic and may be prescribed by a physician for legitimate medical purposes. In addition to its powder form, it can also be purchased in liquid and capsule form.

Manufactured cocaine is not imported into the United States. Only the coca leaf is imported, and the drug is manufactured by drug companies from the imported leaves.

When sold illegally on the street, cocaine comes in small, aluminum foil packets or in small, plastic bags (either ½" × 1" or 1" × 2"). Occasionally a user will inject cocaine into the vein or take it orally, but most often the drug is sniffed through the nostrils, where it is absorbed into the mucous membranes of the nose. An advanced user who injects the drug may do so at intervals as short as ten minutes apart and at times may "shoot" as many as ten times a day.

When officers have reason to believe that they may be dealing with a cocaine user, they should (when permitted by law) examine the money in the suspect's pocket and any matchbooks he may have in his possession. A cocaine user will often roll up a dollar bill or a matchbook to form a tube through which he can sniff the drug. Often, the cocaine crystals will adhere to the paper fibers, thus substantiating a possession charge.

In recent years cocaine ("coke") has become a fashionable drug in certain upper-middle-class circles of society. It is sometimes made available at parties alongside the hors d'oeuvres. Upper-middle-class users don't resort to the dollar bill or matchbook to sniff their coke; they purchase small, jewelled spoons with which to sniff the drug. These spoons have recently made an appearance in fashionable jewelry stores, and can be worn on the outer clothing just like any other jewelled pin.

Cocaine causes the pupils of the eyes to dilate and increases the heartbeat and blood pressure. It can cause nausea, loss of appetite, digestive disorders and, in persons suffering from advanced usage, emaciation. It may produce intense excitation, fear, anxiety, hallucinations, and an exaggerated sense of muscular strength. The user may become paranoid, believing that everyone is an enemy. Thus, officers should be particularly alert when arresting a cocaine user as he is capable of violence when sufficiently motivated by fear. Although the excessive cocaine user is generally incapable of planning a deliberate crime, he may commit crimes of violence out of imaginary fear of perceived danger.

On the drug scene, the "speedball," made of cocaine and heroin, is extremely popular. The cocaine heightens the high produced by the heroin. Cocaine is known by a number of street names, including "corine," "coke," "speedball," "C," "dust," "snowflake," "gold dust," and "girl." Legally purchased cocaine sells for about $60 an ounce. Illegal cocaine may sell for as much as $150 an ounce. Illegal cocaine is manufactured in clandestine South American labs and smuggled into the country on international air flights. Several years ago, a U.S. Customs profile of the cocaine smuggler indicated that most smugglers were South or Central Americans traveling with Italian passports. The cocaine was being smuggled into East Coast cities.

GLOSSARY OF NARCOTICS TERMS*

Technical Terms

ADDICTION. In 1957, the World Health Organization (WHO) defined drug addiction as a state of periodic or chronic intoxication produced by the repeated consumption of a drug. Its characteristics include: (1) an overpowering desire or need (compulsion) to continue taking the drug and to obtain it by any means; (2) a tendency to increase the dose; (3) a psychic (psychological) and generally a physical dependence on the effects of the drug; (4) an effect detrimental to the individual and to society. (Compare with "drug dependence" and "habituation.")

ANALGESIC. Painkiller.

CENTRAL NERVOUS SYSTEM. The brain and spinal cord.

CONVULSION. An involuntary and violent irregular series of contractions of the muscles.

DELIRIUM. A condition characterized by mental excitement, confusion, disordered speech, and, often, hallucinations.

DEPRESSANT. Any of several drugs which sedate by acting on the central nervous system. Medical uses include the treatment of anxiety, tension, and high blood pressure.

DRUG DEPENDENCE. As described in 1963 by WHO, drug dependence is "a state arising from repeated administration of a drug on a periodic or continuous basis." Its characteristics will vary with the agent involved. This is made clear by designating the particular type of drug dependence in each specific case—for example, drug dependence of the morphine type, of the cocaine type, of the cannabis type, of the barbiturate type, etc. (Compare with "addiction" and "habituation.")

HABITUATION. As defined in 1957 by WHO, drug habituation is a condition, resulting from repeated consumption of a drug, which includes these characteristics: (1) a desire (but not a compulsion) to continue taking the drug for the sense of improved well-being that it engenders; (2) little or no tendency to increase the dose; (3) some degree of psychic dependence on the effect of the drug, but absence of physical dependence and, hence, no abstinence syndrome; (4) a detrimental effect, if any, primarily on the individual. (Compare with ADDICTION and DRUG DEPENDENCE.)

HALLUCINOGEN. Any of several drugs, popularly called psychedelics, which produce sensations such as distortions of time, space, sound, color, and other bizarre effects. While they are pharmacologically nonnarcotic, some of these drugs (e.g., marijuana) are regulated under federal narcotic laws.

---

*Reprinted from John B. Williams, *Narcotics and Drug Dependence* (Beverly Hills, Calif.: Glencoe Press, 1974), pp. 405–422, by permission of the author and the publisher.

HYPNOTIC. An agent that induces sleep.

NARCOTIC. This term has two definitions. Medically defined, a narcotic is any drug that produces sleep or stupor and also relieves pain. Legally defined, the term means any drug regulated under the Harrison Act and other federal narcotic laws. Some of these regulated drugs are pharmacologically nonnarcotic (e.g., cocaine).

PHYSICAL DEPENDENCE. Physiological adaptation of the body to the presence of a drug. In effect, the body develops a continuing need for the drug. Once such dependence has been established, the body reacts with predictable symptoms if the drug is abruptly withdrawn. The nature and severity of withdrawal symptoms depend on the drug being used and the daily dosage level attained.

POTENTIATION. Potentiation occurs when the combined action of two or more drugs is greater than the sum of the effects of each drug taken alone. Potentiation can be very useful in certain medical procedures. For example, physicians can induce and maintain a specific degree of anesthesia with a small amount of the primary anesthetic agent by using another drug to potentiate the primary anesthetic agent. Potentiation may also be dangerous. For example, barbiturates and many tranquilizers potentiate the depressant effects of alcohol.

PSYCHOLOGICAL DEPENDENCE. An attachment to drug use which arises from a drug's ability to satisfy some emotional or personality need of an individual. This attachment does not require a physical dependence, although physical dependence may seem to reinforce psychological dependence. An individual may also be psychologically dependent on substances other than drugs.

PSYCHOSIS. A major mental disorder; a serious mental derangement. *Psychosis* replaces the old term *insanity*.

SEDATIVE. An agent which quiets or calms activity.

SIDE EFFECTS. A given drug may have many actions on the body. Usually one or two of the more prominent actions will be medically useful. The others, usually weaker effects, are called side effects. They are not necessarily harmful but may be annoying.

STIMULANT. Any of several drugs which act on the central nervous system, producing excitation, alertness, and wakefulness. Medical uses include the treatment of mild depressive states, overweight, and narcolepsy—a disease characterized by an almost overwhelming desire to sleep.

SYNERGISM. Action of two agents which results in a total effect greater than the sum of the two effects taken independently.

TOLERANCE. With many drugs, a person must keep increasing the dosage to maintain the same effect. This characteristic is called tolerance. Tolerance develops with the barbiturates, with amphetamine and related compounds, and with opiates.

TOXIC EFFECTS (poisoning). Any substance in excessive amounts can act as a poison or toxin. With drugs, the margin between the dosage that produces beneficial effects and the dosage that produces toxic or poisonous effects varies greatly. Moreover, this margin will vary with the person taking the drug.

Slang Terms Associated with Today's Youth and Their Drugs of Abuse

ACAPULCO GOLD. A form of marijuana.

ACID. LSD, lysergic acid diethylamide; DMT.

ACID HEAD. LSD abuser.

ACID TEST. Party at which LSD has been added to the punch.

AMPING; OVERAMPING. See O.D.

ARTILLERY. Equipment for injecting drugs.

(WHERE IT'S) AT. Where (drug) action is taking place.

BAB-O. Nalline: a morphine-related substance used to test for narcotic poisoning from heroin, methadone, or morphine. It is called "Bab-o" since it "takes the user to the cleaners." ("Bab-o" being the trade name of a kitchen cleanser.)

BABYSIT. To guide a person through his drug experience.

BACKTRACK. To withdraw the plunger of a syringe before injecting drugs to make sure needle is in proper position.

BACKWARDS. Term applied to tranquilizers.

BAG. A container of drugs; also, to sniff glue or solvent from a bag.

(FINDING YOUR) BAG. See DOING YOUR THING.

BAGMAN. A drug supplier.

BALL. A party; a good time; blast; gas.

BALLOON. Rubber toy balloon used for storing or delivering narcotics, usually heroin in bulk form but occasionally papered or capped.

BANG. To inject drugs.

BARBS. Barbiturates.

BEAST (THE). LSD.

BEEN HAD. Arrested, or beaten out of something.

BENNIES; BEANS. Benzedrine tablets (brand of amphetamine sulfate, Smith, Kline & French Laboratories).

BERNICE. Cocaine.

BIG D. LSD.

BIG JOHN. The police.

BINDLE. A small paper packet of heroin, morphine, cocaine, or methedrine.

BIZ. Equipment for injecting drugs.

BLACK. Opium.

BLACK-AND-WHITE. A patrol car.

BLANKS. Poor quality narcotic.

BLAST; BLOW. To smoke a marijuana cigarette.

BLASTED. Under the influence of drugs.

BLOTTER ACID. LSD soaked into blotter or paper; high quality LSD.

BLOW A STICK. To smoke a marijuana cigarette.

BLOW YOUR COOL. Loss of self-control while under the influence.

BLOW YOUR MIND. To get high on drugs.

BLUE BANDS. Pentobarbital sodium.

BLUE BIRDS; BLUE DEVILS; BLUE HEAVEN; BLUES. Amobarbital capsules
    (Amytal; amobarbital sodium). Sodium amytal capsules (brand of
    amobarbital, Eli Lilly and Company).

BLUE CHEER. Type of LSD.

BLUE VELVET. Paregoric and an antihistamine.

BOGART. To "Bogart a joint" is either to salivate on or to retain (and not pass
    around) a marijuana cigarette (from Humphrey Bogart).

BOMBED. Intoxicated on drugs.

BOMBIDO. Injectable amphetamine.

BOO. Cannabis.

BOOSTER. Consumption or injection of additional dosage to continue or prolong
    a "trip."

BOTTLE DEALER. A person who sells drugs in 1,000-tablet or capsule bottles.

BOXED. In jail.

BREAD. Money.

BRICK. Kilo of marijuana in compressed brick form.

BRIDGE. Usually alligator clamp or like device used to hold marijuana cigarette
    while smoking it (see CRUTCH).

BROWN SHOES. Name for squares.

BULL. A federal narcotic agent; a police officer.

BUMMER: BUM TRIP. A "bad trip"; bad deal; bad trip on acid or marijuana (see
    FREAK TRIP, FREAK OUT).

BURN. To accept money and give no drug in return, or to give a substance in lieu
    of the drug; also, to burn the skin when injecting.

BURNED. Used to describe the acquisition of bad drugs, diluted drugs, or no
    drugs at all.

BURNED OUT. The sclerotic condition of the vein present in most conditioned addicts.

BUST. An arrest.

BUSTED. Arrested.

BUTTON. Peyote buttons (containing the psychedelic mescaline).

BUY. To purchase drugs.

BUZZ ON. To feel good.

CAN. One ounce of marijuana; term derived from Prince Albert brand tobacco can in which marijuana was commonly sold in the past. Now more frequently observed in small paper or plastic bags (*see* LID).

CANDY. Barbiturates.

CAP. Capsule containing a drug; commonly a No. 5 capsule.

CARGO. Load or supply of narcotics or drugs.

CARRYING. In possession of a drug.

CARTWHEEL. Amphetamine tablet (round, white, double-scored).

CENTS. CCs; cubic centimeters.

CHALK. Methamphetamine.

CHAMP. Drug abuser who won't reveal his supplier even under pressure.

CHARGED UP. Under the influence of drugs.

CHICKEN POWDER. Amphetamine powder for injection.

CHIEF (THE). LSD.

CHIP; CHIPPER; CHIPPING; CHIPPY. To play around with drugs; to use drug sporadically; an abuser taking small, irregular amounts; also, a prostitute.

CHRISTMAS TREE. Tuinal.

CHIVA. Heroin.

CHOCOLATE CHIP. A type of LSD.

CLEAN. To remove stems and seeds from marijuana; also refers to an addict who is free from needle injection marks; also, not holding or possessing any narcotics.

CLEAR UP. To withdraw from drugs.

COASTING. Under the influence of drugs.

COCKTAIL. A regular cigarette into one end of which a partially smoked marijuana cigarette is inserted so as to waste none of the drug.

COKE. Cocaine.

COKIE. A cocaine addict.

COLD. Tough deal, as "cold heart."

COLD TURKEY. Trying to break the habit; "kicking it cold turkey" is breaking the habit of addictive drug use at home, in prison, etc., without the aid of any medication or medical care.

COME DOWN. To come off drugs.

CONNECT. To buy drugs.

CONNECTION. Refers to the peddler or source of supply for the user.

CONTACT HIGH. A feeling of being on drugs or "high" merely from being in contact with someone or something reminding one of drugs.

COOK UP A PILL. To prepare opium for smoking.

COOKER. Bottle cap for heating drug powder with water.

COOL. *See* GROOVY.

CO-PILOTS. Amphetamines.

COP; TO COP. To purchase drugs.

COP OUT. To alibi, confess.

COPE. To handle oneself effectively while under the influence of drugs.

CORINNE. Cocaine.

COTICS. Narcotics.

COTTONS. Bits of cotton saturated with narcotic solution used to strain foreign matter when drawing solution up into hypodermic syringe or eyedropper; these cottons are often saved by addicts for an emergency, as they contain a residual amount of the drug.

CRACKERS. LSD in Boston (from animal crackers).

CRASH. To end a drug experience, particularly from an amphetamine like methedrine; to fall asleep while using drugs, come down hard and fast from a high or a trip.

CRASH PAD. Temporary residence, usually for a night or two, usually communal, often to end a drug experience.

CRAZY. Exciting; in the know, enjoyable.

CRUTCH. Device used to hold marijuana cigarette when it has burned to the point where it will scorch the fingers; usually half of a paper match book; also, a container for a hypodermic needle.

CRYSTAL. Methedrine (methamphetamine), "speed," or other amphetamine.

CRYSTALS. Amphetamine powder for an injection.

CUBE. Sugar cube impregnated with LSD.

CUT. To adulterate a narcotic by diluting with milk sugar, baking powder, etc.

D. LSD.

DABBLE. To take small amounts of drugs on an irregular basis.

DEALER. Drug supplier, peddler.

DECK. A small packet of narcotics.

DEEDA. LSD in Harlem.

DEXIES. Dextroamphetamine sulfate or amphetamine tablets (brand name Dexedrine, Smith Kline & French Laboratories).

DMT. Dimethyltryptamine, a psychedelic, nicknamed "the businessman's LSD," "45-minute psychosis."

DEUCE BAG. A two-dollar container of a drug.

DIME OR DIME BAG. Ten dollars' worth of drugs.

DIRTY. To be in possession of drugs, or to be caught holding.

DOING. May be any "happening" but specifically the taking of a drug.

DOING YOUR THING. Doing what seems best to you; finding your "bag."

DOLLIES. "Dolophine" tablets (brand of methadone hydrochloride, Eli Lilly and Company).

DOMINO. To purchase drugs.

DOPE. Any narcotic.

DOPER. Addict; drug user (also "Dopey").

DOTTING. Placing LSD on a sugar cube.

DOUBLE CROSS. Amphetamine tablets (double scored).

DOUBLE TROUBLE. Tuinal capsule (brand of amobarbital sodium and secobarbital sodium, Eli Lilly and Company).

DO UP. Smoke a joint, or take an injection of heroin.

DOWNER. A depressant drug such as a barbiturate or tranquilizer; also, a "bum trip"; also, to come off drugs.

DREAMER. One who takes opiates or morphine.

DROP. To swallow a pill.

DROPPED. Arrested.

DUBBE. Negro slang for a marijuana roach.

DUST. Cocaine.

EXPLORERS' CLUB. A group of acid heads.

FACTORY. Equipment for injecting drugs.

FAT. Describing someone who has a good supply of drugs.

FINE STUFF. Narcotics of unusually good quality, only slightly adulterated.

FINK. Informer; phony.

FIT; OUTFIT. Equipment for injecting drugs.

FIX; FIX UP. A drug which is about to be injected, or has just been injected; to inject drugs or one dose of a particular drug; see also OUTFIT.

FLAKE. Cocaine.

FLASH. The intense feeling the user has just after "fixing"; to throw up after "fixing."

FLASHBACK. Recurrence of the drug reaction; with LSD, weeks to months later without taking the drug again.

FLEA POWDER. Poor quality narcotics.

FLOATING. Under the influence of drugs.

FLUSH. The initial feeling the user gets when injecting a drug like methamphetamine.

FOOTBALLS. Oval-shaped amphetamines.

FORWARDS. Pep pills, especially amphetamines.

FRANTIC. Nervous, jittery drug user; in need of a fix.

FREAK. One who has flipped, i.e., one who uses drugs to the point of loss of reality; especially used as "speed freak" referring to heavy methedrine user.

FREAK OUT. To have a bad trip; to lose all contact with reality; to have a drug party.

FREAK TRIP. Adverse drug reaction, especially with LSD.

FRESH AND SWEET. Out of jail.

FUZZ. The police; the law.

GAGE. Marijuana.

GARBAGE. Poor quality drugs.

GASSING. Sniffing gasoline fumes.

GATE-KEEPER. One who initiates another into the use of LSD.

GEE-HEAD. Paregoric abuser.

GEETIS. Money.

GEEZE. Injection of drugs.

GEEZER. A narcotic injection.

GET OFF. To get high on speed; also, sexual orgasm.

GHOST (THE). LSD.

GIGGLE-SMOKE. Cannabis, or cannabis smoke.

GIMMICKS. The equipment for injecting drugs.

GLAD RAG (WAD). A cloth material saturated with glue or gasoline, usually a sock.

GLUEY. Glue sniffer.

GO. To participate freely in the drug scene.

GOLD DUST. Cocaine.

GOOD GO. A good or reliable dealer in drugs.

GOOD H. Good quality heroin, approximately 50 percent pure.

GOODS. Narcotics.

GOOFBALLS. Barbiturates; any barbiturate tablet or capsule; may be combined with an amphetamine.

GOOFER. One who uses pills.

GOOFED UP. Under the influence of barbiturates.

GOING UP. Taking drugs for their effects; said of smoking cannabis or injecting "speed," etc.

GOW-HEAD. An opium addict.

GRAM. Gram of heroin, approximately ten capsules.

GRASS. Marijuana in the raw state, such as leaves, stems, seeds.

GRASSHOPPER. Marijuana user.

GRASS BROWNIES. Cookies containing cannabis.

GREENIES. Green, heart-shaped tablets of dextroamphetamine sulfate and amobarbital.

GRIEFO; GRIFFO. Marijuana, cannabis.

GROOVY. Good; "out of sight."

GROUND CONTROL. Caretaker in LSD session.

GUIDE. One who "babysits" with a novice when he goes up on a psychedelic substance.

GUN. Hypodermic syringe.

GURU. Companion on a trip who has tripped before.

H. Heroin.

HABIT. Physically or psychologically dependent on drugs; addiction to drugs.

HALLUCINOGEN. *See* PSYCHEDELIC.

HAND-TO-HAND. Delivery of narcotics person to person.

HANG-UP. A personal problem.

HARD STUFF. Morphine, cocaine, or heroin.

HARRY. Heroin.

HASH; HASHISH. Resin from the *Cannabis indica* plant, which contains a very high tetrahydrocannabinol content.

HASHBURY. Haight-Ashbury, district of San Francisco.

HAWK (THE). LSD.

HAY. Marijuana.

HEAD. Chronic user of a drug or drugs; one who is involved with drugs to the extent that the drug has become an important part of his life.

HEARTS. Benzedrine or Dexedrine (brands of amphetamine sulfate and dextroamphetamine sulfate, Smith Kline & French Laboratories); heart-shaped tablets (orange color).

HEAT. The law; a police officer.

HEAVY. Significant, weighty; highly emotional.

HEMP. Marijuana.

HIGH. Under the influence of a drug, usually a stimulant; a drug user who is "up."

HIP; HEP. To understand; opposite of "square."

HIPPIES. Beatniks.

HIT. One dose of a particular drug; to take a drag off a marijuana cigarette.

HOCUS. A narcotic solution ready for injection.

HOG. An addict who uses all he can get his hands on.

HOLDING. Possessing narcotics.

HOOKED. Addicted; a confirmed addict.

HOPHEAD. Narcotic addict.

HOPPED UP. Under the influence of drugs.

HORNING (SNORTING, SNIFFING). Sniffing narcotics.

HORSE. Heroin.

HOT. Wanted by police.

HOT SHOT. A fatal dosage.

HYPE. One who uses intravenous drugs, specifically heroin or "speed."

HYPE OUTFIT. Equipment for injecting drugs.

ICE CREAM HABIT. Sporadic use of drugs.

J or JAY. "Joint" or marijuana cigarette.

JACKED UP. To be interrogated or arrested.

JAR DEALER. A person who sells drugs in 1,000-tablet or capsule bottles.

JIVE. Marijuana or jive talk.

JIVE STICKS. Marijuana cigarettes.

JOB. To inject drugs.

JOINT. A marijuana cigarette.

JOLT. An injection of narcotics.

JOY POP. Intermittent (rather than continuous) injection of one dose of a drug; one who is "joy popping" only takes an injection now and then.

JOY POWDER. Heroin.

JUG. 1,000-tablet or capsule bottle.

JUNK. Narcotics; heroin.

JUNKIE. A narcotic addict.

KEY. Kilo (2.2 lb.).

KEG. 25,000 amphetamine capsules or tablets, or more.

KICK; KICKING. To stop using drugs (see COLD TURKEY).

KICKS. A drug experience.

KILO. 2.2 pounds.

KIT. Same as "outfit" or narcotic paraphernalia.

L. LSD.

LAB. Equipment used to manufacture drugs illegally.

LAID OUT. Being informed on.

LAME. Not very smart; dumb, or green; not street wise.

LAYOUT. The equipment for injecting drugs.

LEAN. A nonuser of drugs.

LID. *See* CAN.

LID PROPPERS. Amphetamines.

LIPTON TEA. Poor quality narcotics.

LIT UP; LOADED. Under the influence of heroin, marijuana, or alcohol. High on drugs.

LOCOWEED. Marijuana.

LUSH. Alcohol; also an alcoholic.

M. Morphine.

MACHINERY. Equipment for injecting drugs.

MAGIC MUSHROOM. The Mexican species of mushroom containing psilocybin; a psychedelic.

MAIN LINE. To inject drugs directly into a vein.

MAINLINER. One who injects narcotics directly into the veins (intravenously).

MAKE A BUY. To purchase drugs.

MAKE A MEET. To purchase drugs or to leave.

MAKE IT. To buy narcotics; to leave the scene, area.

MAN (THE). The law; the police; or a connection (drug supplier).

MANICURE. Prepare marijuana for use in cigarettes.

MARY JANE. Marijuana.

MATCH BOX. Small container of marijuana; a small amount of cannabis sufficient to make between five to eight cigarettes; about a fifth of a lid.

MDA. A hallucinogen, methyl-3,4-methylenedioxyphenethylamine.

MEET. To buy drugs.

MELLOW YELLOW. Refers to smoking dried banana skins; a hoax, as they contain no mind-altering drugs.

MEZZ. Marijuana.

MICKEY; MICKEY FINN. Chloral hydrate.

MIND BLOWER. Pure unadulterated drugs.

MISS EMMA. Morphine.

MOHASKY; MU; MUGGLES. Cannabis.

MOJO. Narcotics.

MONKEY. A drug habit where physical dependence is present.

MOR A GRIFA. Marijuana.

MOTA. Spanish slang for marijuana.

MULE. A person who delivers or carries drugs for a dealer.

MUTAH. Marijuana.

NARCOTICS. Refers to the natural and synthetic derivatives of opium (morphine, heroin, codeine); not a synonym for drugs.

NARC; NARK. Narcotics agent.

NEEDLE. Hypodermic syringe.

NICKLE BAG (BUY). A five-dollar purchase of narcotics.

NIMBY. Nembutal capsules (brand of pentobarbital, Abbott Laboratories).

NUMBER. Marijuana cigarette.

O.D. Overdose of drugs, usually heroin.

OFF. Withdrawn from drugs.

ON A TRIP. Under the influence of LSD or other hallucinogens.

ON THE NOD. Under the influence of drugs.

ON THE STREET. Out of jail.

OPE. Opium.

ORANGES. Dexedrine tablets (brand of dextroamphetamine sulfate, Smith Kline & French Laboratories).

OUT OF IT. Not in contact; not part of the drug scene.

OUT OF SIGHT. Good; groovy; a positive descriptive term.

OUTFIT; FIT. Equipment for injection by hypodermic method; a "hype" outfit: eyedropper and needle, spoon, pacifier, etc.; hypodermic syringe and needle, safety pin, razor, etc.

OWSLEY'S ACID. LSD purportedly illegally manufactured by Augustus Owsley Stanley, III; also infers that it is good quality LSD.

OZ; OUNCE. Refers to ounce of narcotics, usually heroin or meth.

OZZIE'S STUFF. LSD manufactured by Owsley Stanley.

PG or PO. Paregoric.

PADDY. Caucasian.

PANAMA RED. A potent type of Central American cannabis.

PANIC. A scarcity of drugs usually caused by the arrest of a big peddler.

PAPER. A container of drugs; paper of heroin (bindle); or a prescription for narcotics.

PEACE PILL; PCP. Refers to the drug phencyclidine, originally an anesthetic for dogs.

PEACHES. Benzedrine tablets (brand of amphetamine sulfate, Smith Kline & French Laboratories).

PEANUTS. Barbiturates.

PEDDLER. One who sells narcotics.

PER. A prescription.

PEZ. Candies impregnated with LSD.

PIECE. A pistol, revolver; a container of drugs.

PIG. *See* HOG; also a police officer.

PILL HEAD; PILL FREAK; PILLY. Amphetamine or barbiturate user.

PINKS. Seconal capsules (brand of secobarbital, Eli Lilly and Company).

PLANT. A cache of narcotics.

POINT. Hypodermic needle.

POKE. A puff on a "joint."

POP. A subcutaneous injection, usually referred to as "skin poppin'."

POPPER. Amyl nitrite in ampule form, inhaled.

POT. Marijuana.

POTHEAD. Marijuana smoker.

POT LIKKER. Cannabis tea, usually made with regular tea boiled with cannabis leaves.

POWDER. Amphetamine powder.

PSYCHEDELIC. A drug whose actions primarily affect the mind; "mind-manifesting" (LSD, marijuana, etc.).

PURE (THE). Pure heroin, prior to adulteration, i.e., "This is the pure; you can cut it five or six times at least."

PUSHER. Drug peddler to users; one who seeks more business from regular customers.

PUT DOWN. Stop taking (drugs).

QUARTER. Quarter of an ounce of either heroin or meth, usually 4 to 8 grams.

QUILL. A folded matchbox cover from which narcotics are sniffed through the nose.

RAINBOWS; REDS & BLUES. Tuinal capsules (combination of amobarbital sodium and secobarbital sodium, Eli Lilly and Company brand name).

RAT FINK. Informer for police.

READER. A prescription.

RED; REDS; RED BIRDS; RED DEVILS. Seconal capsules (brand of secobarbital sodium, Eli Lilly and Company).

REEFER. Marijuana cigarette.

REGISTER. To wait until blood comes into the hypodermic before injecting a drug intravenously.

RIGHTEOUS. Good quality drugs.

RIP OFF. To forcibly rob a peddler of his drugs or money.

ROACH. Small butt of marijuana cigarette.

ROACH CLIP. Alligator clip for holding marijuana butt.

ROLL; ROLL DECK. A tinfoil-wrapped roll of tablets.

ROLL DEALER. A person who sells tablets in rolls.

ROPE. Marijuana.

ROSES. Benzedrine tablets (brand of amphetamine sulfate, Smith Kline and French Laboratories).

ROUST. To be interrogated or arrested.

RULER. Judge.

RUN. To take drugs continuously for at least three days.

RUSH. *See* FLASH.

SAM. Federal narcotics agents.

SATCH COTTON. Cotton used to strain narcotics before injection.

SCAT. Heroin.

SCORE; SCORING. Make a drug purchase.

SCRIPT. Drug prescription.

SEEDS. Marijuana seeds.

SEGGY. Seconal capsules (brand of secobarbital, Eli Lilly and Company).

SHIT. Heroin.

SHOOT UP. To inject drugs.

SHOOTING GALLERY. Place where an injection of a drug can be used and/or bought, but which does not permit loitering. Place where users can purchase drugs and inject them.

SHORT. An automobile.

SHORT SLED. Vehicle.

SHOT. An injection of narcotics.

SKIN POPPING. Intradermal or subcutaneous injection.

SLAMMED. In jail.

SLEEPERS. A depressant type drug such as barbiturates.

SMACK. Heroin.

SMASHED. Intoxicated, ''stoned,'' ''high.''

SNIFFING; SNORTING (HORNING). Using narcotics by sniffing through nasal passages, usually heroin or cocaine.

SNITCH. Informer, stoolie.

SNORT. Same as ''sniff.''

SNOW. Cocaine.

SNOWBIRD. Cocaine user.

SOURCE. Where narcotics are obtained; supplier, such as pusher, dealer, connection.

SPACED OUT; SPACED. In a daze, particularly a daze resulting from use of drugs.

SPATZ. Capsules.

SPEED. Methedrine (methamphetamine) or crystal; broadened use in some areas now means any amphetamine or any stimulant.

SPEED FREAKS. *See* FREAK.

SPEEDBALL. A powerful shot of a drug, usually heroin and cocaine combined.

SPIKE. Hypodermic needle.

SPLASH. Speed.

SPLIT. To leave, flee, break up with.

SPOON. A quantity of heroin, theoretically measured on a teaspoon (usually between 1 and 2 grams). 16 spoons per ounce.

SQUARE. A person who does not know what's happening; a nonuser.

STANLEY'S STUFF. LSD purportedly manufactured by Augustus Owsley Stanley, III (*see* "OWSLEY'S ACID").

STARDUST. Cocaine.

STASH. Place where narcotics or "outfit" is hidden; also refers to one's own supply of drugs.

STICK. A marijuana cigarette.

STONED. Under the influence of drugs.

STOOL; STOOLIE. Informer for police (*see* SNITCH).

STP. A drug mixture of methedrine and psychedelic compounds (4-Methyl 2,5, dimethoxy alpha methyl phenethylamine); hallucinogenic drug DOM; "Serenity, Tranquility, Peace."

STRAIGHT. A person holding, or under the influence of, narcotics; teen meanings: (1) under the influence of narcotics; (2) applied to a peddler who gives a good deal.

STRUNG OUT. Heavily addicted or hooked.

STUFF. General term for drugs and narcotics.

SUEDE. Negro.

SUGAR. Powdered narcotics.

SWINGMAN. A drug supplier.

SYNDICATE ACID. STP.

T. Marijuana.

TASTE. A small sample of a narcotic.

TD CAPS. Time disintegrating capsules.

TEA. Cannabis, marijuana.

TEA HEAD. A marijuana smoker.

TEXAS TEA. Marijuana.

THOROUGHBRED. A high-type hustler who sells pure narcotics.

TOKE. A drag on a marijuana cigarette.

TOKE UP. To light a marijuana cigarette; a lighted marijuana cigarette (they burn much more brightly than an ordinary cigarette).

TOOLIES. Tuinal capsules (brand of amobarbital sodium and secobarbital sodium, Eli Lilly and Company).

TORCH. A marijuana cigarette (East Coast).

TORN UP. Intoxicated, stoned.

TRACKED UP; TRACKS. Numerous injection marks along vein; puncture wounds in veins, caused by continued narcotic injections.

TRANKS. Tranquilizers.

TRAVEL AGENT. LSD supplier; pusher of hallucinogenic drugs.

TREY. A three-dollar purchase.

TRICK. Easy mark, sucker, fool.

TRIGGER. To smoke a marijuana cigarette immediately after taking LSD.

TRIP; TRIPPING. The hallucinations and/or feelings experienced by a person after taking a drug, particularly LSD; being "high" on hallucinogens; LSD adventure.

TRUCK DRIVERS. Amphetamines.

TURKEY. A capsule purported to be a narcotic but filled with a nonnarcotic substance.

TURN ON. To use drugs, or to introduce another person to the use of drugs.

"TURN ON, TUNE IN, DROP OUT." Take LSD, learn about the "real" world, and drop out of the nondrugged world.

TURNED OFF. Withdrawn from drugs.

TURNED ON. Under the influence of drugs.

TURNING PEOPLE ON. To give others LSD.

TWENTY-FIVE ('25). LSD.

UNCLE. Federal narcotic agent.

UPPER. Amphetamine.

UP TIGHT. Angry; anxious (may rarely also be used to mean good, as in the words to a song "Everything's up tight, out of sight").

USER. One who uses drugs.

VIBES; VIBRATIONS. Feelings coming from another; may be good or bad vibes.

WAKE-UPS. Amphetamines.

WASHED UP. Withdrawn from drugs.

WASTED. High or drunk; under the influence of drugs.

WEDGES. Small tablets of wedge shape (almost triangular).

WEED. Marijuana.

WEED HEAD. Marijuana smoker.

WEEKEND HABIT. A small, irregular drug habit.

WEIRD. On drugs.

WEST COAST TURN-AROUNDS. Amphetamine tablets or capsules.

WHEELS. Car, automobile.

WHISKERS. Federal narcotic agents.

WHITES. Amphetamine sulfate tablets.

WHITE STUFF. Morphine.

WIG OUT; WIGGING. *See* BLOW YOUR MIND.

WINAMITE. Wine injected into the veins.

WORKS. The equipment for injecting drugs.

YELLOW JACKETS; YELLOWS. Nembutal (brand of pentobarbital sodium, Abbott Laboratories); solid yellow capsules.

YESCA. Spanish term for marijuana.

ZOUNK (ZONK). Under the influence of narcotics.

REFERENCES

Lentini, Joseph R. *Enforcing the Narcotic Drug Laws: A Guide for Customs Inspectors.* Unpublished manuscript, 1969.

Maurer, David W., and Vogel, Victor H. *Narcotics and Narcotic Addiction.* Springfield, Ill.: C. C. Thomas, 1970.

Williams, John B. *Narcotics and Drug Dependence.* Beverly Hills, Calif.: Glencoe Press, 1974.

Chapter 7

Enforcement Techniques

Vice crime presents a particularly difficult control problem for police departments. In most vice crimes, there is no complaining witness; unlike other crimes, the person who would ordinarily be the victim is in fact a cooperative partner in the crime. Vice crimes differ from other types of crimes in one other important respect: although all involved parties contribute to the crime, it is usually only the seller of the illegal service who is arrested—that is, the bookie, the prostitute, or the loan shark. The one exception to this rule is in the area of narcotics in which both the seller and the buyer are arrested, particularly if the buyer has drugs in his possession. There are a number of similarities between the work of the narcotics officer and other vice officers. Therefore, we will study the methods and operations of the narcotics officer with the understanding that these same strategies may also be employed by officers dealing with any of the other vice crimes.

The strategies open to the police in controlling these crimes are limited and consist mainly of the use of informants and undercover officers.

The Use of Informants

There are a number of reasons why the police use informants as part of their drug-control strategy: (1) to furnish information from sources not readily available to the officer. In effect, the informant becomes the eyes and ears of the narcotics officer, developing contacts and obtaining valuable information that would otherwise be inaccessible to the officer; (2) to make observations or perform surveillance assignments in areas in which strangers would be immediately suspect; (3) to conduct undercover negotiations and to make "buys" from narcotic suspects; (4) to gain firsthand intelligence information on drugs, prices, dealers, locations, and vehicles being used in the drug traffic, and (5) to give testimony in legal proceedings (when the evidence cannot be introduced by any other means).

The success of the narcotics officer depends upon his ability to cultivate a number of reliable sources of information. Developing a reliable informant is a sensitive undertaking and one that is usually best accomplished in a one-to-one situation. Above all, the officer must be able to develop a rapport with the prospective informer; he must create an atmosphere of trust that will enable him to gain the confidence of the informer. The officer must know the background of the individual with whom he is attempting to develop a relationship. The officer and the informant must be able to communicate freely and candidly with one another. This requires that the officer be knowledgeable about the drug scene, including conditions on the street and the vocabulary used by the people involved. The officer must always be as truthful and fair with the informant as possible but at the same time he should provide the informant with only as much information as he needs to carry out his end of the bargain.

The officer must make every effort to identify and understand the motives of the informer; he should be particularly aware of the person's reasons for agreeing to act as an informer. Understanding these factors determines to a large extent the methods of control that the officer will employ to manage the informer and his activities. An informer may be motivated by such laudable causes as civic duty, neighborhood pride, or simply the desire to be a good citizen. But on the other hand, his motivations may stem from a desire for revenge (perhaps he or a member of his family was the victim of a crime committed by an addict), or he may inform on a neighbor as the result of a neighborhood feud.

The underworld informer—that is, the individual who is a known law-breaker or who lives on the fringes of the law—has a number of motivations peculiar to his own way of life. He may agree to act as an informer out of fear: fear of certain associates whom he may not trust or fear of the law—particularly if he has already been charged with a petty crime and hopes to gain immunity by providing information to the authorities. He may fear going to prison and be willing to provide information as a means of avoiding punishment. The informer may be seeking revenge against former associates who cut him out of his share of the profits from their joint criminal activities or who informed on him in the past. He may inform out of jealousy over a woman or over the good fortune of one of his friends. Or he may agree to assist the police in order to divert suspicion from himself or to rid himself of his competition on the street.

Other types of informants may provide information to the police because they get a great deal of satisfaction out of associating with the police. The "police buff" often falls into this category of informer. He is interested in everything about the police. He often boasts about his "connections" with the police department and may have an exaggerated sense of the importance of his contributions. This type of informant is dangerous not only to himself but to the officer who uses him. Often his information is false or exaggerated; an officer should never rely on information provided by this type of individual without first checking it out.

Another type of informant is the individual who informs for money. This is the informant who merits the name "stool pigeon" or "snitch." He is abhorred by both the underworld and the police. However, because he is paid, his information must be reliable or he will find himself the target of the officer's wrath. Sometimes, in order to provide information worthy of pay, he will act as an agent provocateur, setting up the action with others and then informing the police. When this type of activity is uncovered in court or by the press, it can be extremely embarrassing to the prosecution and to the police. When informants of this type must be used they should be kept on a short leash.

Finally, there is the informant who for one reason or another wishes to dissociate himself from narcotics. This person may have had a negative personal experience with drugs or he may have been convicted and sentenced on a drug charge. Once such a person has decided to straighten out, he will cooperate with police in order to prove that he is clean.

Whatever the motivation of the informant, the successful narcotics officer knows how to cater to those motivations in a manner that will insure a steady supply of reliable information. The officer who uses an informer should be truthful with him without supplying any more information than is absolutely necessary; he should be fair to the informant and refrain from entrapping him when things get slow. In a recent case in the Midwest, an officer was using two informants who over the course of several months provided him with information which led to a number of important arrests. However, things became slow for a while, and the officer, who was himself posing as a drug dealer, took his informants to another state where they picked up a truck full of marijuana. On return to his home state, the officer arrested both his informants. When this activity was exposed in court, an investigation was made into all of the officer's activities and he was eventually fired. The use of an informant, just like any other police tool, must be properly handled.

The successful use of an informant requires that both the officer and the informant know exactly how their association will work. The informant must be told who or what is being investigated and must work closely with the officer to determine what methods will be used to effect the eventual arrest. The officer must decide in advance what he is willing to pay, in terms of money or favors, and the informant must agree to this arrangement. Decisions must be made as to whether the informant will be arrested along with the other arrests in a particular case, and the control officer must explain the procedure that will be followed in arranging the informant's subsequent release.

Often, it is necessary for the officer to give "buy" money to the informant. Since these are usually department funds, both parties should agree on a policy for handling the money and for its eventual recovery. Informants have been known to accept "buy" money, go in the front door to make a buy, and then exit through the back door with the money, leaving the officer in an embarrassing predicament.

Whenever possible, the officer should arrange to establish probable cause in such a way that he does not implicate the informant. He should establish the informant's reliability by the use of certified records of prior convictions based on information provided by the same informer. In most cases, if the officer does his work properly, the judge will not require the testimony of the informer. Acting as an informant can be an extremely dangerous occupation. Disclosure of the informant's identity can often mean his death, especially in narcotics cases. Thus, the officer should take every legal step to protect the identity of his informer. In the event that it becomes necessary for the informer to testify in court, the police should do everything possible to protect him before, during, and after the trial. Naturally, an informer whose life is in danger provides little information and is difficult to control.

Establishing a good relationship with an informant is important to the officer, for the time may come when the officer's cover or perhaps even his life will depend on this person. Most officers keep the identity of their informers a close secret, even from their colleagues and superiors. This is done as a safety precaution or sometimes as an attempt to prevent others from raiding their sources of information. However, it can be a dangerous practice. All officers should keep records of their informers. These records should include photos and fingerprints of the informer, a copy of his criminal record or rap sheet, and when deemed advisable or required by departmental rules, an official record of all contacts the officer has with the informer. The officer should also document all activities in which the informer is involved.

Keeping these kinds of records provides the officer with a certain amount of protection should the informer prove unreliable or should the officer ever have to explain his association with this individual. If the informer knows that these records exist, he is less likely to act in ways that may prove harmful to the officer. The officer must also let the informer know that should he suddenly become unreliable, he runs the risk of having his activities exposed, losing his police protection, or perhaps having his probation or parole revoked.

When an officer plans to assign an informant to a specific case, he should review the person's motives for involvement in the case, determine his relationship to the principals in the case, and evaluate the chances of success. If the informant is assigned to carry out an undercover mission or to assist an undercover officer, the objectives of the mission must be clearly spelled out in advance so that both the officer and the informant know what end result is expected. A cover story must be concocted and arrangements made to protect the cover should anyone decide to check out the informer or the officer.

If a buy is to be made, the informer should be searched prior to the buy to be certain that he has no narcotics in his possession. Immediately after the buy he should be searched again to ensure that he hasn't held out any of the narcotics or cut the price and is holding out surplus buy money. The informant's statement should be taken as soon as possible after he has made the buy. The statement should include dates, places, persons involved, types of drugs, and amount paid. Obtaining this type of information while it is still fresh in the mind of the informant is important. If the case is a progressive one, requiring a number of buys, each transaction should be documented separately. This ensures that the informant will not become confused in detailing his various activities. Each buy builds up probable cause which will eventually be reduced to writing in an affidavit or complaint. The affidavit must establish probable cause to obtain a search warrant to conduct a raid.

The Drug Search

The act of conducting any type of search, including a drug search, is controlled by the provisions of the Fourth Amendment of the Constitution of the United States:

> The right of the people to be secure in their persons, houses, papers and effects against unreasonable searches and seizures, shall not be violated, and no warrants shall issue, but upon probable cause, supported by Oath or affirmation, and particularly describing the place to be searched, and the persons or things to be seized.

The key phrases governing the issuance of search warrants and the eventual admissibility of the evidence obtained are "unreasonable searches and seizures" and "probable cause." If probable cause is not present, a judge will refuse to issue a search warrant, and if a search is conducted in an unreasonable manner, the evidence will not be admitted at the trial. However, the test of reasonableness is applied to each case individually. There is no accepted definition of a reasonable search. A judge can only decide what is or is not reasonable after hearing the facts at issue. And sometimes what seems reasonable to the arresting officer may not be deemed reasonable in a court of law. The following examples illustrate the lack of consensus on this issue.

Two officers approached an apartment with a search warrant to search for drugs. They knocked on the door and announced their office. After waiting a reasonable amount of time, they forced open the door, and as they entered the living room of the apartment, they saw a suspect swallow a balloon filled with what they suspected to be narcotics. The officers then took the suspect to a hospital, where a doctor pumped his stomach and recovered a balloon filled with cocaine. At the trial the presiding judge ruled that the invasion of the body of the suspect was unreasonable and refused to allow the admission of the evidence.

In 1960, following the robbery of a U.S. mail truck, postal inspectors, armed with a search warrant, went to the home of one of the suspects. They began their search in the garage, where they found $300 and a mailbag which had been aboard the hijacked truck. They continued their search and in the process stripped the plaster off the wall, ripped up floors and ceilings, and dug up a brand new patio. Total damage to the house came to almost $28,000. The suspect and his attorney went to the federal court and, citing the unreasonableness of the search, asked the judge to order the Post Office Department to restore the house to its original condition. The judge refused to grant this request on grounds that the search had been reasonable. It is clear from these examples that the question of reasonableness is not clear cut and can only be determined on the basis of the facts presented in each case.

Probable cause can best be described as a reasonable belief on the part of the police—based on reliable information, knowledge, and corroboration—that a crime has been or is being committed and that evidence can be found in a particular location. Although reasonable belief must go beyond a "mere hunch," it may stop short of actual certainty.

The Search Warrant

Obtaining a search warrant is not an easy matter, nor should it be. Generally, relying on information obtained from a reliable informer whose trustworthiness has been established by presenting to the court evidence that he has in the past provided information that led to indictments or convictions, the police are able to establish a surveillance of the suspected premises. During the surveillance they make note of known criminals entering or leaving the premises, known drug users in the area, and the general reputation of the neighborhood. They look for unusual activity or for anything which corroborates the information given by the informant. If they corroborate his information, the officers then put the informant's statement and the corroboration into writing in the form of an affidavit which they present to a judge who determines whether they have established probable cause to conduct a search. If he decides that probable cause exists, he will issue a search warrant. (See figure 7.1.)

The search warrant will describe in detail the place to be searched and the persons or items to be seized. A warrant should not, for instance, describe the place to be searched as simply "an apartment building, located at 1020 Main Street and owned by Acme Realty Corp." Such a description would be much too general. A more specific description would read as follows: "Apartment 2-B of the Grand Apartments, 1020 Main St., Detroit, Michigan, owned by Acme Realty Corp. and occupied by John Doe. This same type of specificity applies to particular rooms in a hotel, dormitory, or any multiple dwelling units. (See figure 7.2.)

Generally, the warrant will spell out the time of execution of the warrant. (See figure 7.3.) In most states it is required that searches be conducted during the daytime. However, if officers have reason to believe that the search should be conducted at night, they may make a special request. If it can be shown that the evidence is present only during the nighttime hours or that the persons involved in the crime under investigation are present only at certain hours, the court will allow search at that time and will so state in the warrant.

On approaching the premises to be searched, the officers are required to announce their office (identify themselves), demand admittance, and wait a

SAMPLE
AFFIDAVIT

THE COMMONWEALTH OF MASSACHUSETTS

(County), ss.

(Name) Court.

——————, 19

I, (name of applicant) being duly sworn, depose and say:

1. I am (describe position, assignment, office, etc.).

2. I have information, based upon (describe source, facts indicating reliability of source and nature of information; if based on personal knowledge and belief, so state).

3. Based upon the foregoing reliable information (and upon my personal knowledge) there is probable cause to believe that the property hereinafter described (has been stolen, or is being concealed, etc.) and may be found (in the possession of A.B. or any other person) at premises (identify).

4. The property for which I seek the issuance of a search warrant is the following: (here describe the property as particularly as possible).

WHEREFORE, I respectfully request that the court issue a warrant and order of seizure, authorizing the search of (identify premises and the persons to be searched) and directing that if such property or evidence or any part thereof be found that it be seized and brought before the court; together with such order and further relief that the court may deem proper.

_____

Name

Then personally appeared the above-named _____
——————————— and made oath that the foregoing affidavit by him subscribed is true.

_____

Notary Public

Source: Commonwealth of Massachusetts.
Figure 7.1 A sample affidavit.

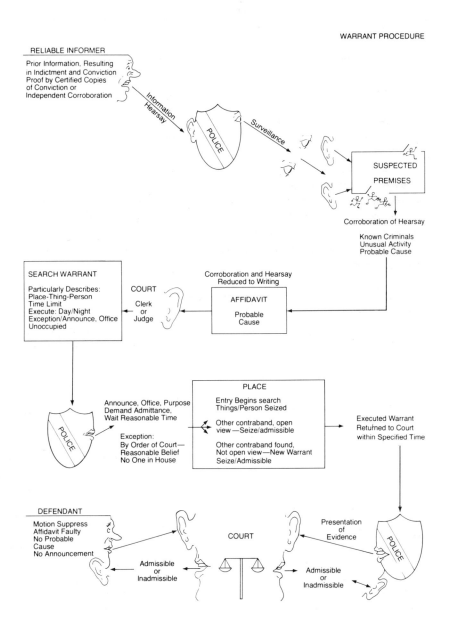

RELIABLE INFORMER

Prior Information, Resulting
in Indictment and Conviction
Proof by Certified Copies
of Conviction or
Independent Corroboration

Information
Hearsay

POLICE

Surveillance

SUSPECTED
PREMISES

Corroboration of Hearsay

Known Criminals
Unusual Activity
Probable Cause

SEARCH WARRANT

Particularly Describes:
Place-Thing-Person
Time Limit
Execute: Day/Night
Exception/Announce, Office
Unoccupied

COURT

Clerk
or
Judge

Corroboration and Hearsay
Reduced to Writing

AFFIDAVIT

Probable
Cause

POLICE

Announce, Office, Purpose
Demand Admittance,
Wait Reasonable Time

Exception:
By Order of Court—
Reasonable Belief
No One in House

PLACE

Entry Begins search
Things/Person Seized

Other contraband, open
view—Seize/admissible

Other contraband found,
Not open view—New Warrant
Seize/Admissible

Executed Warrant
Returned to Court
within Specified Time

DEFENDANT

Motion Suppress
Affidavit Faulty
No Probable
Cause
No Announcement

Admissible
or
Inadmissible

COURT

Presentation
of
Evidence

POLICE

Admissible
or
Inadmissible

Source: William J. Tobin, *Constitutional Law Enforcement,* Commonwealth of
Massachusetts, 1967.

Figure 7.2 Warrant procedure.

SAMPLE
SEARCH WARRANT A

THE COMMONWEALTH OF MASSACHUSETTS

(County), ss.   (Name) Court.

To the sheriffs of our several counties, or their deputies, any State Police Officer, or any Constable or Police Officer of any city or town, within our said Commonwealth.

Proof by affidavit having been made this day before (name of person authorized to issue warrant) by (names of person or persons whose affidavits have been taken) that there is probable cause for believing that (certain property has been stolen, embezzled, or obtained by false pretenses; certain property is intended for use or has been used as the means of committing a crime; certain property has been concealed to prevent a crime from being discovered; certain property is unlawfully possessed or kept or concealed for an unlawful purpose).

We therefore command you in the daytime (or at any time of the day or night) to make an immediate search (identify premises) (occupied by A.B.) and of the person (of A.B.) and of any person present who may be found to have such property in his possession or under his control or to whom such property may have been delivered, for the following property:

(description of property)

and if you find any such property or any part thereof to bring it and the persons in whose possession it is found before (court having jurisdiction) at (name of court and location).

Date at (city or town) this _____ day of _____, 19 .

Clerk.

Source: Commonwealth of Massachusetts.
Figure 7.3 (a/b) Sample search warrants. Note that the location of the premises to be searched, the items to be seized, and the time that the search is to be conducted are all clearly spelled out.

reasonable amount of time to be admitted. There is no definition of "reasonable time." If, for example, officers identified themselves, demanded admittance, and heard sounds indicating attempted escape or possible destruction of evidence, such as water running or a toilet flushing, they would probably be within the bounds of reasonableness if they broke in.

Generally, courts will allow officers to enter the premises without announcing themselves, provided they have sufficient cause to do so. In such cases, a

SAMPLE
SEARCH WARRANT B

STATE OF OHIO)
CUYAHOGA FALLS)   SS
SUMMIT COUNTY)

To any police officer of the City of Cuyahoga Falls in said County, GREETINGS:

WHEREAS, there has been filed with the undersigned an affidavit of which a copy is herewith attached, incorporated herein by reference and made a part thereof.

THEREFORE, you are hereby commanded in the name of the State of Ohio, together with the necessary and proper assistance to enter in the _____ into said
                                                                (daytime or nighttime)
premises, described as aforesaid, and there search for said property as listed aforesaid, and that you bring the same or any part thereof, found in such search before this Court to be dealt with according to law, and further that this warrant shall be returned to this Court within three (3) days from date of issuance.

Given under my hand this 24th day of February, 1975 at _____ _____.
                                                           (time)   (A.M. or P.M.)

_____
John J. Jones, Judge
Cuyahoga Falls Municipal Court

Source: State of Ohio.

special request—based on sound, reliable information—must be made prior to the issuance of the warrant. There are three instances in which such a request might be legitimately made. First, if officers can convince the court that the suspects will more than likely destroy the evidence named in the warrant, they may be allowed to enter without announcement. Second, such permission will most likely be granted if the officers can establish evidence that the suspects or occupants of the premises are armed and that giving notice might result in an attempt to do bodily harm to the officers. And third, if officers can produce information that an announcement of office would cause the suspects to attempt to escape with the evidence, the court will most likely grant them permission to enter the premises surreptitiously.

The search begins upon entry into the premises and ends when the contraband named in the warrant is found. Once the officers have left the premises, the warrant is no longer valid, and they may not return to the premises without first obtaining a new warrant.

During the search, officers may look anywhere on the premises where the named contraband might reasonably be found. Since drugs can often be concealed in very small spaces, officers have license to search in every nook and cranny. Following is a list compiled by Lentini and France (1972, pp. 26–27) of common areas in the home, on the person, and in a vehicle where drugs have been concealed.

DRUG CONCEALMENT IN THE HOME

Telephone base and handle
Sealed cigarette packages
Inside and under wigs
Under washbowls, sinks, or tubs
Closet clothing—waistbands, sleeves, hatbands, shoes, gloves
Flowerpots and window boxes
Light fixtures and lamps
Inside medicine cabinets and prescription bottles
Mattresses and box frames
Behind picture frames, posters, and mirrors
Flashlights
Removable air-conditioning registers
Cat-litter boxes
Light switches
Behind baseboards
Inside hollow doors (removable top)
Underneath carpets
Inside hollow curtain rods, closet rods, and shower curtain rods
Inside stairway posts
Inside door chimes and doorbells
Inside deep-well fryers
Range hoods and filters
Rolled up in window shades
Mailboxes
Inside knife handles
Behind wall phones
Inside transistor radios
Hanging out windows
Sink traps
Dog collars
In and underneath refrigerators, taped under doors, or inside motor compartment
Furniture upholstery

Inside toilet tanks
Magazines and books
Bedposts
Musical instruments and cases
False bottom on radiator covers
Kitchen canisters and containers
Doorknobs
Behind walls, posters, or curtains
Inside television and radio sets
Inside false ceilings, walls, and chimneys
Plumbing inspection doors
Inside crucifixes
In golf bags
In test tubes
Rain gutters and drainspouts
Hot-air ducts
Hems of drapes and curtains
Hollowed-out trees
Shoe-polish containers and equipment
Razor-blade dispensers
Stovepipes
Garbage bags
Pillowcases
Furnaces
Seams of field cots and hollow cap of cot legs
Attic insulation
Inside hassocks
Hidden drawers in tables
Inside television tubes
Inside color television antennas
Inside abandoned plumbing
In toolboxes
Inside letters
Inside and behind vacuum cleaner bags
Inside handle of Kirby vacuum cleaners
Inside patch trap of antique rifle
Inside Christmas-tree decorations

Behind kick plate of sink cabinets
Conduits from fuse boxes
Jewelry boxes
Clothes hampers
In stove insulation, stove exhausts, and
 drip pans
Under lip ring of plastic trash cans
In toothpaste tubes
In surfboards
In electric toothbrush holders
Talcum-powder and cold-cream contain-
 ers
Tea bags
Acoustical-tile ceilings
Bibles (hollow cover)
Inside baked goods—bread, cookies,
 brownies
Candy bars
Art kits
Dolls
Fuel of oil heaters
Psychedelic light housing
Hollowed-out flashlight batteries
Hollowed-out pads of paper
Base of rabbit antennas
Inside eggs
Mixed with tobacco
Taped to hatboxes
Legs of bathtubs
Toaster trays
Plastic rolling pins
Inside cameras
Taped to top of toilet bowls
Neighboring window ledges
In floor drains
False aerosol cans
Fluorescent light tubes
Toys, stuffed animals, and games
Inside Band-Aids and Band-Aid boxes
Above windows, doorsills, and moldings
Fire and water hoses
Cellar beams
Venetian blinds—top and bottom
Inside clocks
Piggy banks
Agitator of washing machines
Chandeliers
Inside trophies
Inside rolled-up newspapers
Electrical sockets
Inside deodorant containers

Taped in dressers and behind drawers
Inside ceramic and clay figurines
Inside candlestick holders
Inside handle of carpenter's toolbox
Taped to moveable clotheslines
Inside pipe-rack stand
Behind exterior brick near windows
Rifle-barrel buttplates
Inside rifle cartridges and shotgun shells
Inside aluminum-foil tubing
Inside paper-towel tubing
Inside toilet-paper roll
Zippered cushions and pillows
Under panels of parquet floors
Inside toilet-bowl floats
Fuse boxes
Fish tanks and bowls
Hollowed-out bars of soap
Hollowed-out furniture legs
Salt and pepper shakers
Hollowed-out fruits and vegetables
Record albums
Spice jars
Wax-paper dispensers
Magnet boxes
Fire-alarm bells
False-bottom baby carriage and cribs
Douche bags
Doghouses
Footlockers
35-mm film cans
Drops on graph paper
Shower-nozzle heads
Hair dryers
Hollow canes
Pay-telephone coin-return slots
Under corner mailboxes
Shaving-brush handles
Miniature chessboards
In clothesline pipes
Ironing-board legs and covers
Bottom half of double broilers
Typewriters and covers
Under number plate on phones
Plastic containers in refrigerator
Bottom of dog-food bags
In bird cages
Inside garbage disposals
Inside tube and barrel of air rifles
Clothespin bag
Electric baseboard heaters

Inside string mops
Inside rabbit hutch
Inside hollow handle of toilet bowl brush
Under tile steps of backyard

Under fence-post tops
LSD on ink blotters
LSD on swiss cheese in refrigerators

DRUG CONCEALMENT ON THE PERSON

Lipstick tubes
Cigarette lighters and packs
Taped under breasts and brassieres
Processed hair, hair buns, and wigs
Parts of the body (rectum, vagina, nose, ears, mouth, and so forth)
Lapels of jackets and coats
Inside and back of watches and other jewelry
Taped behind ears
Cuffs and waistbands
Pockets
Socks and shoes
Pill vials
Inside sanitary napkins or tampons
Hat bands
35-mm film cans
Baby diapers
In corsets
Under dentures
Belts and belt buckles
Behind collars and collar stays
Under Band-Aids and bandages
False limbs
Glass eyes
Hearing-aid glasses
Jockstraps
Swallowed with string attached to teeth
Between toes and taped to feet
Knots of ties
Handkerchiefs
Wallets
Eye-glass cases
Contact-lens cases
Inside pens and pencils
Tobacco tins and pouches

Money belts
Lining of clothing
Hollow end of canes or umbrella handle
Inside chewing gum sticks
Cigarette filters
Compacts
Inside casts
In addressed envelopes
In male girdles
In swimming trunks
In stems of pipes
In chewing gum stuck behind the ear
Pinned to shorts
Inside identification bracelets
Inside feces bags
Inside hollowed-out crutches
Inside neck and wrist lockets, bracelets, and charms
Rings
Earrings
Tie pins, clasps, and cuff links
Inside fly trap of trousers
Hearing-aid battery boxes
Thermos jugs
Inside suitcase lining
Canteens
Inhalers
Lining of change purses
Under insulation in motorcycle helmets
Military cap insignia, lapels, and shoulder patches
Hashish in love beads
False caps on teeth
Hair barrettes
Behind campaign ribbons and uniform brass

DRUG CONCEALMENT IN THE AUTOMOBILE

Domelights, headights, and taillights
Hub caps
Inside horns
Air filters
Oil filters
Spare tires (treads and well)
Windshield-washer bags
Gearshift knobs
Instrument panel and ornamented objects on dashboard
Surplus police cars with double roof
Inside and under ashtrays
Picnic jugs in trunk
False batteries
Under brake and gas pedals
License plates
False heater hoses
Sun visors
Under rugs
Upholstery
Behind bumpers
False dual mufflers
Hollow voltage regulators
Heaters
Vents (air and heater)
Radio speaker grilles
On top of gas tank (suspended or concealed in compartment)
Glove compartment—top of compartment or trap
Convertible tops
False bottom of trunk beds
Fuse box of trunk
Back seat
Floorboard

Trunk
Inside oil caps
Under seats
Cigarette lighters
Carburetor
Pill vials
35-mm film cans
Under tire air-valve caps
Inside motorcycle handlebar tubing
Compartment under floor of older-model Volkswagens
Inside tubing on roof rack
Inside auto surfboard racks
Motorcycle taillights
Rocker panels
Tailpipes
Taped behind bumpers
Insulation under hood
Taxicab roof lights
Under chrome
Key holders
Taped to windows
Service-station travel kits
False radios
Behind Volkswagen battery boxes
Underside of fenders
Armrests
Inside flashlights
Tied to axle
Inside dash knobs
Inside light sockets
Antenna base
Inside floor console
Steering column at transmission indicator (older-model Chevrolets)

Conducting the Drug Search

Officers should exercise caution when searching a home for narcotics. Narcotics is a dirty business, and those who engage in the trade can often be very dangerous. Particular caution should be used when officers are searching electrical appliances such as refrigerators, freezers, washers, dryers, or any other appliance that activates an electrical circuit when the door is opened. For example, when a refrigerator door is opened, an inside light is turned on automatically. The same applies to freezers, some ovens, washing machines, and clothes dryers. Narcotics dealers have been known to hide drugs inside such appliances and to take precautions to destroy the evidence and hurt the searcher when the appliance is opened. This is accomplished by breaking the light bulb on the inside of the appliance and wiring a blasting cap to the exposed electrodes of the bulb. The appliance door is closed and the appliance plugged into a wall outlet. When anyone opens the door of the appliance, the electrical current passes through the electrodes of the broken bulb, detonating the blasting cap. (See figure 7.4.) Needless to say, police officers searching for drugs have been badly injured by these devices.

Naturally, anything named in the search warrant which is found during the search will be seized and used as admissible evidence in court. However, any other contraband that is in open view may also be seized and will be admissible during a trial even though it was not named in the original warrant. For example, officers searching for drugs see an illegal firearm or stolen property sitting

Photo by William Bickett.
Figure 7.4 A booby trap. A blasting cap is wired to a broken refrigerator light bulb. When the refrigerator door is opened, the blasting cap explodes.

on a table in plain sight. Even though these are not named in the search warrant, they may be seized, and they will be admitted as evidence.

Contraband which is not in open view and which is not named in the search warrant, but which is found by officers conducting a search, may be seized; but unless officers obtain a new warrant, the contraband will not be admissible as evidence. If officers wish to use this type of contraband, it is necessary to obtain a new warrant naming the particular contraband. In a case such as this, an officer should be left at the scene to protect the evidence while a new warrant is obtained. If the suspects present attempt to move the contraband, they are then committing a crime in the officer's presence and may be arrested, and the contraband may be seized "incidental to a lawful arrest."

When the search is completed, either by the finding of the articles named in the search warrant or by failure to locate the items, the executed warrant is returned to the court within the time specified by the laws of the state in which it was issued. In most states, the time limit within which a search warrant must be executed is three days. On the back of the warrant is a "Return," which is a statement detailing the actions which were taken by the officers. If officers have seized any items pursuant to the warrant, they should give a receipt to the occupants of the premises or place the receipt with the personal belongings of the suspects who have been arrested. A copy of the receipt should be submitted to the court along with the executed warrant. (See figures 7.5 and 7.6.)

General Enforcement Techniques in Vice Crimes

Enforcement techniques in vice crimes must, because of the nature of these crimes and the absence of complaining witnesses, be somewhat different from the techniques used in dealing with street crimes. Earlier in this chapter, we discussed the use of informants, one of the principal methods of gaining information about individuals involved in any of the vice crimes. In this section, we will discuss other methods of gaining information, establishing probable cause, and enforcing the law against consensual crime. Among the most commonly employed strategies are surveillance, the use of the undercover officer, and the raid.

Surveillance Techniques

Surveillance involves the secretive and continuous watching of suspected persons, vehicles, places, or objects in order to obtain information concerning criminal activities. The objectives of surveillance within this context are: to obtain evidence of a crime; to assist in establishing probable cause for obtaining search warrants; to gather information which can be used later in interrogating suspects; to check on the reliability of informants; to obtain detailed information about a suspect's activities and to keep investigators informed of a suspect's whereabouts at all times; to locate wanted persons by watching their

SAMPLE
RETURN OF SEARCH WARRANT

STATE OF OHIO
        SS

SUMMIT COUNTY

On this _____ day of _____, 19___, I searched for the property described in the within Warrant, at the place therein mentioned, and found the goods as described in the attached inventory.

_____

(Police Officer)

_____

Judge

Pursuant to Section 2933.26 of the Ohio Revised Code, the property listed in the attached inventory has been delivered to me this _____ day of _____, 19___, and I hereby appoint and designate _____ as custodian until further order of a Court of Competent Jurisdiction.

_____

Judge

Source: State of Ohio.
Figure 7.5 Sample of a return of a search warrant.

haunts and associates; to locate contraband material; to prevent the commission of a crime; or to arrest a suspect during the commission of a crime. Some of these objectives are interwoven, and thus an officer on surveillance duty may have several objectives at the same time. Others are singular objectives, carried out in a sequential manner; when one objective is attained, the officer moves on to the next in order to eventually build a completed case. These objectives are achieved in one of two ways: first, by a stationary surveillance in which the officer or officers watch a particular place or person from a fixed location; and second, by means of moving surveillance in which the investigators follow the suspect either on foot or in a vehicle. Regardless of which method is used, it is imperative that the officer make adequate preparations to ensure that the surveillance will be carried out successfully. One of these preparations requires that the officer make himself as familiar as possible with the subject of the surveillance. He should know his name, his address, and what he looks like. This information can be gained from the subject's rap sheet, provided one is avail-

SAMPLE
RECEIPT AND INVENTORY OF PROPERTY
TAKEN BY COMMAND OF SEARCH WARRANT

I, the undersigned being a party to the search ordered at

(1) _____ do this _____ day of _____, 19___, list in the presence

of (2) the applicant for said warrant and (3) _____

the person from whose possession or premises the property was taken and in the presence

of (4) _____

who neither applied for said warrant, nor is he the proprietor nor custodian, nor keeper of the hereon listed property.

I did on the _____ day of _____, 19___, complete this inventory pursuant to the above instruction and did leave one copy with the property owner and did submit for filing one copy to the criminal section of the Office of the Municipal Clerk of _____, Ohio.
(city)

_____
Police officer

I did receive one copy of the above inventory.

_____
Person from whose possession
or premises property taken

1. Address
2. Print name of officer signing affidavity for search warrant.
3. Print name of person from whom property taken, if present.
4. Print name of officer other than the one who signed affidavit if property owner not present.

Source: State of Ohio.

Figure 7.6 A sample receipt and inventory of property taken by command of a search warrant.

able, or from information supplied by an informer. If the department has no photographs of the suspect, the officer should make arrangements to have the suspect pointed out to him. He should also become familiar with the habits of the suspect—does he carry a gun, does he drink, does he use drugs, does he have any peculiar mannerisms? In addition, the officer should be able to recognize the suspect's associates on sight since this knowledge will give him a clearer picture of the kinds of activities the suspect may engage in. Does he have a girl friend? And if so, where does she live?

The officer should get to know the neighborhood in which the surveillance is to take place. What kind of neighborhood is it? How do the people dress? Is it a high-crime area? A low-crime area? What are the general traffic conditions? Are there particular places from which the suspect may be watched without attracting undue attention to the officer? Does the officer feel that a moving surveillance would be accomplished best on foot or in a vehicle?

Most suspects have their favorite bars, restaurants, and meeting places. The officer should become familiar with these places, as well as with the suspect's patterns of moving to and from them. For example, at what time of the day or night does he usually frequent these places? Does he eat at home or does he habitually go to restaurants? Does he spend a lot of time in any one particular place, such as a pool hall or barbershop?

The surveillance officer should also be able to recognize the suspect's car on sight. He should know the make, year, style, and color of the vehicle, its license plate number, and any identifying marks, such as large dents or scratches that would make the car stand out from others of its kind. Most of us are creatures of habit. When we drive from one point to another, we typically take the same route day after day and have our favorite shortcuts. An officer who is intimately familiar with his subject's habits can often make an educated guess as to the destination of the suspect by knowing the various routes he habitually travels to get from one place to another. If, by chance, he should lose the suspect, he can often pick him up again simply by knowing these habits.

Officers chosen for surveillance should be ordinary-looking individuals. An individual having some particularly conspicuous feature should under no circumstances be placed on stakeout, because he or she could be too easily recognized. The officer must have the ability to retain his composure under all circumstances and must be able to blend into his surroundings. He must be alert and resourceful and have good powers of observation and memory. Above all, the officer must have patience and endurance. Sometimes surveillance duty, especially stationary surveillance, can become boring and tiring, which tends to make the officer less alert.

Surveillance officers should dress in the manner of the people in the neighborhood so as not to attract undue attention. For example, an officer in a business suit would stand out in a neighborhood where everyone wears jeans and casual shirts. By the same token, an officer in jeans would be conspicuous in a Wall Street office building. Officers should avoid any idiosyncrasy of dress and should not wear conspicuous jewelry, brightly colored clothing, or anything else that might draw attention to themselves. The officer should be aware that his weapon can make a bulge under his clothing and should take steps to avoid this problem by wearing loose clothing whenever possible. Sometimes, a simple change of attire can give the officer a completely different appearance. Putting on a cap or a hat or donning or removing glasses can alter his appearance to the eyes of a casual observer. These small items, which can be carried in a pocket or briefcase, are excellent tools in situations that require a quick change of identity.

Simple things like having enough change to make a phone call to headquarters can often make the difference between successful and unsuccessful surveillance. An officer should always carry enough money to cover any unexpected or emergency expenses, such as cab fares or subway and bus fares; this is particularly important in cities whose bus companies require passengers to have the exact change. Bills should be carried in small denominations because the time lost waiting for change from a large bill can sometimes mean losing a suspect. Ordinarily, these situations can be avoided by using more than one officer on a surveillance. In fact, one-man surveillance is generally discouraged simply because it requires the officer to remain at such close proximity to the suspect, which can easily arouse suspicion. However, there are times when one-man surveillance cannot be avoided, and in these cases the officer must make several moves that he would not ordinarily employ; he must stay close to the suspect, keeping him in view at all times. If he is following on the opposite sidewalk, he must stay almost abreast of the suspect, and he must be alert enough to react immediately to any evasive action taken by the suspect. For obvious reasons, one-man surveillance is not nearly as efficient as two-man surveillance and should be avoided whenever possible. (See figure 7.7.)

When more than one officer is assigned to a tail, one of the officers should be designated as the lead officer. It is his responsibility to run the job, and the other officers should take their cues from him. The multiple-officer surveillance requires that an efficient system of communications be set up so that the officers can work effectively as a team. Communication can be established through the use of hand signals or electronic devices. Using the walkie-talkie requires a central communicator unless the equipment has enough channels to allow the officers to communicate with one another directly. When several officers are participating in a long-term surveillance operation, arrangements should be made so that each member of the team can be periodically relieved of duty.

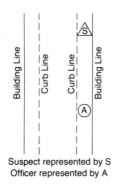

Suspect represented by S
Officer represented by A

Figure 7.7 One-man surveillance.

As stated previously, using more than one officer is usually more successful than using only one officer in a surveillance effort. The major advantage of this arrangement is that it allows one officer to drop back while his partner maintains the surveillance. The second officer can move ahead of the suspect and pick him up from the front. The second officer is also free to communicate with headquarters. Two-man surveillance allows for a combination foot and vehicle surveillance, with one officer following on foot while the other watches from a moving vehicle. This method allows one officer to get fairly close to the suspect while the other trails some distance behind. It also allows officers to work both sides of the street, and, in the event the suspect crosses over, the two officers can change the positions relative to the subject and thus break up any continuous pattern. (See figure 7.8)

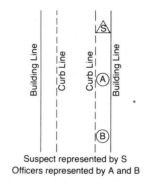

Suspect represented by S
Officers represented by A and B

Figure 7.8 Two-man surveillance on a crowded street.

The use of three officers to tail a suspect (ABC method) provides added insurance that the subject will not be lost. This type of surveillance is particularly efficient in that it not only allows the officers to frequently change positions, but it also allows one officer to drop out of the tail if he suspects that he has been spotted. Under normal traffic conditions, Officer A maintains a reasonable distance behind the suspect. Officer B follows Officer A while Officer C walks on the opposite side of the street. When using this method, Officer B has the responsibility of making sure that the suspect has no other person watching for a tail.

If there is little or no traffic, Officer A can walk in front of the suspect while Officers B and C walk on the opposite side of the street. In very crowded streets, all three officers can walk on the same side of the street as the suspect. Officer A walks very close to the subject, followed by Officers B and C. Officers should alternate their positions from time to time in order to avoid establishing patterns.

The ABC, or three-man, system also allows officers to leapfrog the subject and one another—this technique is typically used when the subject is following a route that is already known to the surveillance team. Officers can move ahead of the suspect, waiting at a fixed point for him to appear and then following him for a distance. Each officer should leapfrog only once to avoid being recognized by the suspect. The disadvantage of this method is that there is no assurance that the suspect will adhere to his habitual route or destination. However, it is valuable in locating meeting places when there is a distinct risk of tipping off the suspect by following him too closely. (See figures 7.9 and 7.10.)

Combined foot and vehicle surveillance may also be used to great advantage. This method allows one or more officers to follow the suspect on foot while the others follow him by car. It has the advantage of providing immediate transportation should the subject take a cab or board a bus. The several officers riding in the car can periodically change places with the officer walking to avoid the chance of being spotted by the suspect. This method also allows officers to leapfrog the suspect and meet him as he walks along. The only drawback of this method is that it can sometimes be too obvious, especially on roads where there is little traffic and where a slow-moving vehicle might attract attention.

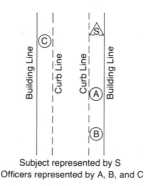

Subject represented by S
Officers represented by A, B, and C

Figure 7.9 ABC method of three-man surveillance under normal traffic conditions.

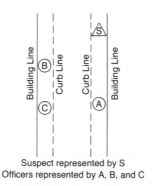

Suspect represented by S
Officers represented by A, B, and C

Figure 7.10 ABC method of three-man surveillance under crowded traffic conditions.

When following a suspect vehicle with only one surveillance car, several precautions should be taken: first, no more than two vehicles should be allowed to come between the suspect vehicle and the surveillance car in city traffic. The surveillance car should be behind and to the right of the suspect vehicle to avoid attracting attention and should take advantage of the blind spots which are built into most cars. The driver of a suspect vehicle ordinarily cannot see to his right rear. And even when he has an outside rear-view mirror, there are blind spots on his left rear where a surveillance car can travel unseen.

In the country or on sparsely traveled roads, officers can allow the suspect a long lead, especially if there are no intersections or forks in the road. From time to time, the suspect vehicle may be lost from view around curves or over hills. If there is other traffic on the road it is best to keep at least one car between the suspect vehicle and the surveillance car. When following at night, occasionally use high beams and then after a while use low beams. From the suspect's position it appears that a different car is behind him. Never use interior lights when following at night.

When using a two-car team, both cars should ordinarily be behind the suspect car. Surveillance cars should travel in different lanes so that if one car becomes caught in an obstructed lane, the other car will be free to move ahead. One surveillance car should be within two cars of the suspect at all times. The other should be farther back in another lane but within sight of the suspect vehicle. Once in a while it is possible for one surveillance car to travel on a parallel street. When using this technique the parallel car should arrive at intersections just before the suspect vehicle so the suspect can be seen down the block and his movements noted. This method requires good communications between the two surveillance cars and a clear channel. It is ideal for use at night or in suburban areas, in which the streets are laid out in symmetrical, rectangular patterns, but it does require that officers be familiar with the area, knowing any dead-end streets which could trap them and thus cause them to lose the suspect.

The use of three cars to follow a suspect is similar to the two-car surveillance but slightly more versatile. One car can follow from the front by leading the suspect and watching through the rear-view mirror. Parallel streets can be used on both sides of the suspect vehicle and surveillance cars can leapfrog the suspect as in foot surveillance. Leapfrogging has the same disadvantages in cars as on foot—there is no assurance that the suspect will follow his regular patterns or go to his usual destinations.

Stationary surveillance—the fixed surveillance of a particular building and its occupants—requires that officers conduct their activities from an operation base which is close enough to the premises under surveillance to allow officers to enter and leave without attracting undue attention. This type of surveillance is typically used when the suspect premises have been identified as a place from which drugs are sold, a prostitute hotel or whorehouse, or a gambling "office." Ordinarily, the surveillance will be maintained for an extended period of time.

The use of the base is necessary when the area does not lend itself to the use of officers on foot or in cars. The base operation requires the use of specialized equipment, such as communications devices, binoculars, still- and motion-picture cameras, and writing materials.

Another type of base operation may be set up in a truck or camper which is parked on the street and from which agents can keep the suspect premises under surveillance. It is important that the type of truck being used is one that will fit into the neighborhood—say, a telephone truck, a plumber's truck, or a milk truck. We would not, for instance, use a motor home in the ghetto. This mobile base has the advantage of being able to move at a moment's notice in the event that the occupants of the premises should decide to move their operation.

Dos and Don'ts of Surveillance Work:

Do act naturally wherever you may be. Always behave as though you belonged there.

Don't arouse the suspicion of uniformed officers in the area who have not been advised of your presence. Once you are seen talking to a uniformed officer, your mission is doomed to failure.

Don't allow yourself to be self-conscious about your presence in the area.

Don't go directly home or to police headquarters if you are spotted—the suspect may follow you to confirm his suspicions.

Don't allow yourself to become the subject of surveillance by the suspect.

Don't peek surreptitiously from doorways or from behind trees or poles. You'll only succeed in calling attention to yourself.

Don't question bartenders, bellhops, or barbers about a suspect until you have made certain that they are not friendly with him.

Don't try any of the movie or TV stunts, such as hiding behind newspapers, unless this is a natural move given the area in which you are working.

The Undercover Officer

The undercover officer is an investigator who uses various identities and pretexts to gain the confidence of criminal suspects for the purpose of determining the nature and extent of any criminal activities in which they may be involved. The undercover officer works in conjunction with informants and surveillance teams to achieve the following objectives: (1) to determine whether a crime is being planned or committed; (2) to identify all persons involved in the ongoing or planned activity; (3) to obtain court evidence or to establish probable cause for a search warrant; (4) to locate contraband or stolen property; and (5) to determine the best time for raiding suspected premises or for arresting the principals in the crime. Undercover officers are used in all types of vice cases—gambling, prostitution, loan sharking, narcotics, and some types of sex crimes. This type of strategy is used because of the nature of the crimes and because, more often than not, complaining witnesses do not come forward. The courts have always recognized the need for this type of police activity, especially in vice cases.

Although undercover work does not require any particular physical attributes or skills, the officer assigned to this type of police work should be an intelligent, resourceful individual who has demonstrated considerable personal initiative. He should be able to work well independently and make decisions without having to constantly rely on his superiors. Since undercover work is sometimes dangerous, the officer should be in good physical condition and be courageous. In a recent discussion with several police administrators, the opinion was put forward that the philosophy of the undercover officer is different from that of the uniformed officer. The general consensus among administrators was that an officer who has spent considerable time in uniform generally has difficulty doing undercover work simply because he is accustomed to making arrests on the spot when he sees a crime being committed and is thus less able to restrain himself from arrest when working undercover. The undercover officer frequently sees crimes being committed and bypasses arrest in order to build a strong case. For this reason, many departments choose their undercover officers from new academy graduates who have not yet acquired the "arrest attitude." These individuals also have the advantage of being unknown on the street. However, use of the untried recruit requires that he be covered rather closely by more experienced officers to ensure his safety and to prevent mistakes which could lead him to reveal his cover. The use of experienced officers from neighboring departments has worked well, especially in MEG units (Metropolitan Enforcement Groups), which have been established around the country to stem the sale of narcotics in wide geographic areas.

The undercover officer should have considerable self-confidence and good judgment. An officer working in an ethnic neighborhood should have at least some knowledge of the language that is spoken in the area. He must also be familiar with the language of the street and the slang terms used within the particular racket he is investigating. Slang often varies from neighborhood to neighborhood, and its misuse can direct suspicion toward the officer. For instance, there are twenty-five to thirty different terms for marijuana—pot, weed, grass, Acapulco Gold, Mary Jane, and so on. Each of these terms has become part of the drug language because of specific neighborhood usage. An undercover officer using the wrong terms in the wrong neighborhood could find that he has inadvertently blown his cover.

Whenever possible, the undercover officer should have the same cultural background as the people he is trying to associate with. If he has any special talents, hobbies, or previous work experience which can aid his cover, they should be used. An officer behaves more normally when he is doing something with which he is familiar. These additional talents also make him more believable. When he goes undercover, he should leave all vestiges of his police identity behind him. He should not carry his badge, official papers, or any other type of police paraphernalia. Unless he is posing as a criminal, he should leave his gun behind, but if he does carry a weapon, it should not be an official issue. He should carry a weapon of a type not associated with police officers. If posing as a particular type of criminal, he should know the method of operation and the particular slang and mannerisms of the people he is emulating.

Regardless of the role he is assuming, the undercover officer must be able to adapt to the particular neighborhood in which he is working. If he is posing as a stranger in town, he should pick a hometown which is unfamiliar to the group he is trying to infiltrate. His cover story should include names, places, and background information which can be checked out, and arrangements should be made to have his cover substantiated should his criminal associates decide to have his story verified. If fictitious information is used for the background, it should be information that cannot be easily checked out. Individuals who are enlisted to corroborate the officer's cover story should be selected for their credibility in the mind of the suspect under investigation.

Often the cover can be reinforced by having the undercover officer appear to be deaf, infirm, or weak. This will make the suspect less suspicious and perhaps cause him to be less cautious in his talk or actions. If the undercover officer is posing as an out-of-towner, feigning ignorance of the language may allow him to learn more than if the suspect knew he could speak the language.

The officer must dress the part. His clothing should reflect the personality and life-style he is assuming. If a certain style, quality, or price of clothing is uniform in a given area, the officer must adhere to these standards so as not to appear out of the ordinary. He should carry all of the usual documents identifying himself—driver's license, social security card, letters—all bearing out his assumed identity. It is always best not to become too dramatic or elaborate in establishing an identity. The simpler the better.

There are several ways that the undercover investigator can make initial contact with the suspect: first, he can rely on an informer to introduce him to the suspect, vouch for him, and set up his cover story; second, he can move into the neighborhood, frequent the suspect's hangouts, make himself known, and gradually work his way into the group; or third, he can create a situation which will draw attention to himself in such a way that he will immediately be accepted as part of the group. Recently, one of my students was assigned to an undercover drug investigation. On his first night in the field, he went into a local drinking place frequented by the drug crowd and proceeded to drink and make a considerable amount of noise. He eventually got into a fight with another patron, and during the fight a lid of grass fell out of his pocket. He recovered the pot and left. One week later he returned and was immediately accepted as part of the group. He went on to break up a large narcotics ring and arrest some big dealers who were subsequently sentenced to long prison terms.

Once the officer has been accepted into the group, he should act naturally and be patient. He should not be too pushy or ask too many questions. Ideally, he should try to manipulate the suspects in such a way that they will come to him with drugs or other contraband. Once he builds the reputation of being "cool," he can work toward identifying the criminals who are running the particular racket he is investigating. He must have a good memory because he cannot be caught writing down the information he acquires. He has to remember the bits and pieces until he is alone and free to write his reports.

Most agencies warn their undercover operatives that it is unwise to show too much interest in a male suspect's wife or girl friend. Although this is probably good advice in most cases, there are times when the undercover officer can gain important information from such contacts. He would probably have a better chance of gaining acceptance if he cultivated a female acquaintance of the suspect—as long as she is not the suspect's girl friend—and allowed others to think of them as a couple. This type of identification tends to blot out individuality and can often be a help to the officer who is operating incognito.

The suspect who accepts the friendship or association of a stranger usually has several reasons for doing so. He may simply like the individual and want his friendship, or he may sense that the stranger may be useful to him in his criminal enterprise or perhaps be a potential customer for contraband goods. But, whatever the reason, the officer is there to gain information and may use a number of strategies to achieve this objective. He should not talk any more than is necessary but should cultivate the habit of being a good listener. When the suspect is talking, the officer should allow him to do so without changing the subject. Conversations with the suspect can be initiated about almost any subject—sports or cars, for example—and then the officer can gradually work the talk around to the area of interest. Often, getting the suspect to drink will loosen his tongue. The officer, however, should not drink if he can avoid it. A physical excuse may be given to explain his not drinking. Once in a while it may be necessary for the officer to drink so that he will not appear out of place in the group.

If the officer finally succeeds in setting up a deal to buy contraband, he should never accept the contraband at the first price offered. He is expected to haggle. He should make every attempt to buy the goods at the lowest possible price. This will avert suspicion that he may have some ulterior motive for wanting to buy the goods. Whatever the officer is buying—whether drugs, guns, or stolen merchandise—he should try to make more than one buy unless he is lucky enough to deal for the whole cache. He should not appear to be too anxious. If possible he can let the deal hang for a few days to give the impression that he is not all that interested. Every so often he should stay away from the neighborhood pretending that he is out of town on a deal.

While an officer is undercover, arrangements must be made to communicate with his headquarters and with fellow officers. Usually arrangements should be made to meet in specified places at certain times, or for the officer to call in at certain times. If the officer misses his calls or appointments, other officers should check up to make sure he is safe.

If arrangements are made for the officer to call, he should use public telephone booths whenever possible. Telephones that go through a switchboard should always be avoided, and he should never call twice from the same phone. Often, it is less dangerous for the officer to call fellow officers at home rather than at headquarters. Call-in times should not form a pattern. Arrangements should be made for the officer to call in at different times on different days of the week. He can pretend to be calling his girl friend or his bookie, just so long as the calls appear to be ordinary.

In meeting with other officers, he need not communicate with them directly but can transmit his message by dropping it in a trash basket, writing it on a matchbook cover, leaving it in a men's room written on toilet paper, or placing it in a newspaper or magazine left in a public restaurant. Meetings should take place in public places unless a long conference is necessary, in which case the undercover man should arrange to be away from his usual locations for a long period of time.

Dos and Don'ts of Undercover Work

Undercover work is an important tool in vice crime enforcement. It should be properly planned to ensure success and to minimize the danger to the undercover officer. There are a number of essential practices which must be carried out in order to attain these goals:

Do determine the history and background of the suspect.

Do determine the past activities of the suspect.

Do determine the present activities of the suspect.

Do determine the type of character you are dealing with.

Do determine the type of crime you are dealing with.

Do determine the type of neighborhood you will be working in.

Do determine the usual type of criminal activity carried on in the neighborhood.

Do study the types of people living in the neighborhood.

Do become familiar with the types of dress, conduct, speech, and occupations commonly found in the neighborhood.

Do concoct an appropriate cover story.

Do memorize the cover story.

Do make every effort to be what you are supposed to appear to be.

Do anticipate questions that may be asked of and about you and prepare plausible answers in advance.

Don't go undercover without permission of your superior except in the most pressing emergencies.

Don't make claims that you cannot prove or back up.

Don't spend more money than your assumed character would ordinarily spend.

Don't (generally) take women on undercover assignments unless they are specifically assigned to the case.

Don't take part in a crime or law violation without the knowledge and approval of your superiors.

Don't (generally) become too friendly with women associated with the suspect.

Don't go to headquarters or associate with fellow officers while undercover.

Don't ever admit your identity.

Don't go to places where you are known as a police officer or where you may meet personal friends who could blow your cover.

Some Additional Points to Remember

Because the undercover officer is dealing with criminals, some of whom are extremely dangerous, it is imperative that he be cautious, skeptical, and alert at all times. Thus, all information about the case should be kept on a "need-to-know" basis. The undercover officer should also remember that not all police officers are honest, and that revealing his identity to such an individual could have dire consequences. When dealing with a suspect, the officer should assume, for his own protection, that the suspect is a clever individual who has been breaking the law for a long time. He is "cop-wise." The officer should never underestimate the suspect's ability to do him harm or to outwit him. He must always be one or two steps ahead of the suspect.

In dealing with the suspect, the officer should not entrap him in the legal sense. Entrapment is defined as an act by a law enforcement officer which induces another person to commit a crime. The officer can provide the suspect with the opportunity to commit a crime but he must never convince or cajole him to commit it. In the subsequent trial, if the defense can show that the officer actually urged the commission of the crime, the case will be thrown out. However, the prosecution can show that the suspect had a reputation for committing such crimes by introducing certified copies of past convictions and witnesses who know the suspect's reputation for committing such crimes. When an officer is directly involved in such a situation, he may participate in a criminal act (with the permission of his superiors) as an accomplice but only for the purpose of obtaining evidence of the crime. He may not participate in criminal acts for his own benefit, to gratify his own personal feelings or desires, or in instances where his activities are not approved by his superior officers after they have discussed his involvement with the prosecutor or district attorney. Once the undercover assignment has resulted in the successful collection of information which will support an affidavit establishing probable cause, the undercover officer can either make the arrest himself or, if the case is a large one involving many people and much contraband, a raid on the suspected premises can be planned and executed.

The Raid

The undercover officer assists his superiors in planning the raid. His role is to provide detailed floor plans of the suspected premises, including all doors, windows, and other means of entry and escape. He should pinpoint, if possible, where the suspects will be, the location of any contraband, and the hiding places of weapons. His assistance is also required in establishing a timetable for the raid. The number and type of officers selected to participate in the raid will be determined by a number of factors: the type of establishment to be raided, the number of doors, windows, and so forth; the location of the property and whether it is under city, county, or state jurisdiction; the type of offense which the raiding party seeks to suppress—for example, town bylaw, city ordinance, state law, or federal statute. When a number of different agencies are involved, raid planning can become complicated and requires complete cooperation between all agencies involved. However, every effort must be made to keep the raid as simple as possible with due regard for everything and every agency involved. The keys to a successful and efficient raid are speed, simplicity, surprise, and legality.

Once the initial movements and logistics of the raid have been determined, it is necessary to select the raid team. Again, we must keep the information about the raid confidential and on a need-to-know basis. Each member of the team must be told of his particular assignment and must memorize the timetable, special signals, and, above all, must understand that he is to take his cue from the raid leader. A successful raid is developed by teamwork, and no unilateral action must be undertaken.

Prior to the raid, proper affidavits establishing probable cause must be submitted to the court and valid search warrant obtained. Raid entry into the suspected premises must be proper and legal. Once entry is made every effort must be made to completely control the premises and the occupants, and then a systematic and thorough search must be made. (Search procedure is discussed earlier in this chapter.) All evidence must be collected and preserved and all contraband seized and controlled in the proper manner. Arrests must be conducted in a legal manner. Any visitors who enter the premises while the raiding party is present should be detained and questioned if legally permissible. Any phone calls into the premises must be screened by the officers for the purpose of gathering additional information about the crimes of the suspects.

It is extremely important that the raiding party adhere to the restrictions placed upon searches and seizures by the Fourth Amendment to the Constitution and by rulings of the United States Supreme Court. Despite the fact that criminals are not required to abide by a particular set of rules, the exclusionary rule applies to the admissibility and nonadmissibility of illegally obtained evidence. If we expect to get convictions in court, we must conduct ourselves according to the guidelines established by the Constitution and the courts.

Electronic Surveillance

Electronic surveillance involves interception of communications by use of telephone wiretaps, secret listening devices, recording devices, or radio transmitters.

Beginning in 1928, the United States Supreme Court handed down a series of decisions applying to listening devices and the introduction of evidence derived from overheard conversations. The decisions may be divided into categories from the point of view of whether the conversations were intercepted with or without the consent of one or the other party to the conversation.*

The following decisions deal with the absence of consent by either party to the conversation:

1928—In *Olmstead* v. *United States,* 277 U.S. 438, 72 L. Ed. 944, the Supreme Court held by a split decision that wiretaps were not within the Fourth Amendment protection against unreasonable search and seizure.

1934—The U.S. Congress imposed restraints on wiretapping by the Federal Communications Act. Section 605 provided in part:

And no person not being authorized by the sender shall intercept any communication and divulge or publish the existence, contents, substance, purport, effect, or meaning of such intercepted communication to any person. . . . (47 U.S.C. Sec. 605)

1937—*Nardone* v. *United States,* 302 U.S. 379, 82 L. Ed. 314, in which the Supreme Court held that Section 605 of the 1934 Federal Communications Act applied to federal law-enforcement officers and that testimony in court would constitute a form of prohibited divulgence thereby excluding testimony about an overheard conversation.

1939—In the second *Nardone* case, 308 U.S. 338, 84 L. Ed. 307, the Supreme Court further held that derivative evidence obtained from the wiretap was likewise barred from admission in a criminal trial (the fruit of the poisonous tree).**

1939–68—Despite the wording of the 1934 Federal Communications Act and decisions in the *Nardone* cases, the Department of Justice and the FBI did not interpret Section 605 as a prohibition against wiretapping but only as a prohibition against "divulgence" outside of government or in courts as evidence.

1952—In *Berger* v. *New York,* 388 U.S. 41, 18 L. Ed. 2d 1040, the Supreme Court of the United States ruled that the New York eavesdrop statute was unconstitutional as it failed to protect Fourth Amendment rights even though it

---

*These decisions and laws were researched by the Bureau of Criminal Investigation Organized Crime Division, State of Ohio.

**Any evidence obtained as a result of an illegal or unconstitutional police act is deemed to be tainted by the original illegal or unconstitutional act, hence, "the fruit of the poisonous tree."

authorized wiretap under court order, finding that the statute failed to particularize a specific crime, permitted eavesdropping for too long a period of time on a single showing of probable cause, and failed to contain a provision for an end of the eavesdropping when the conversation sought was seized.

1967—In *Katz* v. *United States,* 389 U.S. 347, 19 L. Ed. 2d 576, the U.S. Supreme Court discarded the theory that there could be no illegal search and seizure by electronic means unless there had been a technical trespass. *Katz,* the defendant, had made incriminating statements from a public telephone booth outside of which FBI agents had attached a listening and recording device. The court found that even a phone booth was a constitutionally protected area as the Fourth Amendment protects people—not places—and even though there was no physical intrusion, there was, in fact, an illegal search and seizure in that no judicial officer had previously sanctioned the interception of the messages even though probable cause for a warrant for such an interception probably existed.

1968—In *Lee* v. *Florida,* 392 U.S. 378, 20 L. Ed. 2d 1166, the U.S. Supreme Court reversed its prior holding in *Schwartz* v. *Texas* and held that where state officers violated Section 605 of the 1934 Federal Communications Act, the exclusionary rule applied to such conduct on the part of the state officers and such intercepted conversations were not admissible in court.

1968—The Congress adopted broad legislation in the field of wiretaps in the Omnibus Crime Control and Safe Streets Act, Title III. Briefly, Title III prohibits interception or endeavors to intercept wire or oral communications and prohibits their use in state or federal courts as evidence, excepting, however, wiretaps under certain circumstances:

a. When one of the parties in a communication gives prior consent.
b. When intelligence information is gathered in the interest of national security.
c. Upon application of the U.S. Attorney General a federal judge may authorize, upon the showing of probable cause, the interception of a communication where the probable cause testimony or affidavits demonstrate that the suspect has committed or is about to commit one of the enumerated serious offenses.
d. Provided that the state legislature has authorized interception of wire or oral communications by legislation patterned after Title III of the Omnibus Crime Control and Safe Streets Act, the Attorney General or Prosecuting Attorney of any state may also apply for state court authorization on the showing of probable cause to intercept wire or oral communications.

Furthermore, Title III of the 1968 Omnibus Crime Control and Safe Streets Act provided substantial federal penalties for any person, including state and local officials, who engaged in wiretapping without the authority of a federal or state court order. There are still some states whose legislatures have not adopted a wiretap or eavesdropping act since Congress adopted the 1968 Omnibus Crime Control and Safe Streets Act so that no local or state police officer in those states has permission to engage in wiretapping or other type of electronic surveillance when neither party to the communication consents. To the contrary, such an act is a violation of federal law and subjects the violator to imprisonment and fine. Only federal officers working through the United States attorney general or the United States district attorney and as expressly authorized by a federal judge have the authority, in those states which have not passed an eavesdropping law, to engage in wiretapping or other types of electronic eavesdropping where neither party to the communications has previously consented to such interception.

There are also a number of decisions related to eavesdropping in which only one party to the conversation has given consent to the interception or recording of the communication:

1952—In *On Lee* v. *United States*, 343 U.S. 747, 96 L. Ed. 1270, the Supreme Court of the United States upheld a conviction in which the trial judge permitted the testimony of a narcotics agent who monitored by radio equipment an incriminating discussion between a government informant and the defendant. The trial court permitted the narcotics agent to testify despite the fact that the informant was no longer available to testify and rejected the claim of trespass by either the inside informant or by the narcotics agent stationed outside who monitored and recorded the conversation. Specifically, the court rejected the proposition that eavesdropping on a conversation with the connivance of one of the parties constituted an unreasonable search and seizure.

1957—In *Rathbun* v. *United States*, 355 U.S. 107, 2 L. Ed. 2d 134, the Supreme Court of the United States affirmed a conviction in which the defendant was charged with transmitting an interstate communication which threatened the life of another. The Supreme Court found no error committed by the trial judge who permitted the testimony of police officers, stating that, with the consent of the person threatened, they listened to the defendant make threats over a regularly used telephone extension. The court held that the content of the communication overheard on the regularly used telephone extension with the consent of one party to the conversation was admissible and that the overhearing did not violate the provisions of Section 605 of the Federal Communications Act of 1934.*

1963—In *Lopez* v. *United States*, 373 U.S. 427, 10 L. Ed. 2d 462, the defendant was tried on charges of having attempted to bribe an Internal Revenue agent. Testimony of the Internal Revenue Service agent was supported by a wire recording which documented the bribe attempt. The court held that the wire recording of the conversation was properly admitted into evidence since the agent was in the office of the defendant with his consent and the recording device was used only to obtain the most reliable evidence possible of the conversation and that the use of the device did not violate the Fourth Amendment. Justices Brennan, Douglas, and Goldberg strongly dissented, contending

---

*The 1934 Federal Communications Act has been replaced by the 1968 Omnibus Crime Control and Safe Streets Act, but interception is permissible when one of the parties to the communication gives prior consent (18 U.S.C. 255 (2) (c)).

that electronic surveillance by federal agents was subject to the warrant provisions of the Fourth Amendment.

1966—In *Osburn* v. *United States,* 385 U.S. 323, 17 L. Ed. 2d 394, Osburn, attorney for the defendant, was charged and convicted of attempting to bribe a member of a jury panel (Vick) in a federal criminal trial involving Jimmy Hoffa. Osburn hired Vick to investigate prospective jurors and then raised the issue of bribery. Vick reported this to federal authorities. Two judges of the district court authorized by warrant the recording of further conversations between Vick, the informer, and Osburn, the attorney. Such recordings were made and received as part of the evidence in Osburn's trial.

In affirming the conviction, the court indicated that this was a case similar to *Lopez* v. *United States* but not subject to the arguments of the dissenting justices in *Lopez* because the tape recording was obtained within the narrow compass of the warrant authorized and issued by the two federal judges permitting the recording of the subsequently received conversations that incriminated Osburn.*

1971—*United States* v. *White,* 401 U.S. 745, 28 L. Ed. 2d 453, in which the conversations of the defendant (White) with a government informant were overheard by agents using radio equipment. The informant did not testify at the trial because the prosecutor was unable to locate him. However, government agents testified as to the conversations they overheard by monitoring the radio transmitter concealed on the informant's person. There was concern that the *Katz* decision (the Fourth Amendment protects people, not places) and the warrant procedure followed in *Osburn* would result in the exclusion of the evidence obtained in *White*. However, the court reaffirmed the propriety of using statements made to undercover agents as evidence and expressly upheld the situation in the *Lopez* case. The court did not disturb the *On Lee* decision and observed:

> If the conduct and revelations of an agent operating without electronic equipment do not invade the defendant's constitutionally justifiable expectations of privacy, neither does a simultaneous recording of the same conversation made by the agent or by others from transmission received from the agent to whom the defendant is talking and whose trustworthiness the defendant necessarily risks.**

As a general rule, if one party to the communication consents to the interception or recording of the conversation, based on existing statutory and constitutional interpretation by the courts, there is no violation and the court will receive the evidence.

---

*The question that Osburn raised was whether, in the future, agents were going to be required to obtain warrants under the provisions of the Fourth Amendment before recorded conversations with one-party consent would be admissible in a subsequent trial.

**U.S. v. *White,* 401 U.S. 745, 28 L. Ed. 2d 453.

While one may argue from the *White* case that the care taken in *Osburn* by obtaining a warrant prior to the recording of the bribery attempt is not needed, where time permits, it is suggested that the obtaining of a search warrant to tape or record the bribery attempt would be the preferred way to proceed.

ADDENDUM

In 1973 Thomas Avdeef, investigator for the Orange County, California, district attorney's office, developed a set of uniform regulations outlining the responsibilities of the various law-enforcement agencies in setting up and utilizing informers. This format might well become a national model for the use of defendant informants.

The following rules and regulations were devised for the express purpose of establishing standard guidelines for the handling of defendant informants by both the utilizing enforcement agency and the local district attorney. Such standardization, it is hoped, will help avoid some of the more common pitfalls that often accompany defendant informant agreements—for example, the informant who acts as a double agent, regardless of whether he is under investigation or arrest by another agency, or has been blackballed by another department.

Nothing contained within these rules and regulations is meant to circumvent or undermine the well-established procedures that are currently being used by the various law-enforcement agencies.

UNIFORM REGULATIONS GOVERNING INFORMANTS*

PART 1
DEFENDANT INFORMANTS

INDEX

---

*Thomas Avdeef, Internal Document, District Attorney's Office, Orange County, Calif., 1973.

Chapter 1—Purpose and General Provisions

Section 100—Purpose.   The purpose of the regulations set forth herein are to bring within the scope of the District Attorney's Office a uniform guide for the handling of defendant informants.

Such regulations shall apply to all defendant informant cases whether such is a misdemeanor and/or felony.

Section 110—Compliance with Provisions and Regulations.   Defendant informant agreements shall comply with the provisions of this part and regulations adopted by the District Attorney pursuant thereto.

The provisions of this part and regulations adopted pursuant thereto shall apply throughout the county to all defendant informant agreements.

The provisions of this part shall not preclude further additions, or deletions, reasonably prescribed to the regulations set forth.

Section 120—Adoption of Regulations.   The District Attorney may adopt regulations to interpret and make specific the provisions of this part.

Chapter 2—Definitions

Section 200—Construction.   The definitions contained in this chapter shall govern the construction of this part, unless the context otherwise requires.

Section 205—Approved.   ''Approved'' means compliance with the provisions of this part and the regulations adopted thereto as determined by the District Attorney.

Section 210—Burden of Compliance.   ''Burden of Compliance'' means the obligation of the enforcement agency to produce sufficient evidence of adherence to the regulations set forth.

Section 215—Burden of Responsibilities.   ''Burden of Responsibilities'' means those areas of responsibility designated specifically to the District Attorney or enforcement agencies.

Section 220—City and County.   ''City'' means any city. ''County'' means any county.

Section 225—Defendant Informant.   That person who has pending a criminal complaint, information or indictment issued against him charging him with a crime or crimes specific.

Section 230—District Attorney. "District Attorney" means prosecutor or the elected officeholder of the position in the County.

Section 235—Enforcement Agency. "Enforcement Agency" means that agency concerned primarily with the enforcement of laws within its authority.

Section 240—Genders. "Genders" means the masculine gender includes the feminine and neuter.

Section 245—Magistrate. "Magistrate" means Justice of the Peace.

Section 255—Prospective Effect. "Prospective Effect" means no part of it is retroactive unless expressly so disclosed.

Section 260—Shall and May. "Shall" is mandatory and "may" is permissive.

Section 265—Singular and Plural. The "singular" number includes the plural; and the "plural," the singular.

Section 270—Tenses. Present tense includes the past and future tense; and the future, the present.

Section 275—Effective Dates. The regulations become operative October 1, 1973. Effect on pending proceedings.

The uniform informant regulations shall become operative on October 1, 1973, and shall govern proceedings in actions brought on or after that date and, further proceeding in actions pending on that date.

Chapter 3—Responsibilities of the Enforcement Agency

Section 300. The utilizing Enforcement Agency shall, at the very earliest opportunity, evaluate and examine the Informant's abilities, truthfulness, security, nature and history of his criminal activity, and the degree of his prior public exposure.

Section 305. The Informant must be able to provide information which, when examined and utilized, will result in uncovering crime which is of a more serious proportion than that with which the informant is being charged.

Section 310. The Enforcement Agency shall not make promises or representations, express or implied, to the informant which have not been concurred with by the District Attorney nor shall the Enforcement Agency act on behalf of the District Attorney without the express written or oral authorization of the District Attorney.

Section 312.   Any representations made to the Defendant Informant prior to utilizing him shall be put in writing and signed by the Defendant Informant and witnessed by two persons.

Section 315.   The informant shall not be advised that he will not have to testify in court.

Section 320.   It shall be the duty of the Enforcement Agency to notify the Informant's attorney of his pending cooperation.

Section 325.   The Enforcement Agency's commanding officer shall be appraised of the identity and activities of the Informant.

Section 330.   The utilizing Enforcement Agency shall submit to the District Attorney's Office, prior to utilization of the Defendant Informant, a complete, up-to-date file on the defendant before any consideration to use the informant will be made.

Section 335.   Such files shall contain not less than or limited to the following items:
   a.   A current, up-to-date rap sheet on the informant;
   b.   A current photograph of the informant;
   c.   A fingerprint card of the informant;
   d.   A complete record check on the informant, including the listing of outstanding warrants;
   e.   The prior work record of the informant with the same or other Enforcement Agencies;
   f.   A complete identification sheet on the informant;
   g.   A complete copy of the informant's arrest and investigation reports;
   h.   A written statement from the Defendant Informant as to the reason for his cooperation.

Section 340.   The informant shall not be allowed to continue in criminal activity under color of a police or other Enforcement Agency.

Section 342.   The utilizing Enforcement Agency will submit a request to the District Attorney before utilization of the Defendant Informant. Such request shall include the completed informant file and a duplicate 3 × 5 card.

Section 343.   Such 3 × 5 card shall reflect the name, address, CII number, FBI number, driver's license number, social security number, telephone number, description of information to be provided or services to be performed, and present cases pending against the Defendant Informant.

DOE, John	CII No._____
4423 Fifth Street	FBI No._____
Santa Ana, Ca.	DL No._____
Phone: (714) 835-4422	SS No._____

(Include description of information to be provided or services and present cases.)

Section 345.   When an agency wishes to use as an informant, a person who is (a) under *arrest* by another agency or agencies; (b) under investigation by another agency or agencies; or (c) under prosecution by another agency or agencies, that agency will contact such other agency or agencies *prior to* the use of such informant. At which time, *all* concerned agencies will then participate in an evaluation of the proposed use of the informant.

Section 350.   The utilizing Enforcement Agency shall maintain the current activities of the informant.

Section 355.   The utilizing Agency shall maintain a documented work record on the informant containing not less than or limited to the following items:
    a.   The amount of evidence seized;
    b.   The number of persons arrested;
    c.   The number of cases pending.

Section 360.   The Enforcement Agency shall keep the District Attorney advised of the current status of the informant's activities so that proper time and arrangements may be made in advance by the District Attorney for court appearances and trial continuations.

Section 365.   It shall be the responsibility of the specific Enforcement Agency concerned to develop and operate within its own practical guidelines in the general handling of informants.

Section 370.   The utilizing agency shall have the burden of compliance with the uniform regulations governing informants by producing sufficient evidence of its adherence to the regulations as set forth herein.

Section 375.   Nothing contained within these rules and regulations are to supersede those rules and regulations which have been adopted by the particular Enforcement Agency in the handling of Informants.

Chapter 4—Responsibilities of the District Attorney

Section 400.   It shall be the duty of the District Attorney to maintain a separate system of files, with limited and controlled access for security for all Defendant Informants.

Section 405.   Such access shall be limited to the custodian of such reports, the Enforcement Agency concerned, and the District Attorney at the time of the trial.

Section 407.   Should the informant fail to produce or he becomes unreliable, the District Attorney shall make such appropriate entries on the informant's 3×5 card.

Section 410.   The District Attorney shall, where appropriate, obtain search and seizure on the Defendant Informant at the time of his probation and sentencing hearing.

Section 414.   The District Attorney shall, with the concurrence of the utilizing agency, review the Defendant Informant's case and make a determination as to whether a certified plea is to be taken prior to the utilization of the informant.

Section 415.   The District Attorney shall maintain a written or recorded record of all Defendant Informant agreements.

Section 420.   The District Attorney shall, at the Defendant Informant's hearing, represent to the court whether or not the Defendant Informant has fulfilled his contract between the parties.

Section 422.   The District Attorney shall, at the time of the Defendant Informant's sentencing, present to the magistrate in his chambers, a complete, updated Defendant Informant file containing his work performance.

Section 425.   No misdemeanor offense which the Defendant Informant has incurred shall be dismissed without the knowledge of the District Attorney or the deputy in charge of Municipal Court operations and until all cases upon which the Informant has worked have been disposed of.

Section 430.   No felony offense which is pending against an Informant shall be dismissed under any circumstances without the knowledge of the District Attorney or the deputy in charge of Superior Court operations.

Section 435.   All agreements and commitments shall have been completed by the parties prior to the sentencing of the Defendant Informant. Further, no agreements shall be honored by the District Attorney which have been made after the Defendant Informant has been sentenced.

Section 505.

CONFIDENTIAL

Name _____Age _____ Date of Birth _____
Address _____City and State _____
Telephone Number _____

State the reasons why you wish to assist this agency by disclosing known criminal activity:

Do you understand that you are not privileged to break any laws during the period of time that you are assisting this agency? _____

Do you understand that you are to keep in constant contact with this agency while assisting us? _____

_____
                                   Signature

Witness: _____

Witness: _____

Date: _____

Source: Thomas Avdeef, "Uniform Regulations Governing Informants." Internal document of the Office of the District Attorney, Orange County, CA.

REFERENCES

Avdeef, Thomas. *Uniform Regulations Governing Informants.* Orange County, Calif.: Office of the District Attorney, 1973. Internal Document.

Lentini, Joseph R., and France, James G. *Ohio Peace Officer's Manual.* Cincinnati: W. H. Anderson Co., 1972.

Tobin, William J. *Constitutional Law Enforcement.* Boston: Commonwealth of Massachusetts, 1967.

Chapter 8

The Role of Organized Crime in Vice and Narcotics

Organized crime has been defined in many different ways, but perhaps the most comprehensive definition—and the one that takes into account all the many varied activities attributed to organized crime—is the definition developed by the Ohio Organized Crime Prevention Council (1975, p. 1).

> Organized crime is a conspiracy which involves the active or passive participation of a group of individuals to achieve a common criminal goal. Its activities encompass isolated or related criminal transactions and/or legal business enterprises or organizations subverted to a criminal purpose. The existence of an organization for the carrying out or facilitating the commission of one crime or different crimes is differentiated from other types of crime or simple criminal conspiracies.

The scope of this definition allows for the inclusion of at least three types of criminal enterprises within the general category of organized crime. They are:

1. Any criminal enterprises directly associated with a criminal structure or syndicate.
2. Any independent criminal enterprises existing under the umbrella of a criminal structure.
3. Any criminal enterprises which result from a conspiracy, as noted above, but which are free from association with a criminal structure.

This definition also takes into account the basic characteristics and behaviors associated with the criminal structure in this country. Some examples of the traits cited by the Ohio Organized Crime Prevention Council (1975, p. 1) are:

> The communication, yet detachment, between upper levels and the levels of management and entrepreneurship.

> The permanent management functions for review of the risk/return relationship and planning for new markets.

> The infiltration of business, unions and other social systems.

> The protection provided upper-level members.

The Kefauver Commission (1951; cited by the President's Commission on Law Enforcement and the Administration of Justice 1967, p. 1) declared that:

1. There is a nationwide crime syndicate known as the Mafia, whose tentacles are found in many large cities. It has international ramifications which appear most clearly in connection with the narcotics traffic.
2. Its leaders are usually found in control of the most lucrative rackets in their cities.
3. There are indications of a centralized direction and control of these rackets, but leadership appears to be in a group rather than in a single individual.
4. The Mafia is the cement that helps to bind the Costello-Adonis-Lansky syndicate of New York and the Accardo-Guzik-Fischetti syndicate of Chicago as well as smaller criminal gangs and individuals throughout the country. These groups have kept in touch with Luciano since his deportation from this country.
5. The domination of the Mafia is based fundamentally on "muscle" and murder. The Mafia is a secret conspiracy against law and order which will ruthlessly eliminate anyone who stands in the way of its success in any criminal enterprise in which it is interested. It will destroy anyone who betrays its secrets. It will use any means available—political influence, bribery, intimidation, etc. to defeat any attempt on the part of law enforcement to touch its top figures or to interfere with its operations.

Whether we refer to organized crime as "the syndicate," "the Mafia," "the mob," "the confederation," "La Cosa Nostra," or any one of a number of generally descriptive appellations, we can safely assume that a group of crimes, committed by individuals and groups who fall within the parameters of our definition, are being perpetrated. These crimes can be distinctly separated from the group of crimes which are unorganized—for example, muggings, robberies, burglaries, and rapes. The unorganized crimes are still being carried out by criminals having no organized criminal affiliations. At one time, the crimes with which this text concerns itself were also carried out by individuals, but in many cases, because of their nature, have lent themselves to organization and structure.

Certainly, the crimes committed by the ethnic street gangs in nineteenth-century America bore more resemblance to unorganized crime than to organized crime. Street robbery, extortion, and theft by the street gangs—protected as they were by corrupt ward politicians and police, for whom they often carried out the job of voter intimidation and political assassination—gradually evolved into neighborhood criminal hierarchies that were virtually immune to the law. Hammer (1974, p. 92) describes the origins and growth of the early street gangs that led to the development of widespread, organized crime:

While most gangs were narrowly local, the province of the young and concerned with small, indiscriminate depredations, some, though retaining the ethnic balance, broke the pattern. They were not native to America at all but were brought over by immigrants who had come of age at home and had received their training there. They adapted their groups to the new environment and, in some cases, even spread across the country, though until the development of fast and widespread communication their links with one another tended to be rather hit or miss. Among them were the Mafia, the Camorra and similar secret terrorist societies brought to the States from Sicily, Naples, Calabria, and elsewhere in Italy, and the Chinese Tongs.

The Origins of Organized Crime—Historical Perspectives

Following the Civil War, great waves of immigrants hit the American shores: Irish, Italians, Northern Europeans, Chinese, and many others. These were the people who made up the great melting pot, people who came to America in search of a new freedom and a dream of prosperity. With the arrival of these groups came a number of diverse cultures, each of which had its own criminal subculture. Settling into the new land, these groups of immigrants established their own ethnic conclaves, "shantytown," "Chinatown," "Little Italy." Frightened, hopeful, but distrustful of what they could not understand, these people became the prime targets for exploitation by their own kind. And because they were unable to speak the new language, they could not—and often would not—complain to the authorities. Thus they were forced to rely on their own community leaders for jobs, handouts, representation in the courts of law, and advice. Unwittingly they provided their exploiters with a political base of power in return for favors received.

One by one, each of these immigrant groups achieved a formidable degree of power in the sphere of local politics, and gradually the bases for what we now know as organized crime began to emerge. Ethnic control of crime seems to depend on several variables, including geographic location, cultural tradition, and perception of the criminal activity. Gerald M. Caplan, director of the National Institute of Law Enforcement and Criminal Justice (cited in Ianni 1973, p. i), has described the changing relationship between ethnicity and organized crime:

> Recent books and films have made the phrase "organized crime" synonymous with specific ethnic stereotypes. In reality, however, the racial and ethnic composition of American crime syndicates has varied from city to city and year to year. During this century, a succession of ethnic groups has dominated crime in many cities, with control passing from the Irish to the Jews to the Italians and more recently, to blacks and Spanish-speaking groups.

The beginning of the metamorphosis of the urban street gangs into the crime syndicate can be dated from the ratification, in January, 1919, of the Eighteenth Amendment to the Constitution, which provided for the prohibition of the legal manufacture, sale, or transportation of alcoholic beverages in the United States. Prohibition provided the fertile soil that was necessary for the success of organized crime: by criminalizing alcoholic beverages, the government created a void that gave the street gangs an opportunity to take the first step toward organizing what today are multibillion-dollar crime syndicates. Encyclopaedia Britannica describes these beginnings:

> Prohibition brought into being a new kind of criminal—the bootlegger. The career of Al Capone was a dramatic instance of the development of bootlegging on a large scale. His annual earnings were estimated at $60,000,000. The rise of the bootlegging gangs led to a succession of gang wars and murders. . . . Historians of the underworld, however, suggest that by the late 1920's bootlegging was on the verge of semi-monopoly control and that the end of gang wars was approaching.

From "Prohibition," *Encyclopaedia Britannica,* 14th Edition (1973), 18:611. Reprinted by permission.

Originally, the bootlegging gangs established illegal drinking places (speakeasies), liquor delivery routes, and small-time operations to bring booze to a thirsty public. Gradually, they developed smuggling operations and eventually established their own stills to manufacture the illegal liquor. Competition increased as gangs sought to broaden their areas of control of the illegal business, resulting in a number of gang wars. Killings, machine-gunnings, bombings, and planned assassinations turned the major cities of the United States into veritable battlegrounds. Innocent people were killed and maimed, money flowed freely, and crooked politicians and police aided and abetted the gangs in their criminal activities.

As they organized their own territories, the gangs—the Capones, the O'Bannions, the Gennas, the Valley Gang, the Ragan Colts, and others—controlled most of the crime which took place in the area under their control. Bootlegging, gambling, and prostitution operations were conducted much like any legitimate business—for profit. However, the warfare between the gangs produced a public outcry, especially in Chicago, the city which had become the crime capital of the country. In an effort to bring peace to Chicago, a New York mob leader named Johnny Torrio was brought in to arbitrate the problem between the mobs.

Torrio suggested that only by cooperating among themselves could the gangs put an end to the killings and the bad publicity. He argued for an end to the street crimes of robbery, safecracking, and other violent crimes, and for confining gang activities to bootlegging, gambling, and prostitution. He proposed that each gang have complete control over its own territories without infringement on the territories of other gangs. The gang leaders might have been venal and vicious, but they weren't stupid. They saw wisdom in Torrio's suggestions and agreed to his proposal. But the ensuing peace lasted only three years. Al Capone, who was originally one of Torrio's henchmen, eventually became his chief aide. At one point, an attempt was made to assassinate Torrio but failed. Torrio eventually went to prison on a federal bootlegging charge, leaving Capone as the boss of Chicago. Capone's ascension to the throne and his subsequent attempts to control the entire city of Chicago led to a revival of the gang-war era. Although police were unsuccessful in arresting Capone for any of his multiple crimes, finally in 1931 he was indicted by the federal government on charges of income tax evasion and was eventually convicted.

One organizational structure had come out of the Capone era in Chicago. Since the gangs still clung to their ethnicity, Capone had fallen back on an old-country establishment, the Mafia. In striving to control Chicago, he had included the control of L'Unione Siciliano, which had a large following in Chicago. The L'Unione had organization, a code of silence, and a long history of crime and assassination. By the time Capone was jailed, he was recognized as the Capo of the Chicago branch of L'Unione.

The Crime Families

While Chicago was moving slowly toward organization, New York was also moving in the same direction. The gangs in New York were experiencing their own brand of growing pains. One big-time gambler, bootlegger, and friend of high-placed politicians was Arnold Rothstein. Rothstein had made a fortune in bootlegging but had never been part of a gang structure. He hired his underlings as he needed them and then paid them off. He made no permanent alliances and maintained that the activities of the gangs were "stupid." Among those who worked for Rothstein from time to time were Meyer Lansky, Charles "Lucky" Luciano, Bugsy Seigel, and Frank Costello. These up-and-coming young hoodlums listened attentively to the words of the rich and successful Rothstein. Hammer (1973, p. 121) tells us:

> Rothstein had enough ego to be flattered by their respect and by their willingness to listen, ask questions, follow his advice. They were his pupils and he taught them well. He lectured constantly on the need for organization. . . . But Rothstein's ideas about organization far exceeded those commonly understood and practiced in the underworld. As they stood, he said, the gangs were ridiculous; ethnic exclusivity and rivalry were both stupid and wasteful. Make use of the best, organize the best.

He cautioned that the garish dressers and headline hunters, like Capone, were cutting their own throats. He advocated a quiet, orderly, respectable life completely separate from "business." He pointed to Torrio, who had amassed a fortune but who was hardly known. Rothstein's pupils followed his advice, and as the 1930s progressed, each rose, using Rothstein's principles, to high places in the ranks of the underworld. Luciano eventually was able to convince the gang leaders from across the country to establish a true organization based on the "family" structure of the Mafia. Costello became boss of a New York family; Lansky ran Florida and organized gambling operations between the United States and Batista's Cuba; Seigel was sent west to organize the "open territory" of Nevada, where gambling was legal, and to establish a foothold in that mecca of money.

The repeal of the Volstead Act produced turmoil in the ranks of the criminal gangs. Legalization of alcohol shut off the money spigot. And the gangs had to find a new place to invest the millions they had amassed during Prohibition. This crisis was what precipitated Luciano into the national limelight. Using the organizational principles set down by Rothstein, he organized the crime families across the nation. He incorporated the ideas of Torrio, Capone, and Rothstein to weld together a powerful network of crime families.

Like Torrio, he advocated complete territorial control by a particular family; like Capone, he instituted the family organization of the Mafia; and like Rothstein, he stressed organization, cooperation, and subtlety. Because of his efforts he emerged as *Capo di Tutti Capi,* the "Boss of All Bosses." Crime was finally organized. Luciano also established "The Commission," a group of leaders representing each family who made decisions affecting national problems between the families. For instance it was the commission that decided that Nevada and Miami should be "open territory" in which all the families could invest their funds. Lansky was sent to Florida to handle everyone's interest and to keep peace in the open territory.

In its *Task Force Report: Organized Crime,* The President's Commission on Law Enforcement and the Administration of Justice diagrammed the internal structure of an organized crime "family." (See figure 8.1.)

From this diagram, one can see that the "Boss" is far removed from any direct involvement in actual illegal activity. He is buffered by the underboss, the lieutenants, and the soldiers. Actual criminal activity is carried out by soldier members of the families and nonmembers who act as fronts for such activity. At the level of lieutenant we may find an individual who has complete control of all the rackets in an entire city or a particular section of the city. In families whose activities are multi-state, the lieutenant may be responsible for all the activity in one entire state. In most instances, no one below the level of lieutenant has ever met the Boss, and to some the underboss is a complete stranger.

Soldiers may serve in a number of different capacities. At the higher level they may control a single racket, such as gambling or loan sharking, in one particular section of the city. At the lower levels they may be errand boys and small-time hoods. Movement up the ladder to the control of a racket or even to a small piece of the action may depend on a number of variables—reputation for loyalty, willness to take orders, brains, and so forth. In the soldier ranks we find the specialists, the hit men or button men, the enforcers, the corrupters, and the lawyers and business types.

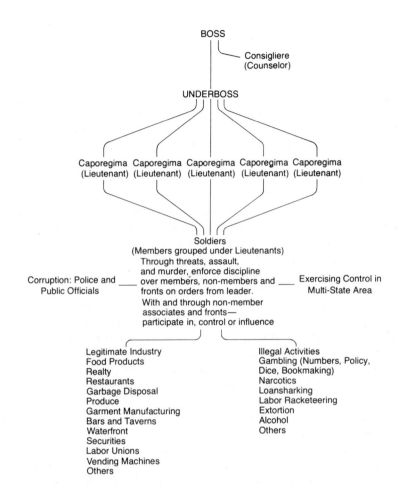

BOSS

Consigliere
(Counselor)

UNDERBOSS

Caporegima   Caporegima   Caporegima   Caporegima   Caporegima
(Lieutenant) (Lieutenant) (Lieutenant) (Lieutenant) (Lieutenant)

Soldiers
(Members grouped under Lieutenants)
Through threats, assault,
and murder, enforce discipline

Corruption: Police and ___ over members, non-members and ___ Exercising Control in
Public Officials   fronts on orders from leader.   Multi-State Area
                          With and through non-member
                          associates and fronts—
                          participate in, control or influence

Legitimate Industry   Illegal Activities
Food Products   Gambling (Numbers, Policy,
Realty   Dice, Bookmaking)
Restaurants   Narcotics
Garbage Disposal   Loansharking
Produce   Labor Racketeering
Garment Manufacturing   Extortion
Bars and Taverns   Alcohol
Waterfront   Others
Securities
Labor Unions
Vending Machines
Others

Source: The President's Commission on Law Enforcement and the Administration of
Justice, *Task Force Report: Organized Crime,* 1967.
Figure 8.1 An organized crime family.

The Role of Organized Crime in Unions and Business

We have already discussed illegal activities of organized crime syndicates as
they relate to vice crimes. Here we will only mention several other criminal
activities, among which are labor racketeering, extortion, and alcohol violations.

Several major unions, such as the Teamsters Union, the East Coast
Longshoremen's Workers Union, and several of the craft unions, are under
suspicion of being syndicate controlled. The federal government is presently
investigating the Teamsters Union's association with known organized crime

figures. It is alleged that Teamster funds have been illegally channeled into mob projects, and that the money has never been repaid. In New England and New York it is well known that longshoremen from several locals do not work unless they are willing to "kick back" a portion of their wages for the privilege to work. Control of these locals is in the hands of syndicate "goons" who control elections with "muscle." This also puts the controlled unions at the mercy of their officers, who have established "sweetheart contracts" with their employers. A "sweetheart contract" is one in which the union officers guarantee freedom from labor problems in return for bribes. The losers, of course, are the rank-and-file union members. Many of these unions were delivered into the hands of the criminals in return for "amortizing" debts to loan sharks.

Organized crime experts have estimated that most of our East Coast ports could be shut down by unions whose officers have long criminal records or who are suspected of being members of crime families. The average taxpayer pays for this kind of criminality, not only in higher prices for goods imported through East Coast ports, but also in terms of goods stolen from the docks and business delays which force prices up.

Extortion takes the form of force applied to legitimate businessmen to force them out of business or to convince them that they should do business with operations owned by crime figures. One glaring example was the attempt made by New Jersey criminals to force the Great Atlantic and Pacific Tea Co. to stock a soap powder manufactured by a small syndicate-owned company. The product did not meet A&P quality standards and was refused a place on the supermarket shelves. Each refusal by A&P was met with a rash of fires and robberies, and one of its market managers was even killed. A&P alerted the FBI and the extortion plot was broken up.

Organized criminals have also continued their activities in the bootlegging racket, not in the same manner as during Prohibition but in ways just as profitable. Smuggling alcohol, producing counterfeit tax stamps, and running cheap liquor from low-tax states to high-tax states without paying the appropriate taxes are among these activities.

An article appearing in *Newsday* magazine February 20, 1975, reported the following:

> The Cosa Nostra has become New York State's biggest wholesaler of cigarets and, because of its illegal operation, the State and City are losing an estimated $133 million in tax revenues a year, authorities say.
>
> From Montauk Point to Buffalo, mob smugglers using sophisticated electronic equipment and traffic managers bring in an estimated 128,964 cartons of illegal cigarets daily. They come by trailer, truck, rented van, car, airplane or train.
>
> The cigarets disappear into warehouses and suburban homes rented by the mob. Within hours they are distributed by an army of mob peddlers who take orders in advance. Special mob outlets include gas stations, vending machines and bookmakers.

According to police and legislative estimates, the lost state and local sales taxes totaled $133 million last year. "We've had bookmakers take cigaret orders with their bets," said a New York City detective. "As fast as you hit them, they're back on the street taking their orders."

We've seen the figures—$50 billion from gambling, $20 million from loan sharking, and untold millions from narcotics. Obviously, one of the biggest problems facing the crime syndicates is how to explain this money. How is it possible to accumulate that much money legitimately? Does one pay taxes and write "gambling" or "loan sharking" on the tax return? The mob learned early and well that they can get away with the crimes they commit simply because law-enforcement agencies are not as well organized as they, especially in the area of vice crime. They also learned that the IRS is a powerful agency that puts people in jail if they don't pay taxes. Therefore, they had to devise a way to "clean" the money and explain its sources. They chose to invest in legitimate business, because it not only produces more money but is also legal. There are a number of advantages to investing in legitimate business:

1. It gives the criminal the appearance of being a quiet, upstanding member of the community (Rothstein's Law).
2. It explains the source of so much money.
3. Legitimate business can be used as a "laundry" to clean dirty money.
4. Legitimate business can be used as a front for racket operations.
5. Legitimate business provides an explanation for "mode of living."
6. It allows the payment of taxes to allay the suspicions of the Internal Revenue Service.
7. It allows for the eventual takeover of other legitimate businesses.

Organized crime figures have invested heavily in legitimate business for all of the above reasons. As shown in figure 8.1, the most popular business investments are in food products, realty, restaurants, garbage disposal, produce, garment manufacturing, bars and taverns, waterfront business, securities, labor, unions, vending machine businesses, and others. All of these different types of businesses have one thing in common: they produce a rapid turnover in funds; most of them are small to medium in size; and all are fairly high-risk ventures. The risk factor makes it easier to take over, especially when the businessman finds himself in financial difficulty.

Combating Organized Crime

The local police department, no matter how big, is incapable of mounting an effective campaign against organized crime. Granted, the local police can

Commitment of Political Leaders

26 Federal Investigative Agencies

Federal Prosecutors' Units

Federal Regulatory Agencies

Joint Congressional Investigative Committee

Commitment of Political Leaders

Local Police Special Units

Local Prosecutors' Units

Government Crime Commissions

Grand Jury Reports

Commitment of Political Leaders

State Police Investigations

State Attorney General Intelligence Units

State and Regional Intelligence Groups

State Prosecutors' Units

State Regulatory Agencies

Government Crime Commissions

Commitment of Citizens

Private Crime Commissions

Press and News Media

Social Scientists

Private Trade Associations

Source: The President's Commission on Law Enforcement and the Administration of Justice, *Task Force Report: Organized Crime*, 1967.

Figure 8.2 Coordinated effort against organized crime.

enforce the laws against individual crimes, the revenue from which goes into the coffers of organized crime, such as gambling, organized prostitution, or narcotics, but most police departments do not have the specialists necessary to investigate the entire problem. We know from experience that merely arresting the bookie or the occasional controller doesn't stop gambling. The penalties are too weak, the fines are too small, and the criminal is back in business before we have even finished writing our reports. Arresting the prostitute or the pimp does not stop prostitution, and very few loan sharks are ever arrested at the local level. Organized crime can only be controlled by bringing to bear the combined strength of local, city, and state agencies in cooperation with federal agencies. Only by a process of information sharing, analysis, communication, and combined enforcement can we ever hope to stop the crime syndicates. (See figure 8.2.)

Only by establishing organized crime units at the local level, which will work with other departments in the gathering and coordinating of intelligence information, can we hope to gain an overall picture of organized crime operations in a given area. Once such intelligence is gathered, it must be analyzed statistically by experts. We need the cooperation of businessmen, accountants, statisticians, and mathematicians, in addition to the investigative expertise of our police departments, in order to pull down the structure which we call organized crime.

Salerno (1969, p. 5) elaborates on the problems of controlling organized crime:

> No state has yet enacted a set of effective laws for controlling organized crime; the police can establish a fine record of arrests and still ignore organized crime; prosecutors can have an enviable record of convictions and not concern themselves with organized crime; judges can build a reputation for being "tough" without ever imposing a penitentiary commitment on any operator of organized crime; and probation departments, correctional institutions and parole boards appear to regard organized crime as totally outside their area of responsibility.

Things are, however, beginning to change. Federal organized crime strike forces have been established. Local police officers are being trained. And newer and more efficient methods are being developed to coordinate the law-enforcement effort against organized crime. Perhaps it will be only a matter of time before control of organized crime becomes a viable possibility.

REFERENCES

Hammer, Richard. "Playboy's History of Organized Crime." *Playboy* 20 (August 1973):92–172.

Ianni, Francis A. *Ethnic Succession in Organized Crime*. Washington, D.C.: U.S. Department of Justice, Law Enforcement Assistance Administration, 1973.

Ohio Organized Crime Prevention Council. *System One*. Columbus, Ohio, 1975.

President's Commission on Law Enforcement and the Administration of Justice. Task Force Report: Organized Crime. Washington, D.C.: U.S. Government Printing Office, 1967.

Salerno, Ralph F. "Organized Crime: An Unmet Challenge to Criminal Justice." *Crime and Delinquency* (July 1969):5.

Index

Abstinence syndrome. *See* Withdrawal
Adamism. *See* Exhibitionism
Addict, identification of, 108, 126
Adler, Polly, 68
Alkaloid, defined, 107
Amphetamines: abuse of, 112;
    types of, 112–13
Analgesic, defined, 107
Anexoria, defined, 108
Annilingus. *See* Sodomy
Anthropophagy, defined, 92
Apomorphine, characteristics of, 123
Auletrides, in ancient Greece, 59

Barbiturates: abuse of, 111;
    types of, 111–12
Berger v. *New York,* 176
Bestiality, defined, 85
Betting information, transmission of, 24
B-girl, method of operation, 70–71
Bisexuality, defined, 79
Bondage, defined, 81
Buggery. *See* Sodomy

Call Girls, methods of operation, 64–66
Cannabis Sativa. See Marijuana
Cannibalism. *See* Anthropophagy
Child molesting. *See* Pedophilia
Cocaine: characteristics of, 127–28;
    sale of, 128;
    speedball, 128;
    symptoms of abuse of, 128
Codeine, characteristics of, 123
Crime: consensual, 1, 5;
    victimless, 1–7
Cunnilingus. *See* Sodomy

Demerol, characteristics of, 123
Dicteriades, in ancient Greece, 59
Dilaudid, characteristics of, 123

Dionin, characteristics of, 123
Dolophine, characteristics of, 123–24
DOM. *See* STP
Dream book, use of, 14–17
Drugs: abuse of, and peer-group
    pressure, 108;
    classification of, 109;
    habituation to, defined, 107;
    hallucinogenic, 113–21;
    hypnotic, 110–11;
    over-the-counter (OTC), 109;
    prescription, 109;
    searches for, 150–55;
    somnifacient, 111
Drunkenness, cost of in Washington,
    D.C., 4

Enforcement: discretionary, 3;
    techniques, for gambling, 26
Eukodal, characteristics of, 123
Euphoria, defined, 108
Exhibitionism, defined, 81
Exhibitionists: control of, 82;
    types of, 82

Federal Communications Act,
    provisions of, 176
Fellatio. *See* Sodomy
Fetishes, types of, 94–95
Fetishism, defined, 94
Finder's fee, in loan-sharking, 51
Fire-water complex. *See* Sex pyromania
Flash paper, use of in gambling, 19
Frottage, defined, 84
Fund for the City of New York,
    gambling survey, 8, 29–31

Gambling: and the Knapp Commission,
    25;
    legal, in Nevada, 25;